Lecture Notes in Artificial Intelligence   9266

Subseries of Lecture Notes in Computer Science

Vladimír Mařík · Arnd Schirrmann
Damien Trentesaux · Pavel Vrba (Eds.)

Industrial Applications of Holonic and Multi-Agent Systems

7th International Conference, HoloMAS 2015
Valencia, Spain, September 2–3, 2015
Proceedings

 Springer

Editors
Vladimír Mařík
Czech Technical University in Prague
Prague
Czech Republic

Arnd Schirrmann
Airbus Group Innovations
Hamburg
Germany

Damien Trentesaux
University of Valenciennes
and Hainaut-Cambresis
Valenciennes
France

Pavel Vrba
Czech Technical University in Prague
Prague
Czech Republic

ISSN 0302-9743   ISSN 1611-3349 (electronic)
Lecture Notes in Artificial Intelligence
ISBN 978-3-319-22866-2   ISBN 978-3-319-22867-9 (eBook)
DOI 10.1007/978-3-319-22867-9

Library of Congress Control Number: 2015946576

LNCS Sublibrary: SL7 – Artificial Intelligence

Printed on acid-free paper

Springer International Publishing AG Switzerland is part of Springer Science+Business Media
(www.springer.com)

Preface

It is real pleasure to state that the research activities around holonic and multi-agent systems for industrial applications have continued and even increased their importance during the last decade. The number of both the scientific topics and the achievements in the subject field is growing steadily, especially because of their direct relevance to the Industry 4.0 initiative. The influence of the multi-agent and holonic system philosophy on the Industry 4.0 visions is more than clear.

Besides HoloMAS, which has been the pioneering event in the subject field, there are other conferences such as the IEEE SMC annual conference, INDIN, ETFA, or INCOM that focus their attention on advanced industrial solutions, some of which are based on intelligent agents. But the HoloMAS conference keeps its orientation, character, and flavor and it remains strongly industry oriented.

This year's conference was the tenth in the sequence of HoloMAS events. The first three (HoloMAS 2000 in Greenwich, HoloMAS 2001 in Munich, and HoloMAS 2002 in Aix-en-Provence) were organized as workshops under the umbrella of DEXA society. Starting with 2003 HoloMAS achieved the status of an independent conference organized biyearly on odd years, still under the DEXA patronage (HoloMAS 2003 in Prague, HoloMAS 2005 in Copenhagen, HoloMAS 2007 in Regensburg, HoloMAS 2009 in Linz, HoloMAS 2011 in Toulouse, and HoloMAS 2013 in Prague). The HoloMAS line of scientific events has created a solid community of researchers and practitioners who are active in the subject field. They have started to cooperate in large EU projects, for example, in the EU Integrated Project ARUM (2012–2015), and have jointly elaborated on several new project proposals since the last HoloMAS event.

The research of holonic and agent-based systems has attracted the interest of industry and receives increasing support from both the public sector and private institutions. We witnessed the increased interest from the IEEE System, Man, and Cybernetics Society (http://ieeesmc.org/), namely, from its Technical Committees on Distributed Intelligent Systems and on Cybernetics for Intelligent Industrial Systems, which was established early this year. Another IEEE body – Industrial Electronics Society – supports the related R&D field through its Technical Committee on Industrial Agents (http://tcia.ieee-ies.org/). Its mission is to provide a base for researchers and application practitioners for sharing their experiences with applications of holonic and agent technologies in the industrial sector, especially in assembly and process control, planning and scheduling, and supply chain management. There are a number of impacted journals that provide space for articles dealing with industrial agents such as *IEEE Transactions on SMC: Systems, IEEE Transactions on Industrial Informatics, Journal of Production Research, Journal of Intelligent Manufacturing,* or *JAAMAS*.

We are proud to announce that the HoloMAS 2015 conference was held again under the technical co-sponsorship of the IEEE SMC Society.

For HoloMAS 2015 there were 27 papers submitted, from which the Program Committee selected 17 regular papers and two surveys to be included in this volume.

The surveys are aimed at software engineering methods for intelligent manufacturing and at standards and ontologies for process automation. The regular papers are organized into four sections. Conceptual and design issues are the focus of the first section (three papers). The next section is aimed at intelligent manufacturing systems exploring holonic and multi-agent principles (five papers). There is also one specific section summarizing the intermediate results of the EU Integrated Project ARUM aimed at adaptive production management, planning, and scheduling, which explores the latest principles in the domain (four papers). The last section is dedicated to the very hot field of smart grids, networks, and big data (five papers). This application area seems to have grown in importance in the last few years, because some of the results could be easily applied to industrial practice.

There were two invited talks specifically targeted toward HoloMAS 2015:

- Stamatis Karnouskos (SAP): Industrial Cyber-Physical Systems and Their Implications for Modern Enterprises
- Amro M. Farid (Masdar Institute of Science and Technology & MIT): Designing Multi-Agent Systems for Resilient Engineering Systems (the extended abstract is included in this volume)

In general, we are very pleased that the papers accepted for publication as well as the keynotes and surveys follow the main innovation trends in the field of holonic and multi-agent systems and display the current state of the art keeping the industrial orientation of the research in mind. Thus, HoloMAS 2015 reflected the progress in the field, but kept its original character and focus.

The HoloMAS 2015 conference represented another successful scientific event in the HoloMAS history and created highly motivating environment, challenging future research and fostering the integration of efforts in the field. This conference offered – as usual — information about the state of the art in the MAS industrial application field to specialists in neighboring research fields covered by the DEXA multi-conference event.

We are very grateful to the DEXA Association for providing us with this excellent opportunity to organize the HoloMAS 2015 conference within the DEXA event. We would like to express many thanks to Gabriela Wagner and Jitka Seguin for all their organizational efforts, which were of key importance for the success of our conference.

We would like to thank to IEEE SMC Society, and especially the Technical Committees on Distributed Intelligent Systems and on Cybernetics for Intelligent Industrial Systems of this Society, for their technical contributions.

June 2015

Vladimír Mařík
Arnd Schirrmann
Damien Trentesaux
Pavel Vrba

HoloMAS 2015

7th International Conference on

Industrial Applications of Holonic and Multi-Agent Systems

Valencia, Spain, September 2–3, 2015

Conference Co-chairs

Vladimír Mařík	Czech Technical University in Prague, Czech Republic
Arnd Schirrmann	Airbus Group Innovations, Germany
Damien Trentesaux	University of Valenciennes and Hainaut-Cambresis, France
Pavel Vrba	Czech Technical University in Prague, Czech Republic

Program Committee

José A. Barata	Universidade Nova de Lisboa, Portugal
Theodor Borangiu	University Politehnica of Bucharest, Romania
Vicent Botti	Universitat Politècnica de València, Spain
Robert W. Brennan	University of Calgary, Canada
Patrikakis Charalampos	Technological Education Institute of Piraeus, Greece
Armando W. Colombo	University of Applied Sciences Emden - Schneider Electric, Germany
Adriana Giret	Universitat Politècnica de València, Spain
William A. Gruver	Simon Fraser University, Canada
Kenwood H. Hall	Rockwell Automation, USA
Toshiya Kaihara	Kobe University, Japan
Martin Klíma	Certicon, a.s., Czech Republic
Kari Koskinen	Aalto University, Finland
Jose Luis Martinez Lastra	Tampere University of Technology, Finland
Paulo Leitão	Polytechnic Institute of Bragança, Portugal
Wilfried Lepuschitz	Practical Robotics Institute Austria, Austria
Bjorn Madsen	Multi Agent Technology Ltd., London, UK
César A. Marín	University of Manchester, UK
Luis M. Camarinha-Matos	Universidade Nova de Lisboa, Portugal
Francisco Maturana	Rockwell Automation, USA
Duncan McFarlane	Cambridge University, UK
Nikolay Mehandjiev	University of Manchester, UK
Lars Moench	University of Hagen, Germany
Ngoc Thanh Nguyen	Wroclaw University of Technology, Poland
Marek Obitko	Rockwell Automation, Czech Republic

Stuart Rubin	SSC Pacific, San Diego, USA
Ilkka Seilonen	Aalto University, Finland
Paulo Shakarian	Arizona State University, USA
Petr O. Skobelev	Rocket and Space Corporation "Energia," Russia
Alexander Smirnov	SPIIRAS, Russia
Václav Snášel	Technical University of Ostrava, Czech Republic
Thomas Strasser	AIT Austrian Institute of Technology, Austria
Pavel Tichý	Rockwell Automation, Czech Republic
Valeriy Vyatkin	Lulea University of Technology, Sweden
Alois Zoitl	fortiss, Germany

Organizing Committee

Jitka Seguin	Czech Technical University in Prague, Czech Republic
Gabriela Wagner	DEXA Society, Austria

Contents

Invited Talk

Designing Multi-agent Systems for Resilient Engineering Systems   3
   Amro M. Farid

Surveys

Software Engineering Methods for Intelligent Manufacturing Systems:
A Comparative Survey.   11
   Adriana Giret and Damien Trentesaux

A Survey on Standards and Ontologies for Process Automation   22
   Wilfried Lepuschitz, Alvaro Lobato-Jimenez, Emilian Axinia,
   and Munir Merdan

Conceptual Design and Validation

From Conception to Implementation of Reconfigurable and Distributed
Manufacturing Control System   35
   Robson Marinho da Silva, Diolino J. Santos Filho, and Paulo E. Miyagi

The Designing Process for a HMES Used for the Management
of Radiopharmaceuticals Production   47
   Andrei-Octavian Silisteanu

Behavioural Validation of the ADACOR^2 Self-organized Holonic
Multi-agent Manufacturing System   59
   José Barbosa, Paulo Leitão, Emmanuel Adam, and Damien Trentesaux

Digital Factories and Manufacturing Control Systems

A Service-Oriented Architecture Implementation in the Digital Factory
of the University.   73
   Jeffrey Wermann, Eduardo Cardoso Moraes,
   and Armando Walter Colombo

A Volatile Knowledge Approach to Improve the Autonomy of Holons:
Application to a Flexible Job Shop Manufacturing System   84
   Emmanuel Adam

Invariant-Based Production Control Reviewed: Mixing Hierarchical
and Heterarchical Control in Flexible Job Shop Environments   96
    Henning Blunck and Julia Bendul

An Approach for Characterizing the Operating Modes in Dynamic Hybrid
Control Architectures.   108
    Jose Fernando Jimenez, Abdelghani Bekrar, Damien Trentesaux,
    and Paulo Leitão

Interacting Holons in Evolvable Execution Systems: The NEU Protocol.   120
    Paul Valckenaers and Patrick A. De Mazière

ARUM: Adaptive Production Management

Adaptive Production Management Using a Service-Based Platform   133
    Usman Wajid, Vadim Chepegin, Despina T. Meridou,
    Maria-Eleftheria Ch. Papadopoulou, and José Barbosa

Agent-Based Production Scheduling for Aircraft Manufacturing Ramp-up . . .   145
    Pavel Vrba, Ondřej Harcuba, Martin Klíma, and Vladimír Mařík

Adaptive Production Management for Small-Lot Enterprise   157
    Daria Kazanskaia, Yaroslav Shepilov, and Bjorn Madsen

Approach to the Solution of Aerospace Product Lifecycle Management
Problem Based on Network-Centric Principles   169
    P.O. Skobelev, O.I. Lakhin, A.S. Polnikov, and E.V. Simonova

Smart Grids, Complex Networks and Big Data

Towards a Design Methodology for Agent-Based Automation of Smart
Grid   181
    Gulnara Zhabelova and Valeriy Vyatkin

An Open Source-Based and Standard-Compliant Smart Grid Laboratory
Automation System: The AIT SmartEST Approach.   195
    Filip Andrén, Georg Lauss, Roland Bründlinger, Philipp Svec,
    and Thomas Strasser

Applying Agents and Genetic Algorithms for Reducing Peak Consumption
in District Heating.   206
    Petr Kadera and Martin Macaš

Big Data Semantics in Industry 4.0   217
    Marek Obitko and Václav Jirkovský

Agent Simulation of Traffic Optimisation with the Use of Complex
Networks Analysis and Voting   230
    Jarosław Koźlak and Małgorzata Żabińska

Author Index   243

Invited Talk

Designing Multi-agent Systems
for Resilient Engineering Systems

Amro M. Farid[✉]

MIT Mechanical Engineering Department, Cambridge, MA, USA
amfarid@mit.edu

Abstract. Our modern life has grown to depend on many and nearly ubiquitous large complex engineering systems. Many disciplines now seemingly ask the same question: "In the face of assumed disruption, to what degree will these systems continue to perform and when will they bounce back to normal operation". This presentation argues that multi-agent systems (MAS), as decentralized and intelligent control systems, have an indispensable role to play in enabling the overall resilience of the combined cyber-physical engineering system. To that effect, it first draws from recently published work that provides measures of resilience for large flexible engineering systems. These measures define the system's actual & latent resilience as it goes through physical disruptions. The role of a multi-agent system is then introduced so as to intelligently bring about reconfigurations that restore the system performance back to its original level. Naturally, the implementation of such a multi-agent system requires a distributed architecture. To this effect, the recent literature has used the quantitative resilience measures to distill a set of principles that design resilience into the multi-agent system. These are specifically discussed in the context of production systems and power grids. The presentation concludes with several avenues for advancing multi-agent systems to support resilient engineering systems.

1 Introduction

Our modern life has grown to depend on many and nearly ubiquitous large complex engineering systems [24]. Transportation, water distribution, electric power, natural gas, healthcare, manufacturing and food supply are but a few. These systems are characterized by an intricate web of interactions within themselves [17] but also between each other [25]. Our heavy reliance on these systems coupled with a growing recognition that disruptions and failures; be they natural or man-made; unintentional or malicious; are inevitable. Therefore, in recent years, many disciplines have seemingly come to ask the same question: "How *resilient* are these systems?" Said differently, in the face of assumed disruption, to what degree will these systems continue to perform and when will they be able to bounce back to normal operation [21]. Furthermore, the major disruptions of 9/11, the 2003 Northeastern Blackout, and Hurricanes Katrina and Sandy have caused numerous agencies [3, 14, 28] to make resilient engineering systems a policy goal.

© Springer International Publishing Switzerland 2015
V. Mařík et al. (Eds.): HoloMAS 2015, LNAI 9266, pp. 3–8, 2015.
DOI: 10.1007/978-3-319-22867-9_1

2   Static Resilience Measures in Engineering Systems

Given the growing importance of designing resilient engineering systems, the literature has stressed the need for formal quantitative definitions, frameworks and measures [3–5,13,16,21,23,29,30]. While many works measure resilience as an output in response to a disruption as an input, ultimately such approaches effectively treat the physical system as a "black-box" that does not necessarily shed light as to *why* a particular disruption leads to a particular change in performance[]. Many other works approach resilience from a graph theoretic perspective where nodes represent physical locations and edges represent their interconnections [1,2,6,15,18–20,22,26,27,30]. And yet such works neglect the natural functional *heterogeneity* found in many engineering systems. More recently, a set of static resiliece measures have been developed on the basis of Axiomatic Design for Large Flexible Engineering Systems (LFES) where the system function and form are succinctly captured in a LFES knowledge base [8,9,11]. These measures explicitly consider the presence of sequence dependent and sequence independent constraints, and the possibility of multi-valued service paths. They also distinguish between actual and latent resilience where the former considers the drop in performance due to a disruption and the latter measures how the overall system "health" has degraded. In all, these resilience measures allow for heterogeneous function, form, and operands to support a wide class of engineering systems.

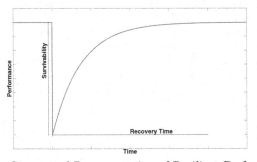

Fig. 1. Conceptual Representation of Resilient Performance

3   Enabling Dynamic Resilience with Multi-agent Systems

Once resilience measures for the physical engineering system have been established, the attention shifts to enabling grater dynamic resilience with multi-agent systems. Such a MAS constitutes a decentralized control system. It is decentralized so to continue operation as one or more parts of the system suffer disruption. It is intelligent in that it can make decisions to reorganize and reconfigure the physical system in response to measurements of system structure *and* performance. Consequently, the MAS (like other control systems) must be designed specifically for the restrictions imposed by the structure and behavior of the physical system.

4   Multi-agent System Design Principles

From this foundation of resilience measurement and the specific characteristics of physical systems that multi-agent system design principles may be developed. The recent literature has followed such a process and provides such design principles for multi-agent systems in power systems [7,10] and production systems [12]. As both systems may be classified as large flexible engineering systems, they have several design principles in common (restated here with application neutral terminology).

Principle 1. *Application of Independence Axiom: The agent architecture must be explicitly described in terms of the physical system's structural degrees of freedom.*

Principle 2. *Existence of Physical Agents: As a decision-making/control system, the multi-agent system must maintain a 1-to-1 relationship with the set of physical capabilities that* **exist** *in the system.*

Principle 3. *Functional Heterogeneity: The structural degrees of freedom within the agent architecture must respect the heterogeneity of capabilities found within the physical system be they stochastic or deterministic processes or their various types: transformation or transportation.*

Principle 4. *Physical Aggregation: The agent architecture must reflect the physical aggregation of the objects that they represent.*

Principle 5. *Availability: The agent architecture must explicitly model the potential for sequence independent constraints that impede the availability of any given structural degree of freedom.*

Principle 6. *Interaction: The agent architecture must contain agent interactions along the minimal set of physical sequence-dependent constraints (i.e. nearest neighbor interactions).*

Principle 7. *Maximum Reconfiguration Potential: Aside from the minimal set of physical sequence-dependent constraints, the agent architecture should avoid introducing any further agent interactions (which may impose further constraints).*

Principle 8. *Scope of Physical Agents: Agents' scope and boundaries should be aligned with their corresponding physical resources and their associated structural degrees of freedom.*

Principle 9. *Encapsulation: Physical system information should be placed in the agent corresponding to the physical entity that it describes.*

These nine design principles are common to production and power systems and are likely to find application in other large flexible engineering systems. That said, each type of LFES has its unique characteristics that customize the MAS design. In production systems, the system operands (i.e. the products & delivered services) are generally quite complex in their own right and require significant informatic description. Managing such heterogeneous information either within the product (in the form of "intelligent products") or amongst the resources that operate on them is a central challenge and directly affects system reconfiguration. Therefore, for production systems, an additional principle is added:

Principle 10. *Reconfiguration Method: The same reconfiguration process can require significantly different effort (measured in time, cost, or energy) depending on the method used to conduct the reconfiguration (and not just the reconfigured resources).*

Power systems are distinguished by the many time scales in their dynamics. Naturally, power system operation & control techniques are specifically tailored to one or more of these time scales. Therefore, for power systems, several MAS design principles are added to address these dynamic characteristics:

Principle 11. *Scope of Physical System Model & Decision Making: The physical system model must describe the physical system behavior at all time scales for which resilient decision-making/control is required. These time scales are described by characteristic frequencies for continuous dynamics and characteristic times for discrete (pseudo-steady-state) processes.*

Principle 12. *Temporal Scope of Execution Agent/Real-time Controller: The characteristic frequencies in the physical system model must be controlled by at least one execution agent/real-time controller capable of making decisions 5x faster than the fastest characteristic frequency.*

Principle 13. *Temporal Scope of Coordination Agent: A coordination agent may not take decisions any faster than 5x slower than the slowest characteristic frequency in the physical system model.*

Principle 14. *Equivalence of Agent Hierarchy & Time Scale Separation: If the physical system model has two or more characteristic frequencies or times that are (mathematically proven or practically assumed to be) independent then the associated agent may be divided into an equal number of hierarchical agents each responsible for decision-making/control for the associated characteristic frequency or time.*

Together, these MAS design principles can help to support resilience in large complex engineering systems. The MAS itself is decentralized and therefore should be able to continue operation in spite of disruption,

5   Conclusion and Future Work

This extended abstract summarizes the presentation given at HoloMAS 2015 where it is further detailed with the underlying mathematics and practical examples. In all, the presentation draws together several recent research contributions in resilience measurement and multi-agent system design. Because the design principles are based upon the resilience measures, they directly support quantitatively driven design decisions as the MAS is developed and is likely to support resilience in many types of complex engineering systems. The production and power system cases further illustrate the need for methods to customize MAS design to their respective application domain.

References

1. Albert, R., Jeong, H., Barabasi, A.L.: Error and attack tolerance of complex networks. Nature **406**(6794), 378–382 (2000)
2. Ash, J., Newth, D.: Optimizing complex networks for resilience against cascading failure. Physica A: Statistical Mechanics and its Applications **380**, 673–683 (2007)
3. Ayyub, B.M.: Systems resilience for multihazard environments: Definition, metrics, and valuation for decision making. Risk Analysis, 1–16 (2013)
4. Barker, K., Ramirez-Marquez, J.E., Rocco, C.M.: Resilience-based network component importance measures. Reliability Engineering and System Safety **117**, 89–97 (2013)
5. Bhamra, R., Dani, S., Burnard, K.: Resilience: the concept, a literature review and future directions. International Journal of Production Research **49**(18), 5375–5393 (2011)
6. Colbourn, C.: Network Resilience. SIAM Journal on Algebraic Discrete Methods **8**(3), 404–409 (1987)
7. Farid, A.M.: Multi-agent system design principles for resilient operation of future power systems. In: IEEE International Workshop on Intelligent Energy Systems, San Diego, CA, pp. 1–7 (2014)
8. Farid, A.M.: Static resilience of large flexible engineering systems : part I - axiomatic design model. In: 4th International Engineering Systems Symposium, Hoboken, N.J., pp. 1–8 (2014)
9. Farid, A.M.: Static resilience of large flexible engineering systems : part II - axiomatic design measures. In: 4th International Engineering Systems Symposium, Hoboken, N.J., pp. 1–8 (2014)
10. Farid, A.M.: Multi-Agent System Design Principles for Resilient Coordination & Control of Future Power Systems. Intelligent Industrial Systems **1**(1), 1–9 (2015). (in press)
11. Farid, A.M.: Static Resilience of Large Flexible Engineering Systems : Axiomatic Design Model and Measures. IEEE Systems Journal **1**(1), 1–15 (2015). (in press)
12. Farid, A.M., Ribeiro, L.: An axiomatic design of a multi-agent reconfigurable manufacturing system architecture. In: International Conference on Axiomatic Design, Lisbon, Portugal, pp. 1–8 (2014)
13. Francis, R., Bekera, B.: A metric and frameworks for resilience analysis of engineered and infrastructure systems. Reliability Engineering and System Safety **121**, 90–103 (2014)
14. Haimes, Y.Y., Crowther, K., Horowitz, B.M.: Homeland security preparedness: Balancing protection with resilience in emergent systems. Systems Engineering **11**(4), 287–308 (2008)
15. Harary, F., Hayes, J.P.: Edge fault tolerance in graphs. Networks **23**(2), 135–142 (1993)

16. Henry, D., Ramirez-Marquez, J.E.: Generic metrics and quantitative approaches for system resilience as a function of time. Reliability Engineering and System Safety **99**, 114–122 (2012)
17. Hollnagel, E., Woods, D.D., Leveson, N.: Resilience Engineering: Concepts and Precepts, kindle edi edn. Ashgate Publishing Limited, Aldershot (2006)
18. Holme, P., Kim, B.J., Yoon, C.N., Han, S.K.: Attack vulnerability of complex networks. Physical Review E (Statistical, Nonlinear, and Soft Matter Physics) **65**(5), 56101–56109 (2002)
19. Hwang, F.K., Najjar, W., Gaudiot, J.L.: Comments on Network resilience: a measure of network fault tolerance [and reply]. IEEE Transactions on Computers **43**(12), 1451–1453 (1994)
20. Ip, W.H., Wang, D.: Resilience and Friability of Transportation Networks: Evaluation, Analysis and Optimization. IEEE Systems Journal **5**(2), 189–198 (2011)
21. Madni, A.M., Jackson, S.: Towards a conceptual framework for resilience engineering. IEEE Systems Journal **3**(2), 181–191 (2009)
22. Najjar, W., Gaudiot, J.L.: Network resilience: a measure of network fault tolerance. IEEE Transactions on Computers **39**(2), 174–181 (1990)
23. Pant, R., Barker, K., Zobel, C.W.: Static and dynamic metrics of economic resilience for interdependent infrastructure and industry sectors. Reliability Engineering & System Safety **125**(92–102) (2013)
24. Reed, D.A., Kapur, K.C., Christie, R.D.: Methodology for assessing the resilience of networked infrastructure. IEEE Systems Journal **3**(2), 174–180 (2009)
25. Rinaldi, S.M., Peerenboom, J.P., Kelly, T.K.: Identifying, understanding, and analyzing critical infrastructure interdependencies. IEEE Control Systems **21**(6), 11–25 (2001)
26. Rosenkrantz, D.J., Goel, S., Ravi, S.S., Gangolly, J.: Resilience Metrics for Service-Oriented Networks: A Service Allocation Approach. IEEE Transactions on Services Computing **2**(3), 183–196 (2009)
27. Salles, R.M., Marino Jr., D.A.: Strategies and Metric for Resilience in Computer Networks. Computer Journal **55**(6), 728–739 (2012)
28. The White House: Office of the Press Secretary: Presidential Policy Directive: Critical Infrastructure Security and Resilience (PPD-21). Tech. rep., The White House, Washington, D.C. United states (2013)
29. VanBreda, A.D.: Resilience Theory : A Literature Review by. Tech. Rep. October, Military Psychological Institute, Pretoria, South Africa (2001)
30. Whitson, J.C., Ramirez-Marquez, J.E.: Resiliency as a component importance measure in network reliability. Reliability Engineering & System Safety **94**(10), 1685–1693 (2009)

Surveys

Software Engineering Methods for Intelligent Manufacturing Systems: A Comparative Survey

Adriana Giret[1]([✉]) and Damien Trentesaux[2]

[1] Dpto. Sistemas Informáticos y Computación,
Universidad Politécnica de Valencia, Valencia, Spain
agiret@dsic.upv.es
[2] LAMIH UMR CNRS 8201, University of Valenciennes
and Hainaut-Cambrésis, 59313 Valenciennes, France

Abstract. In order to survive, manufacturing systems need to adapt themselves at an ever-increasing pace to incorporate new technology, new products, new organizational structures, etc. Distributed intelligent manufacturing systems are very large and complex systems that require appropriate technologies and tools, not only to operate but also to be designed. In the specialized literature there is a large number of approaches to develop this kind of systems, but not all of them are suitable to deal with the requirements of the new manufacturing era. In this paper we make a deep analysis of the different approaches reported in the field and make a comprehensive analysis on the appropriateness of every approach for coping with the requirements of today's Intelligent Manufacturing Systems.

Keywords: Intelligent manufacturing system · Design · Engineering methodologies

1 Introduction

The manufacturers success is no more measured by their ability to cost-effectively produce a single product, success now seems to be measured in terms of flexibility, agility and versatility. But manufacturing systems are often very large-scale and complex systems [9]. Despite this complexity, appropriate technologies and tools are required to make them operate efficiently to meet the introduced manufacturer' success. An approach consists in designing distributed intelligent manufacturing system that breaks this complex system into smaller manageable systems. This approach has motivated researchers in academia and industry to create and exploit new production paradigms on the basis of autonomy and co-operation because both concepts are necessary to create flexible behaviour and thus to adapt to the changing production conditions. Distributed intelligent manufacturing systems (or for short Intelligent Manufacturing Systems - IMS), and Holonic Manufacturing Systems (HMS) are considered as important approaches for developing industrial control systems. In the specialized literature

© Springer International Publishing Switzerland 2015
V. Mařík et al. (Eds.): HoloMAS 2015, LNAI 9266, pp. 11–21, 2015.
DOI: 10.1007/978-3-319-22867-9_2

there is a large number of approaches to develop this kind of systems, but not all of them are suitable to deal with the requirements of the new manufacturing era. In this paper we make a deep analysis of the different approaches reported in the field and make a comprehensive analysis on the appropriateness of every approach for coping with the requirements of today's IMSs.

Section 2 overviews the features of IMSs, identifying the key technologies used in the field. Section 3 identifies the modelling requirements for IMS that will guide the analysis presented in Section 4. Section 5 summarizes the analysis with a discussion. Finally some conclusions are drawn.

2   Intelligent Manufacturing Systems

It is well known that manufacturing systems are large-scale and complex systems for a number of operational and structural reasons [9]. This complexity makes such systems difficult to control and predict[1]. The rapidly changing needs and opportunities of todays global market forces to fully integrated enterprises to be replaced by business networks in which each participant provides others with specialized manufacturing services [24]. Probably the most important reason for a collaborative environment and the need to interconnect different systems is that the market has extended and became global. This means that a new kind of integration is required with third party partners that are not even known in advance or that are subject to change. Providing personalized, high-quality and low-cost product has brought challenges to the traditional production paradigm.

Techniques from Artificial Intelligence have already been used in Intelligent Manufacturing for more than twenty years. However, the recent developments in multi-agent systems have brought new and interesting possibilities. The holonic manufacturing approach (HMS) for IMS is based on the concept of *"holonic systems"*, developed by Arthur Koestler [16]. In the HMS field the manufacturing system is viewed as consisting of autonomous modules (holons/agents) with distributed control. For an extensive review of the different theoretical developments and applications of industrial agents see [19].

Over the last few years, new technologies are revolutionizing the way manufacturing and supply chain management are implemented. The convergence of Internet and manufacturing control systems provides the basis for the creation of a new generation of computing solutions that can dramatically improve the responsiveness of organizations to better communicate with their customer and suppliers. This new approach is called Service Oriented Manufacturing Systems. This new situation makes possible the rapid and easy on-demand creation of virtual manufacturing enterprises (open manufacturing systems) made up of different manufacturing partners that collaborate by means of services in order to fulfill the customer needs. Moreover, the areas of Service Oriented Architecture

---

[1] In order to coupe with the complexity of manufacturing systems, researchers and practitioners have used successfully the "divide and concur" approach in which the large system is decomposed into smaller and simpler components that are more easily manageable reducing the overall system complexity.

(SoA)/Service Oriented Computing (SoC) and Multi-agent Systems (MAS) are getting closer and closer, this fact leads to think on these two technologies as good candidates to achieve the requirements of the factories of the future.

3 Modeling Requirements for Intelligent Manufacturing Systems

3.1 Functional Requirements

Manufacturing control systems are large-scale complex systems designed to carry out a clearly defined task in a standardized and well structured environment. Although manufacturing processes undergo several changes and disturbances, the levels of uncertainty and unpredictability are not comparable to spacial, traffic, or service application systems.

The modules, or entities (agents/holons), which implement the control of these systems should cooperate in order to achieve the global manufacturing objectives. With regard to these objectives, a module never rejects the cooperation of another module deliberately. It only rejects their execution, when the actions requested are impossible or strongly unfavorable for the manufacturing process. In this sense, manufacturing entities are semi-autonomous. In order to implement semi-autonomous entities the specialized literature has used agent technology (made up by autonomous entities) together with some engineering constraints/requirements in order to have semi-autonomous components. The engineering constraints used successfully, by researchers and practitioners, to restrict the full autonomous execution of agents are: organization regulations (such as: master-slave and/or client-server relationships, explicit norms/regulations that restrict the scope of the agents' actions), temporal hierarchical structures and communication constraints, among others. These issues impose the following functional requirement.

(R1): Manufacturing control systems require autonomous entities to be organized in hierarchical and heterarchical structures.

The second requirement is related to the kind of behavior that the control unit at factory level should exhibit. Manufacturing control units are continually handling a high number of repeated events which are known, but unpredictable. This flow of events should be handled in an effective way and with temporal constraints. The handling of the events can consequently be fixed a-priori by routines, while the beginning and execution of these routines should be performed in real-time. The set of events and their occurrence patterns change over time.

(R2): Manufacturing control units require routine-based behavior which is both effective and timely [4].

The third requirement is related with standardization. The standardization is pointed out by industry as a major challenge for the industrial acceptance of any technology. The large number of different components, different layers, different communication and controlling protocols, impose this requirement to any technology used in a manufacturing control system.

(R3): Manufacturing control systems require standardized structures, standardized functional units that can be connected to the different levels in the system by means of standardized interfaces and communication protocols [19].

The fourth requirement is related with sustainability. Sustainability in manufacturing systems is an urgent requirement for todays manufacturing companies due to several established and emerging causes: environmental concerns, diminishing non-renewable resources, stricter legislation and inflated energy costs, increasing consumer preference for environmentally friendly products, etc. Efforts to develop sustainable manufacturing systems must consider issues at all relevant levels (product, process, and system), and not just one or more of these in isolation. The information systems that manage and control the different levels in manufacturing systems must take into account sustainability issues of the solutions proposed, executed and controlled.

(R4): Manufacturing control systems require sustainable production processes [26].

3.2   Software Engineering Requirements

Besides functional requirements, any control system (which is used in a manufacturing environment) should satisfy general industrial standards (as is stated by *R3*). These standards specify, among other things, requirements for reliability, fault tolerance, diagnosis, and maintenance. The control systems should achieve certain reliability levels which guarantee a continuous operation. This is also true for the control software. However, product dependability is only achieved if the software development process is carried out following an engineering methodology, instead of developing it in an ad-hoc way with no engineering methods or techniques.

From fundamental Software Engineering principles the following requirements are derived:

(R5): Programming methods should provide data and process encapsulation[2].

(R6): Control programs should have clear semantics.

---

[2] It is important to point out that this requirement is fulfilled automatically by almost all of todays' programming languages, since the great majority of them follows a class-based approach. This fact is demonstrated in the analysis we present in next section, see Table 1. Nevertheless, it is important to keep this requirement as an important one when developing complex systems.

Specialized literature in the field of intelligent manufacturing basically takes two approaches to problem decomposition. (i) Physical decomposition (the most obvious): agents are used to represent the entities of the physical world, such as workers, machines, tools, schedules, products, orders, attributes and operations. This approach defines different sets of state variables that should be handled by the agents in an efficient way and with a limited number of interactions. However, with this approach a great number of agents per resources are required. A common example of this approach is the use of order agents and machine agents for the planning and scheduling of manufacturing [8]. (ii) In the functional decomposition approach the agents are used for encapsulating functionalities such as work order acquisition, planning, scheduling, material handling, logistic, etc. In this approach the agents do not have an explicit relationship with the physical entities. Moreover, in last recent years, the Service Oriented Manufacturing System research community tackled the problem decomposition in terms of services. In this approach any manufacturing ability that may/or may not be associated with a resource is virtualized as a service and made available to consumers by means of a new computation paradigm, Cloud Computing. In it Service Oriented Architectures (SoA) are used to implement the computational components to execute the system. From these approaches the following requirement is derived.

(R7): A methodology for IMS should lead straight-forward translation from the control task on a factory resource or factory function to autonomous entities [15], that can encapsulate and provide to consumers their functionalities and abilities as services [18].

In the field of intelligent manufacturing a kind of "loosely" hierarchical aggregation for real world systems has been recognized. These systems have to remain readable while they are expanded into a wide range of temporal and spatial scales. For example, a modern automobile factory, incorporates hundreds of thousands of individual mechanisms (each of which can be an agent) into hundreds of machines which are grouped into dozens or more production lines. Engineers can design, build, and operate such complex systems by shifting from the mechanism, to the machine or to the production line (depending on the problem at hand) and by recognizing the higher-level agents as aggregations of lower-level agents. This implies the following requirement:

(R8): A methodology for IMS should define a development process which is guided by abstraction levels, and should also provide modeling artifacts, tools and guidelines to manage this process.

The traditional methods and techniques for manufacturing system modeling, such as CIM, are mainly based on a top-down approach. The user's requirements and the global conceptual design constitute the whole set of modeling constraints. With these approaches very rigid hierarchical architectures are built [15]. On the other hand, traditionally IMS were characterized as being bottom-up. Nevertheless, in order to coupe with the complexity of the distributed system made up by a network of intelligent entities, IMS modeling requires a mixed development process, bottom-up and top-down depending on the level being modeled. It is not necessary to define the whole set of constraints at the beginning. A mixed development process allows the generation of reconfigurable and scalable architectures. This characteristic implies the following requirement.

(R9): A methodology for IMS should define a mixed top-down and bottom-up development process.

Finally the following requirement is inferred from the characteristics of "new manufacturing".

(R10): A methodology for IMS should integrate the entire range of manufacturing activities (from order booking through design, production, and marketing) to model the agile manufacturing enterprise [15].

Taking these requirements into account we will now analyze the different methodologies reported in the specialized literature. The goal of this study is to determine to what extend these methodologies take into account the requirements for modeling IMS. Firstly, we present a brief summary of the different methodologies (more details can be found in specialized literature). Finally, we will make a comparative summary based on the requirements we have cited in this section.

4   Methodologies for Engineering Intelligent Manufacturing Systems

In IMS specialized literature there are few studies on IMS development methods. There is a recognized need, however, for design methodologies which provide clear, specific and unambiguous development processes and guidelines [22]. In this section we summarize the most relevant approaches of the field. The methods presented in this section deals with the development of systems that are made up by intelligent entities, holons or agents.

The first proposals in the specialized literature were focused on the identification and specification of the agents/holons that made up the system. The first pioneering work is from Van Brussel et al. [27]. Most of the ideas proposed in this work where adopted by other approaches in the field. For example the method for the identification of agents in a manufacturing system of Ritter et al. [23]. Also, Colombo et al. [5] extended the approach of Petri Net based modeling [10] for the modeling of agent based manufacturing systems. Bussmann et al. [4] propose the methodology DACS (Methodology for the Design of Agent Based Manufacturing Control Systems), which, among other things, includes a specification of the manufacturing components to be controlled and their physical behavior. Leitão and Restivo in [20], attempt to formalize the structure and behavior of an IMS, combining UML notation for the static aspects of the system, and Petri Nets to model behavioral aspects. Another proposal is [11].

Here an agent organization is proposed for modeling each holon/holarchy. In [21] Martinez-Lastra and Colombo propose an engineering framework for simulation and visualization of agent societies in an IMS. In ANEMONA [13], the manufacturing system is specified by a top-down recursive analysis phase, followed by a bottom-up design stage to produce the system architecture. The Agent Development Environment (ADE) [29] is an integrated tool in which the user designs the templates of holonic agents from which automatic code is generated to implement the system.

Over the last few years the focus of the different proposed approaches where mainly targeted to service oriented manufacturing systems, reconfiguration, self-adaptation, sustainability, among others. In [24] the authors use agent-based service-oriented approaches for the business level of virtual enterprise cooperation. Shin et al. [25] propose a conceptual framework for self-evolutionary manufacturing system. Borangiu et al. [2] propose an engineering approach for intelligent manufacturing systems in which the system is characterized by a flow of active entities which run on a guided network. In [18] Leitão presents a Service Oriented MAS approach in order to engineer Service Oriented Manufacturing Systems. Autonomous Cooperative System (ACS) [28] is a platform of Rockwell Automation Logix controllers that enable the control system developers to run the holonic agents directly on PLCs. The method proposed in [6,7] aims to expand the scope of analysis beyond functional boundaries to apply sustainability at factory level. ROMAS [12] is a methodology that addresses the open problem of engineering normative open systems using the multi-agent paradigm. ANEMONA-S + Thomas [14] is a service oriented framework for the development of Service Oriented Intelligent Manufacturing Systems. Self-adaptation is a very important feature when engineering Intelligent Manufacturing Systems. In [17] the authors make an interesting review of the key aspects to take into account for self-adapting systems and also a large review of the state of the art in terms of models, methods and tools.

5   Comparative Overview

In this section we provide an analysis of the different approaches presented in previous section with respect to the requirements for engineering IMS described in Section 3. Table 1 shows the studied methodologies, indicating, for each one, how it copes with the different IMS modeling requirements.

The proposals of Ritter et al. [23], Colombo et al. [5], Leitão and Restivo [20] and Fischer et al. [11] only take into account a small phase of the development process of manufacturing systems. They are focused on the control of production processes and the identification of agents that will control the process. DACS [4] is focused on the controlling elements of the manufacturing system. The output of this method is an agent-based design, but it does not offer development guidelines or a tool for the implementation of the system. On the other hand, ANEMONA [3] is a complete and specific methodology for IMS that provides the designer clear and manufacturing-specific modeling guidelines.

Table 1. Development Methods and Modeling Requirements for IMS. Note: $\sqrt{}$ means complete coverage, $\sim$ means partial coverage, and S refers to services identification for $R7$

Method	Requirements									
	R1	R2	R3	R4	R5	R6	R7	R8	R9	R10
Van Brussel et al. Method	√	√			√	√	√	√	√	√
Ritter et al. Method	√				√	√	~			
Colombo et al. Method	√				√	√	~			
DACS	√				√	√	~			
Leitão and Restivo Method	√				√	√	√			
Fischer et al. Method	√				√	√	√			√
Martinez-Lastra and Colombo Method	√	√			√	√	√	√		√
ANEMONA	√	√			√	√	√	√	√	√
ADE	√	√			√	√	√	√		√
Shen et al. Framework	√	√			√	√	√S	√		√
Shin et al. Framework	√	√			√	√	√	√		√
Borangiu et al. Approach	√	√			√	√	√S	√		√
Leitão's SoMAS Approach	√	√	√		√	√	√S	√		√
ACS	√	√			√	√	√	√		√
Despeisse et al. Method		√		√	√	√				√
ROMAS	√	~			√	√	~ S		~	
ANEMONA-S + Thomas Framework	√	√	√		√	√	√S	√	√	√

The second group of analyzed approaches show a more complete coverage of the requirements. Nevertheless, there are some requirements ($R3$, $R4$ and $R9$) that need urgent attention since they are not considered by most of the approaches. From Table 1 we can conclude the following.

- Requirement $R3$ refers to the need in industrial environments to enforce the usage of standardization for implementation, communication protocols and control. This requirement is only taken into account by two approaches, the SoMAS proposal of Leitão and ANEMONA-S + Thomas. Both approaches define components and process guidelines to connect with layers of the ISA'95 standard [1].
- Requirement $R4$ is the sustainability requirement for manufacturing systems. Only one approach deals with this requirement. Nevertheless, in the specialized literature there is a large list of different proposals for specific isolated components/layers of a manufacturing system [26]. There is an urgent need to include sustainability aspects in the engineering methods of the whole manufacturing system in order to assure a correct and complete coverage of it through out the complete components and layers.
- Requirement $R9$ refers to mixed development methods (bottom-up and top-down). Almost all of the methods analyzed follow one approach or another without combining them, except for Van Brussel et al. method, ANEMONA, ANEMONA-S +Thomas which have mixed top-down and bottom-up development process.

6   Conclusions

The modeling of Intelligent Manufacturing Systems constitutes the fundamental interest of this paper. Intelligent Manufacturing Systems are large and complex systems that require appropriate methods and tools to design and operate. In the specialized literature we can find many proposal for engineering manufacturing systems. Nevertheless, some of them do not cope appropriately with the specific and complex requirements of this kind of systems. These facts motivated us to study the main development methods of the specialized research field, and to compare them in order to obtain a qualitative measure of the adequacy of each one for today's Intelligent Manufacturing System development. To carry out this comparison we have defined ten modeling requirements for the factories of the future. These requirements have been divided into two groups: functional requirements and software engineering requirements. The first ones refer to the type of programs that should be developed applying a methodology, while the second refers to the properties of the software engineering method. All of these requirements are specific for Intelligent Manufacturing Systems. We have carried out the comparison based on the ten modeling requirements and the different methods. The result is Table 1. From this analysis we can conclude that there are three requirements that are not well treated by most of the methods in the research field and are identified as open problems: (i) Standardization, (ii) Sustainability and (iii) Mixed top-down and bottom-up development process. From our review it was also faced that the maturity and the available quantity of theoretical and applied (specialized) models in IMS enable now researchers to address in depth methodological and software engineering aspects. A step beyond these existing developments would be to propose to the whole community a set of IMS-oriented software development kits and software tools as a basis for holonic and multi-agent control of manufacturing systems, including a robust performance evaluator based on the generic and dynamic emulation of various manufacturing systems to be tested. This would also speed-up the development of proof-of-concepts and help industrialists and researchers to design, test and evaluate different IMS-friendly strategies and control architectures. Indeed, evaluating a single control architecture on a single manufacturing system will never convince industrialists. Researchers must then now address methodological aspects and software engineering of IMS-oriented control systems.

References

1. Wbf Book. THE WBF BOOK SERIES-APPLYING ISA 95. Implementation Experiences. Wbf Book Series. World Batch Forum, Wbf, Momentum Press (2010)
2. Borangiu, T., Raileanu, S., Stocklosa, O., Tahon, C., Berger, T., Trentesaux, D.: Service oriented control framework for a holonic system characterized by a guided flow of entities. In: Borangiu, T., Thomas, A., Trentesaux, D. (eds.) SOHOMA 2011. SCI, vol. 402, pp. 21–34. Springer, Heidelberg (2012)
3. Botti, V., Giret, A.: ANEMONA: A Multi-agent Methodology for Holonic Manufacturing Systems. Springer Series in Advanced Manufacturing. Springer (2008)

4. Bussmann, S., Jennings, N., Wooldridge, M.: Multiagent Systems for Manufacturing Control. A design Methodology. Springer, Berlin (2004)
5. Colombo, A.W., Neubert, R., Sussmann, B.: A coloured Petri net-based approach towards a formal specification of agent-controlled production systems. In Proceedings of the IEEE International Conference on Systems, Man and Cybernetics, Tunisia (2002)
6. Despeisse, M., Ball, P.D., Evans, S., Levers, A.: Industrial ecology at factory level: a prototype methodology. Inst. Mech. Eng. Part B J. Eng. Manuf. **226**, 1648–1664 (2012)
7. Despeisse, M., Oates, M.R., Ball, P.D.: Sustainable manufacturing tactics and cross-functional factory modelling. Journal of Cleaner Production **42**, 31–41 (2013)
8. Duffie, N., Prabhu, V.: Real-time distributed scheduling of heterarchical manufacturing systems. Journal of Manufacturing Systems **13**(2), 94–107 (1994)
9. Efthymiou, K., Pagoropoulos, A., Papakostas, N., Mourtzis, D., Chryssolouris, G.: Manufacturing systems complexity review: challenges and outlook. In: (CIRP- CMS2012) 45th CIRP Conference on Manufacturing Systems, Procedia CIRP, vol. 3, pp. 644–649 (2012)
10. Feldmann, K., Colombo, A.W.: Material flow and control sequence specification of flexible production systems using coloured Petri nets. International Journal of Advanced Manufacturing Technology **14**, 760–774 (1998)
11. Fischer, K., Schillo, M., Siekmann, J.: Holonic multiagent systems: a foundation for the organisation of multiagent systems. In: Mařík, V., McFarlane, D., Valckenaers, P. (eds.) HoloMAS 2003. LNCS (LNAI), vol. 2744, pp. 71–80. Springer, Heidelberg (2003)
12. Garcia, E., Giret, A., Botti, V.: ROMAS A Multi-Agent Approach for Designing Normative Open Systems. Springer (2014)
13. Giret, A., Botti, V.: Engineering Holonic Manufacturing Systems. Computers in Industry **60**(6), 428–440 (2009)
14. Giret, A., Botti, V.: ANEMONA-S + thomas: a framework for developing service-oriented intelligent manufacturing systems. In: Borangiu, T., Thomas, A., Trentesaux, D. (eds.) Service Orientation in Holonic and Multi-agent Manufacturing. SCI, vol. 594, pp. 61–70. Springer, Heidelberg (2015)
15. HMS. HMS Requirements. http://hms.ifw.uni-hannover.de/ (accessed 2014)
16. Koestler, A.: The Ghost in the Machine. Arkana Books, London (1971)
17. Krupitzer, A.C., Roth, F.M., VanSyckel, S., Schiele, G., Becker, C.: A survey on engineering approaches for self-adaptive systems. Pervasive and Mobile Computing **17**, 184–206 (2015)
18. Leitão, P.: Towards self-organized service-oriented multi-agent systems. In: Borangiu, T., Thomas, A., Trentesaux, D. (eds.) Service Orientation in Holonic and Multi Agent. SCI, vol. 472, pp. 41–56. Springer, Heidelberg (2013)
19. Leitão, P., Marik, V., Vrba, P.: Past, Present, and Future of Industrial Agent Applications. IEEE Transactions on Industrial Informatics **9**(4), 2360–2372 (2013)
20. Leitão, P., Colombo, A.W., Restivo, F.: An approach to the formal specification of holonic control systems. In: Mařík, V., McFarlane, D., Valckenaers, P. (eds.) HoloMAS 2003. LNCS (LNAI), vol. 2744, pp. 59–70. Springer, Heidelberg (2003)
21. Martinez-Lastra, J.L., Colombo, A.W.: Engineering framework for agent-based manufacturing control. Engineering Applications of Artificial Intelligence **19**, 625–640 (2006)
22. McFarlane, D.C., Bussmann, S.: Holonic manufacturing control: rationales, developments and open issues. In: Deen, S.M. (ed.) Agent-Based Manufacturing. Advances in the Holonic Approach, pp. 301–326. Springer, Berlin (2003)

23. Ritter, A., Baum, W., Hopf, M., Westkamper, E.: Agentification for production systems. In: Second International Workshop on Integration of Specification Techniques for Applications in Engineering, Grenoble (2002)
24. Shen, W., Hao, Q., Wang, S., Li, Y., Ghenniwa, H.: An agent-based service-oriented integration architecture for collaborative intelligent manufacturing. Robotics and Computer-Integrated Manufacturing **23**(3), 315–325 (2007)
25. Shin, M., Muna, J., Jung, M.: Mself-evolution framework of manufacturing systems based on fractal organization. Computers & Industrial Engineering **56**, 1029–1039 (2009)
26. Trentesaux, D., Prabhu, V.: Sustainability in manufacturing operations scheduling: stakes, approaches and trends. In: Grabot, B., Vallespir, B., Gomes, S., Bouras, A., Kiritsis, D. (eds.) APMS 2014, Part II. IFIP AICT, vol. 439, pp. 106–113. Springer, Heidelberg (2014)
27. Van Brusel, H., Bongaerts, L., Wyns, J., Valckenaers, P., Ginderachter, P.V.: A Conceptual Framework for Holonic Manufacturing: Identification of Manufacturing Holons. Journal of Manufacturing Systems **18**(1), 35–52 (1999)
28. Vrba, P.: Review of industrial applications of multi-agent technologies. In: Borangiu, T., Thomas, A., Trentesaux, D. (eds.) Service Orientation in Holonic and Multi Agent. SCI, vol. 472, pp. 327–338. Springer, Heidelberg (2013)
29. Vrba, P., Tichy, P., Marik, V., Hall, K., Staron, R., Maturana, F., Kadera, P.: Rockwell Automation Holonic And Multi-agent Control Systems Compendium. IEEE Transactions on Systems, Man and Cybernetics, Part C: Applications and Reviews **41**(1) (2011)

A Survey on Standards and Ontologies for Process Automation

Wilfried Lepuschitz[1]([⊠]), Alvaro Lobato-Jimenez[1], Emilian Axinia[2], and Munir Merdan[1,3]

[1] Practical Robotics Institute Austria, Vienna, Austria
{Lepuschitz,Lobato,Merdan}@pria.at, Munir.Merdan@ait.ac.at
[2] COPA-DATA GmbH, Salzburg, Austria
EmilianA@copadata.com
[3] Austrian Institute of Technology, Vienna, Austria

Abstract. Agent technology and model-based engineering have proven potential in various prototypical implementations and academic environments but are not yet well accepted in industrial practice. However, it is evident that upcoming manufacturing systems need to integrate more rigorous foundations of semantics than currently applied data models and architectures but the conformance with industrial standards is crucial for their acceptance.

This paper presents a survey on standards and ontologies for the process domain carried out during the first phase of the project BatMAS, which aims at the integration of a system ontology for providing an extensive knowledge base. On the one hand, the knowledge base should be accessed by an agent-based system for batch process automation and on the other hand, it should provide access for various functionalities of a complete automation solution.

Keywords: Ontology · Standard · Batch process · Survey

1 Introduction

Domains such as the food and beverage industry are considered to be very dynamic due to changing market demands, product innovations, new types of packaging as well as new production technologies and equipment. Consequently, flexibility is a key requirement for production plants in such domain, even though the oftentimes historical development of production infrastructure results in a heterogeneous and complex automation landscape. Moreover, the applied industrial software used for process control, human machine interface, supervisory control and data acquisition (SCADA) systems, building automation, management information systems, etc., tends to be very diverse. Typically, the needed functionalities are implemented in various types of software solutions, ranging from pure "island"-solutions, focused on a certain service with limited extensibility, to packages offering interconnectivity, modularity and a development

© Springer International Publishing Switzerland 2015
V. Mařík et al. (Eds.): HoloMAS 2015, LNAI 9266, pp. 22–32, 2015.
DOI: 10.1007/978-3-319-22867-9_3

platform. Even though the same data sources from the production floor are commonly taken as basis, these different systems incorporate numerous information flows and functionalities, e.g. for data pre-processing, archiving, filtering, processing and presentation. Hence, any changes of the production infrastructure will require the update of the various functionalities in all these different systems, resulting in extensive engineering time and costs.

As a consequence, automation solutions need to evolve in response to the rapidly changing demands to new production processes but also to their growing complexity. Intelligent process control systems are required, which offer a direction towards solving the interoperability problems within the manufacturing life cycle as well as between software applications. In this context, introducing concepts such as artificial intelligence is regarded as promising for the process industry [1]. The aim of applying semantic and agent technologies is thus to increase the flexibility in industrial control [2]. Most reported agent-based approaches focus on discrete processes but agent technology is also well usable in the process domain according to the analysis presented in [3].

The general ideas of agent technology for increasing the flexibility of production systems already range back several decades [4]. Together with other approaches like ontologies for model-based engineering, they are part of the evolution into endeavors nowadays denoted as cyber-physical systems [5] or Industry 4.0 [6]. However, despite the potential benefits of applying such approaches, the industrial environment has not yet broadly adopted these actually old but finally feasible ideas. Concerning the application of model-based engineering, an obstacle is seen in the required data and information. Instead of having these available in standardized data formats involving an according formalization, they are mostly organized in classical office documents such as Word, PDF or Excel, which impedes automatic analysis processes or model creation [7].

Accordingly, upcoming manufacturing systems need to integrate more rigorous foundations of semantics than currently applied data models and architectures [8]. Besides, as standards represent a consensus on the semantics of terms and definitions in a domain, being compliant with them results in an increased reusability and applicability in industrial practice [9]. Generally, the issue of standardization is considered to be a major challenge concerning the industrial acceptance of semantic and agent technologies [10].

This paper gives an overview on standards and ontologies for the process domain. The literature research represents the first phase of the recently started project BatMAS (Batch Process Automation with an Ontology-driven Multi-Agent System) for not reinventing the wheel during the process of creating a knowledge base for the project's envisaged agent-based system and the typically attached functionalities of a complete automation solution.

This paper is structured as follows. Section 2 briefly introduces the project BatMAS and its requirement for a system ontology. An overview of relevant standards and their according Extensible Markup Language (XML) realizations is given in Section 3. Section 4 presents reported ontologies with a focus on the process domain. Finally, the paper is concluded in Section 5 with a summary.

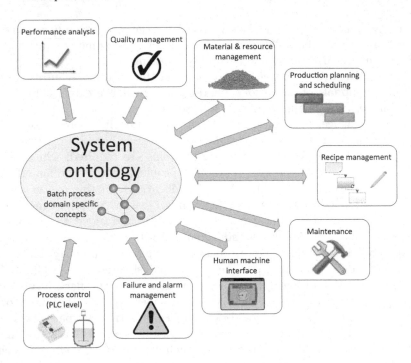

Fig. 1. BatMAS system architecture with a system model and an agent approach for batch process automation.

2 The Project BatMAS

The project BatMAS shall cover two aspects: a system ontology offering extensive data for various functionalities in conjunction with an agent-based approach for batch process automation. Moreover, for reducing the application engineering efforts of the agent system, control code generation mechanisms are investigated.

Fig. 1 presents the typical functionalities of a process control system on various control levels. They were provided by industrial project partner Copa-Data, which possesses broad experience regarding industrial control systems in various domains including batch process automation. Commonly, the shown functionalities rely on data sources located on the production floor and thus data stored in Programmable Logic Controllers (PLCs). However, for achieving flexible SCADA software that integrates these functionalities, it is of interest to develop an extensive and adaptable system model as a core data source with more flexibility than the typically rigid PLC data structures.

In general, the system ontology shall incorporate a representation of the batch process domain concepts. The aim is to achieve an extensive semantic data model for vertical and horizontal data integration and interoperability between the various physical and virtual components. Moreover, it shall represent a universal and consistent data structure to be accessed by typical functionalities and services such as performance analysis or recipe management besides from providing data also in an understandable format for human operators. The project Bat-MAS is based on previously carried out research on agent technology for the batch process domain [11,12] but shall enhance the concepts concerning compliance towards industrial standards as well as applicability and integration in engineering processes and commercial tools.

3   Standards for Process Automation

A range of industrial standards exists, which represent a consensus on the semantics of terms and definitions covering various levels and scopes of industrial automation. In the following, relevant standards for process automation and their realizations in XML are presented.

The standard IEC 61512 [13], based on ANSI/ISA-88 Batch Control, introduces a framework for the specification of requirements for the batch process domain and for their translation into application software. IEC 61512 provides reference models and structures as well as definitions concerning processes (process model), physical equipment (physical model) and control software (procedural control model) as well as recipes in the domain of process automation.

BatchML [14] is an XML implementation of ANSI/ISA-88. It consists of a set of XML schemas using the XML Schema language (XSD) that implement the models and terminology of the standard. It provides a set of type and element definitions such as master recipes, control recipes, recipe building blocks, equipment elements, batch list, and enumeration sets.

Based on ANSI/ISA-95, the multi-part standard IEC 62264 [15] describes an information exchange framework for the integration of enterprise-control systems aiming to achieve the implementation of enterprise systems and control systems that interoperate and easily integrate. Part 1 focuses on the characterization of hierarchical models and terminology in the operational management and control domain claiming to improve the communication between mentioned entities. On this basis, the scope of Part 2 is the definition of object models and attributes of the exchanged information including personnel, equipment, physical assets, materials, and process segment information. A generic specification of the mentioned models assures the applicability in a wide field of domains.

As an implementation of ANSI/ISA-95, MESA introduced Business To Manufacturing Markup Language (B2MML) [16]. It consists of a set of XML schemas using XML Schema language (XSD) that implement the data models described in the ISA-95 standard.

The standard ISO 15926 [17] titled "Industrial automation systems and integration – Integration of life-cycle data for process plants including oil and gas production facilities" describes a generic data model and reference data library for process plants. Its seven parts cover the classification of data and information, plant or facility reference data, a format for information exchange as well as query and transfer protocols. The reference data library (RDL) is a publicly maintained class collection comprising technical equipment items such as pipes, instruments, buildings, or activities used in process facilities.

With XMpLant [18], an ISO 15926 complying framework was introduced, that includes an XML schema implementing the classes defined in the reference data library. Comprising interfaces to and from the major process plant applications it enables the integration of information across these applications. This integration is accomplished by the use of a mapping subsystem which defines the relationships between external and ISO 15926 inherent models.

The standard IEC 62424 [19] defines a graphical representation of process plants in pipe and instrumentation (P&I) diagrams focusing on the functional requirements instead of the technical realization, as well as a format for data exchange between process engineering P&I tools and process control engineering tools. The described format CAEX (Computer Aided Engineering Exchange) is a neutral, object oriented, XML-based data format for storing hierarchical plant information.

AutomationML (Automation Markup Language) [20], also denoted as IEC 62714, is a dataformat based on CAEX for the storage and exchange of plant engineering information. Referenced in the IEC 62424 standard, the aim of AutomationML is to interconnect engineering tools in various disciplines, including electrical design, process engineering, process control engineering, PLC programming, robot programming, etc. The specification includes the characterization of topology, logic, behavior, geometry and kinematic models.

Table 1 shows the aptitude of the analyzed standards for the typical functionalities and services of an automation solution. Of course none of the standards is designed for covering all aspects but by taking several standards into account, a solution could be designed for maximizing vertical and horizontal data integration and interoperability.

Table 1. Aptitude of the analyzed standards in regard to typical automation solution functionalities.

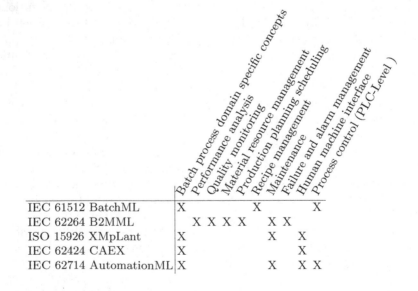

	Batch process domain specific concepts	Performance analysis	Quality monitoring	Material resource management	Production planning scheduling	Recipe management	Maintenance management	Failure and alarm management	Human machine interface	Process control (PLC-Level)
IEC 61512 BatchML	X					X				X
IEC 62264 B2MML		X	X	X	X		X	X		
ISO 15926 XMpLant	X					X		X		
IEC 62424 CAEX	X					X				
IEC 62714 AutomationML	X					X			X	X

4 Ontologies for Process Automation

The previous section elaborated on a range of standards for process automation. However, inconsistencies can and do exist within the definitions and relations within various standards, which is exacerbated by extensions defined by individual manufacturers. In this context, Deshayes et al. propose a general architecture for designing ontologies for standards integration and conformance [8]. The architecture is composed of four levels with different sets of ontologies. While the vendor ontologies are defined by individual companies, the standards ontologies represent a more generic definition of the terms or concepts. According to their name, the domain ontologies are used for describing a specific domain and can be used for checking the consistency between standards ontologies. Finally, core ontologies incorporate generic concepts crossing multiple domains with the aim for maximized shareability and reusability.

Regarding the fact, that most agent-based approaches rather focus on discrete processes [3], also the majority of reported ontologies have been developed for the corresponding domain of manufacturing systems. A small selection of such ontologies is given in the following before presenting more details on ontologies for the process domain.

The ADACOR ontology integrates concepts for manufacturing components with physical resources (machines, tools, etc.) as well as for production orders, operations and disturbances [21]. The MASON ontology focuses on likewise aspects representing thus an upper ontology for the manufacturing domain [22]. An equipment module ontology with the focus on the functions and behaviors of equipment entities and their connections is presented in [23]. A further ontology for manufacturing processes comprising also the concept of controllers is reported in [24].

Regarding the process domain, Batres et al. provide a set of ontologies for describing plants, processes and products [25]. The concepts are arranged in a formalism as structural, behavioral, and operational interrelated objects for achieving simulation models of physicochemical behaviors.

Furthermore, Batres et al. report of work on an upper ontology for the standard ISO 15926 [26]. As such, the ontology defines top-level concepts for supporting the development of domain ontologies.

OntoCAPE is a formal ontology specified for computer-aided process engineering (CAPE) [27]. Its creators consider it to be a so-called "heavyweight ontology" and thus an ontology that involves axiomatic definitions and restrictions concerning the domain semantics. The ontology has been developed according to six design principles, which are coherence, conciseness, intelligibility, adaptability, minimal ontological commitment, and efficiency. OntoCAPE is separated into several abstraction layers ranging from the Meta Layer on top for describing fundamental modeling concepts down to the Application-Specific Layer providing classes and relations for individual applications in the domain of chemical process engineering. The ontology consists of more than 60 modules that are freely available for download. OntoCAPE has been used already in several projects as for instance concerning chemical plants in the development of a knowledge-based software prototype for the integration and management of scattered engineering design data [28].

Further work extends OntoCAPE in regard to modeling operational processes. The Work Process Modeling Language (WPML) [29] allows the representation of behavioral and funcional aspects of a process making use of Onto-CAPE concepts in conjunction with additional concepts defined for operational processes. Moreover, the authors demonstrate the possibility of integrating the structural concepts of ANSI/ISA-88 in WPML.

Process supervision represents another aspect not covered by OntoCAPE itself. However, an ontology denoted as OntoSafe [30] provides the means for representing states and conditions and thus including faults of plant components but also of process sections. With this ontology it is possible to specify the dependencies between process descriptors such as flowsheets with a supervision system. OntoSafe utilizes a set of partial models of OntoCAPE extended by another partial model for describing the afore mentioned concepts. OntoSafe has been evaluated in conjunction with an agent-based system in several simulations in the frame of a case-study concerning the domain of oil and gas production.

The Purdue Ontology for Pharmaceutical Engineering (POPE) is an ontology specifically made for the pharmaceutical process domain [31, 32]. Its aim is to provide guidelines and support decision making during the product and process development. As a consequence, concepts for defining materials, formulations as well as operations are pivotal for this ontology and its usage. Besides, also mathematical models and their usage are covered by POPE in the framework of OntoMODEL, which is a tool for mechanistic mathematical model management [33].

Based on concepts taken from OntoCAPE as well as POPE, the ontology OntoReg introduces a regulatory domain for automating the regulatory compliance in pharmaceutical production due to the tight legislation in this domain [34]. By applying this approach, the regulatory requirements can be translated into tasks to be carried out using a reasoner and an according rule engine.

Muñoz et al. present an ontology for batch process automation denoted as BaPrOn [35]. The ontology is mainly based on the standard ANSI/ISA-88 integrating its structural models for processes and physical equipment. Moreover, a focus in the ontology is laid on representing recipes according to the standard. It is designated for handling diversity in scheduling problem representation as well as for allowing an effective data sharing and information flow [9]. Combined with a scheduling algorithm, the ontology has been utilized in several use-cases for showing its reusability. Further work is concerned with integrating also other hierarchical levels according to the standard ANSI/ISA-95.

In a previous project denoted as PrOnto, the authors of this paper developed an ontology for representing the physical components of a process plant [12]. On the basis of this ontology, a path finding algorithm is employed for dynamically calculating routes from one component of the system to other ones taking criteria such as failure states of components into account.

Table 2 shows the aptitude of the reported ontologies for the typical functionalities and services of an automation solution. It can be seen that none of the presented ontologies provide concepts for all of these functionalities. However, nearly all of them are covered by one or more ontologies with the exception of human machine interfaces for process automation.

Table 2. Aptitude of the reported ontologies in regard to typical automation solution functionalities.

	Batch process domain specific concepts	Performance analysis	Quality monitoring	Material resource management	Production planning scheduling	Recipe management	Maintenance management	Failure and alarm management	Human machine interface	Process control (PLC-Level)
MASON		X	X		X					X
ADACOR			X	X	X		X			X
Lohse et al. 2006			X							X
Alsafi & Vyatkin 2010			X							X
Batres et al. 2002	X		X							
Upper Ontology ISO 15926	X		X				X	X		X
OntoCAPE	X	X	X	X						X
WPML	X			X	X					X
OntoSafe	X		X					X		X
POPE	X		X		X					
OntoReg	X	X	X							
BaPrOn	X	X	X	X	X					
PrOnto	X		X					X		X

5   Conclusion

The ideas of agent technology and model-based engineering have shown potential in various prototypical implementations and academic environments. However, they have not yet found a broad acceptance and application in industrial practice. Regarding model-based engineering, a potential lies in formalizing information for a broad vertical and horizontal data integration and interoperability. In this context, the conformance with industrial standards is crucial for a concept's reusability as well as applicability and thus acceptance.

This paper presented a survey on standards and ontologies for the process domain carried out during the first phase of the project BatMAS, which aims at the integration of a system ontology for providing an extensive knowledge base. On the one hand, the knowledge base should be accessed by an agent-based system for batch process automation and on the other hand, it should provide access for various functionalities of a complete automation solution.

Regarding information models for these functionalities, none of the analyzed standards and ontologies alone is sufficient. However, a satisfying solution could be achieved by combining their concepts and ideas. Therefore, further research will be concerned with merging the concepts towards a unifying solution.

Acknowledgement. The authors acknowledge the financial support from the "IKT der Zukunft" program by the Austrian Research Promotion Agency under contract FFG 845626.

References

1. Jämsä-Jounela, S.L.: Future trends in process automation. Annual Reviews in Control **31**(2), 211–220 (2007)
2. Vrba, P., Mařík, V.: Capabilities of dynamic reconfiguration of Multiagent-Based industrial control systems. IEEE Transactions on Systems, Man and Cybernetics, Part A: Systems and Humans **40**(2), 213–223 (2010)
3. Metzger, M., Polaków, G.: A survey on applications of agent technology in industrial process control. IEEE Transactions on Industrial Informatics **7**(4), 570–581 (2011)
4. Shen, W., Norrie, D.H.: Agent-based systems for intelligent manufacturing : A state of-the-Art survey. Knowledge and Information Systems, an International Journal **1**(2), 129–156 (1999)
5. Sanislav, T., Miclea, L.: Cyber-Physical Systems - Concept, Challenges and Research Areas. Journal of Control Engineering and Applied Informatics **14**(2), 28–33 (2012)
6. Bauernhansl, T., ten Hompel, M., Vogel-Heuser, B. (eds.): Industrie 4.0 in Produktion, Automatisierung und Logistik. Springer, Wiesbaden (2014)
7. Christiansen, L., Hoernicke, M., Fay, A.: Modellgesttztes Engineering. atp edition - Automatisierungstechnische Praxis **56**(3), 18–27 (2014)
8. Deshayes, L., Foufou, S., Gruninger, M.: An ontology architecture for standards integration and conformance in manufacturing. In: Tichkiewitch, S., Tollenaere, M., Ray, P. (eds) Advances in Integrated Design and Manufacturing in Mechanical Engineering II, pp. 261–276. Springer (2007)
9. Munoz, E., Capn-Garca, E., Espuna, A., Puigjaner, L.: Ontological framework for enterprise-wide integrated decision-making at operational level. Computers & Chemical Engineering **42**, 217–234 (2012)
10. Leitao, P., Mařík, V., Vrba, P.: Past, Present, and Future of Industrial Agent Applications. IEEE Transactions on Industrial Informatics **9**(4), 2360–2372 (2013)
11. Merdan, M., Lepuschitz, W., Axinia, E.: Advanced process automation using automation agents. In: Proceedings of the 5th International Conference on Automation, Robotics and Applications, pp. 34–39 (2011)

12. Lepuschitz, W., Groessing, B., Axinia, E., Merdan, M.: Phase agents and dynamic routing for batch process automation. In: Mařík, V., Lastra, J.L.M., Skobelev, P. (eds.) HoloMAS 2013. LNCS, vol. 8062, pp. 37–48. Springer, Heidelberg (2013)
13. International Electrotechnical Commission: IEC 61512 Batch Control - Parts 1–4, Geneva (2000–2010)
14. Manufacturing Enterprise Solutions Association International: Business To Manufacturing Markup Language - BatchML, Chandler (2013)
15. International Electrotechnical Commission: IEC 62264 Enterprise-control system integration Parts 1–5, Geneva (2007–2013)
16. Manufacturing Enterprise Solutions Association International: Business To Manufacturing Markup Language - B2MML, Chandler (2013)
17. International Organization for Standardization: ISO-15926: Integration of lifecycle data for process plants including oil and gas production facilities - Part 1 - Overview and fundamental principles, Geneva (2003)
18. Nextspace: XMpLant Overview (accessed March 2015)
19. International Organization for Standardization: IEC 62424 - Representation of process control engineering - Requests in P&I diagrams and data exchange between P&ID tools and PCE-CAE tools, Geneva (2008)
20. AutomationML consortium: Whitepaper AutomationML - Part 1 - Architecture and general requirements (accessed March 2015)
21. Leitao, P.: An Agile and Adaptive Holonic Architecture for Manufacturing Control. PhD thesis, University of Porto, Portugal (2004)
22. Lemaignan, S., Siadat, A., Dantan, J.Y., Semenenko, A.: MASON: a proposal for an ontology of manufacturing domain. In: IEEE Workshop on Distributed Intelligent Systems: Collective Intelligence and its Applications, pp. 195–200 (2006)
23. Lohse, N., Hirani, H., Ratchev, S.: Equipment ontology for modular reconfigurable assembly systems. International Journal of Flexible Manufacturing Systems 17(4), 301–314 (2006)
24. Alsafi, Y., Vyatkin, V.: Ontology-based reconfiguration agent for intelligent mechatronic systems in flexible manufacturing. Robotics and Computer-Integrated Manufacturing 26(4), 381–391 (2010)
25. Batres, R., Aoyama, A., Naka, Y.: A life-cycle approach for model reuse and exchange. Computers & Chemical Engineering 26(4–5), 487–498 (2002)
26. Batres, R., West, M., Leal, D., Price, D., Masaki, K., Shimada, Y., Fuchino, T., Naka, Y.: An upper ontology based on ISO 15926. Computers & Chemical Engineering 31(5–6), 519–534 (2007)
27. Morbach, J., Wiesner, A., Marquardt, W.: Ontocape-a (re)usable ontology for computer-aided process engineering. Computers & Chemical Engineering 33(10), 1546–1556 (2009)
28. Morbach, J., Marquardt, W.: Ontology-based integration and management of distributed design data. In: Nagl, M., Marquardt, W. (eds.) Collaborative and Distributed Chemical Engineering. LNCS, vol. 4970, pp. 647–655. Springer, Heidelberg (2008)
29. Hai, R., Theien, M., Marquardt, W.: An ontology based approach for operational process modeling. Advanced Engineering Informatics 25(4), 748–759 (2011)
30. Natarajan, S., Ghosh, K., Srinivasan, R.: An ontology for distributed process supervision of large-scale chemical plants. Computers & Chemical Engineering 46, 124–140 (2012)

31. Venkatasubramanian, V., Zhao, C., Joglekar, G., Jain, A., Hailemariam, L., Suresh, P., Akkisetty, P., Morris, K., Reklaitis, G.: Ontological informatics infrastructure for pharmaceutical product. Computers & Chemical Engineering **30**(10–12), 1482–1496 (2006)
32. Zhao, C., Jain, A., Hailemariam, L., Suresh, P., Akkisetty, P., Joglekar, G., Venkatasubramanian, V., Reklaitis, G.V., Morris, K., Basu, P.: Toward intelligent decision support for pharmaceutical product development. Journal of Pharmaceutical Innovation **1**(1), 23–35 (2006)
33. Suresh, P., Hsu, S.H., Akkisetty, P., Reklaitis, G.V., Venkatasubramanian, V.: OntoMODEL: Ontological Mathematical Modeling Knowledge Management in Pharmaceutical Product Development, 1: Conceptual Framework. Industrial & Engineering Chemistry Research **49**(17), 7758–7767 (2010)
34. Sesen, M.B., Suresh, P., Banares-Alcantara, R., Venkatasubramanian, V.: An ontological framework for automated regulatory compliance in pharmaceutical manufacturing. Computers & Chemical Engineering **34**(7), 1482–1496 (2010)
35. Munoz, E., Espuna, A., Puigjaner, L.: Towards an ontological infrastructure for chemical batch process management. Computers & Chemical Engineering **34**(5), 668–682 (2010)

Conceptual Design and Validation

From Conception to Implementation of Reconfigurable and Distributed Manufacturing Control System

Robson Marinho da Silva[1,2]($\boxtimes$), Diolino J. Santos Filho[2], and Paulo E. Miyagi[2]

[1] Universidade Estadual de Santa Cruz, Ilhéus, BA, Brazil
rmsilva@uesc.br
[2] Escola Politécnica da Universidade de São Paulo, São Paulo, SP, Brazil
{Diolinos,pemiyagi}@usp.br

Abstract. Currently, the design of the manufacturing control systems must assure reconfiguration flexibility for agile reaction to unexpected occurrences in components in the shop-floor control level or business processes in enterprise and factory control levels. Other requirement of these control systems is ensuring collaboration and integration of heterogeneous, autonomous and distributed manufacturing subsystems to take advantages of local facilities. The combination of Holonic and Multi-Agent System (HMAS) and Service-Oriented Architecture (SOA) techniques is effective to design this Reconfigurable and Distributed Manufacturing Control System (RDMCS). However, there are few methods based on formalisms which ensure a systematic workflow to implement a RDMCS considering since its abstraction phase. Therefore, this paper proposes the use of Petri net in a hybrid bottom-up and top-down design approach to combine HMAS and SOA techniques. Application examples demonstrate the modeling and effectiveness of the proposal using tools for edition, debug, simulation and generation of controller languages from the proposed models.

Keywords: Holonic system · Agent-based system · Service-oriented architecture · Design methodology · Petri net

1 Introduction

The growing competitiveness and technological evolution impose changes requiring a migration of manufacturing paradigm to be "adjustable" to abnormal transitory situations and business and market interests. An example is the distributed manufacturing system composed by subsystems in disperse geographic location with heterogeneous businesses processes that must interact each other to take advantages of their local facilities [6,11]. These challenges restrict the implementation of the manufacturing paradigm [17] which depend of a control system that ensures the adequate use of the new technologies [10].

Control functions are usually organized into hierarchical control levels, such as enterprise control, factory control, and shop-floor control levels [6]. However,

© Springer International Publishing Switzerland 2015
V. Mařík et al. (Eds.): HoloMAS 2015, LNAI 9266, pp. 35–46, 2015.
DOI: 10.1007/978-3-319-22867-9_4

to ensure that a Reconfigurable and Distributed Manufacturing Control System (RDMCS) meets all its purpose, a global vision of the system goal must integrate with autonomous decision of each subsystem. Furthermore, a RDMCS must consider reconfiguration flexibility [15], to be updated for agile reaction both for unexpected variations of shop-floor control level (such as fault occurrence, addition, replacement or exclusion of resources) as for variations of enterprise and factory control levels (such as new businesses processes to attend new demands or quality control. Therefore, a breach in traditional methods must be considered to model and implement a RDMCS.

For efficient use of resources, a method to implement a RDMCS must avoid repetition of tasks and overlapping of project scope through reuse models and ensuring through a formalism the implementation of design specifications, interoperability and collaboration among related entities. Holonic Multi-Agent System (HMAS) is a way to conceive an intelligent control components for a RDMCS. Moreover, the agent-based control software can be endowed with communications and information processing capabilities, transforming it into a self-reconfiguring element. The result is a modular and distributed intelligent automation system associating hierarchical and heterarchical control structure [11]

The Service Oriented Architecture (SOA) is an effective way to assure collaboration among distributed subsystems. Based on SOA, an integration level is introduced among the factory control and shop-floor control levels. Despite some studies [4,13] present new perspectives and tools about how to combine the SOA and HMAS concepts, there are few publications proposing a method based on formalisms.

In most holonic architecture, production order and manufacturing resource holons make decisions; however, other holons should be autonomous for this. The development of mechanisms to the holarchy composition that accomplish a productive process can be more explored. Some architectures have a product-oriented vision and pay more attention to scalability and generic components of the system. Other have a machine-oriented vision, paying more attention to an optimal utilization of the machine level than to the specific product performance. However, a combined vision of business processes, product and machine-orientation is more adequate. Furthermore, patterns to facilitate the development of new control solutions and a suitable semantic for RDMCS must be integrated into the design phases. The workflow of itself method should be described using tools, such as PN extensions that facilitate the communication among different design staffs, following a cloud engineering vision [16].

In the light of the foregoing, this paper presents a method using Petri net (PN) [7,8] to specify a RDMCS based on combination of HMAS and SOA, exploring strength aspects and good practices of the aforementioned and others related works, such as [1,3,5,13]. In Section 2 the proposed implementation method of RDMCS is presented. The phases of the method, and the PN formalism are also described. Models of an application example are presented in Section 3. The Section 4 has the main conclusions.

2 Modeling and Implementation of Reconfigurable and Distributed Manufacturing Control System

Figure 1 illustrates the elements of the adopted control architecture in which holarchies represent the productive processes[1] which are composed by services of the atomic holons. Thus, holarchies can represent the different control levels and a holon can belong to different holarchies. The holons are as follows: (i) *Product Holon (PrH)* which forms the production plan holarchy which in turn represents a recipe of how to join raw materials and intermediate products where operations (such as machining and assembly) are performed to obtain the final products; (ii) *Task Holon (TH)* which represents the business processes strategies to attend the product order. The *TH*s are also requested for the reconfiguration strategies; (iii) *Supervisor Holon (SuH)* which manages the operations and the messages exchange between holons; and (iv) *Operational Holon (OpH)* which represents the physical resources and the human. In implementation phase, MAS platforms are used to implement an agent which represents a atomic holon.

Several works in the area of reconfigurable manufacturing system [6,11,13,15] demonstrate that PN is an adequate technique for description of discrete event systems [12], its productive processes and control systems. According to [8], an approach based on extensions and proper interpretation of PN allows the modeling in a more simplified and transparent manner.

As this work considers a solution that facilitates the practical use, two PNs extensions are adopted: (i) a channel/agent PN type called Production Flow Schema (PFS) [8], and (ii) a non-autonomous PN model named Input Output Place Transition (IOPT) [7]. The PFS describes the RDMCS at abstraction level and the workflow of the method itself. Successive refinements are applied and the initial PFS model is detailed at each level. Then, the functional and operational dynamic behavior is described by a IOPT technique and its associated tools are used for dynamic edition and analysis of the models which is a way to specify the control functions. The advantage is that these models/ specification can be the input of some software for generation of C code for programs of industrial controllers.

According to [12], the place transition PN is a 5-tuple (P, T, A, W, M) in which: (i) $P = P_1, P_2, P_3, ..., P_r$ is a finite set $(r \in \mathbb{N}^*)$ of places[2]; (ii) $T = T_1, T_2, T_3, ..., T_s$ is a finite set $(s \in \mathbb{N}^*)$ of transitions; (iii) $A = PXT \bigcup TXP$ is the oriented arcs set; (iv) $W : A, I, H \rightarrow \mathbb{N}^*$ is a function weight associated to arcs, in which the absence indicates an unitary weight; and (v) $M = M_o, M_1, M_2, ..., M_n$ is the marking, in which $M = m_1, m_2, ..., m_r$ is defined by the vector of these markings involving the number of marking m_i in the place P_i. M_0 is the initial marking of the net. The IOPT is a 12-tuple $(P, T, A, M, W, TA, WTest, priority, isg, ie, oe, osc)$ where: (i) the definition of P, T, A, M and W is the same of the place transition PN; (ii) TA is a set of Test Arcs, such that $TA \subseteq (PxT)$; (iii) $WTest$ is a weight function

---

[1] An ontology is proposed and its terms are in Sans Serif font.
[2] The terms related to PN are in Courier font.

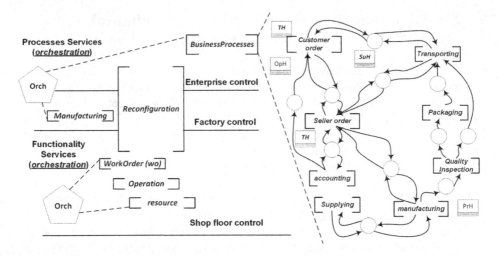

Fig. 1. Control architecture and the refinement of *TH*-[Business processes] task holon.

associated to `test arcs`, $WTest : TA \to \mathbb{N}^*$; (iv) *priority* is a partial function applying non-negative integers to `transitions`, $priority : T \to \mathbb{N}^*$; (v) *isg* is an `input signal guard` partial function applying Boolean Expressions (BE) composed only by `input signals` (IS) to `transitions`, $isg : T \to BE$, where $\forall BE \in isg(T), Var(BE) \subseteq IS$; (vi) *ie* is an `input event` partial function applying `input events` (IE) to `transitions`, $ie : T \to IE$; (vii) *oe* is an `output event` partial function applying `output events` (OE) to `transitions`, $oe : T \to OE$; and (viii) *osc* is an output signal condition function from `places` into sets of rules, $osc : P \to P(RULES)$, where $RULES \subseteq (BESxOSxIN_o)$, $BES \subseteq BE$ and $\forall e \in BES, Var(e) \subseteq ML$, with ML being the set of identifiers for each `place marking` after a given execution step. Each `place marking` has an associated identifier, for executing the generated code.

The proposed method is represented in Fig. 2, where elements of Unified Modeling Language (UML), HMAS, SOA and PFS are combined. The method is divided into five *phases*[3] (represented by a UML element named package) and their *sub-phases* (represented by`activities`). Into each *phase*, actors[4] (staffs are represented by UML *actor*), and the utilized and generated artifacts (these are represented by UML *notes*) of each *phase* are described.

The *conceptual modeling phase* is performed by the *requirements analyst* actor. The used artifact is the *requirements list*, and the generated artifacts are the *use case diagrams*. The *ontology specification sub-phase* is made based on specifics modules which should be defined for each domain. In *holons identification sub-phase*, the elements of the control architecture are identified. Figure 1 (on the right) also shows a specification of ontology using a PFS refinement of *THs* which represent internal workflow of a Business Processes involving

---

[3] Terms related elements of the method are in *italic*.

[4] Terms related to SOA technique are underlined.

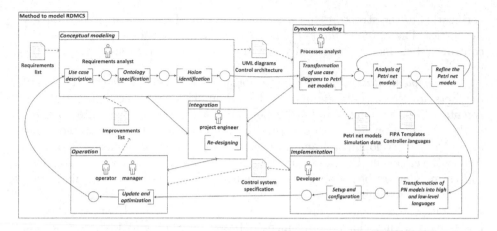

Fig. 2. Schema of the method using PFS and UML to model RDMCS.

customer order, seller order, accounting, transporting, packaging, manufacturing, quality inspection and supplying.

The *dynamic modeling phase* is performed by the process analyst actor. The used artifacts are *UML diagrams* and the *control architecture;* and the generated artifacts are PN models and the *simulation data.* The UML diagrams created in preview *sub-phase* is transformed into PN models. For this, the productive processes is modeled by a *holon* that is represented by an `activity` or `distributor` of the PFS relating the workflow (represented by `arcs`) among them. Modeling *PrHs* details the workflow which performs one or more `operations` generating products that may be intermediate or final. Modeling *THs* details the strategies for composition of Business Processes. Modeling *SuH* details the management activities, workflow of resources abilities and messages exchange among holons. Modeling *OpHs* represents the control objects with an `activity` associated only for identification, and they are modeled directly in IOPT considering the set of possible states including fault (represented by `places`), and conditions (represented by `transitions`) for the change of states. The synchronization is made with `input event`, `output event`, `guard expression`, `asynchronous channels` and `auxiliary places`, e.g., to synchronize the functioning of a valve and its electric actuator. In this phase, mechanisms for reconfigurable control are also modeled which are called "diagnoser" and the "decider", to fulfill the requirements of the diagnosis and decision phases. To model the "diagnoser", process analyst defines observable and non-observable events, according to [14]. The steps for this modeling are: (i) "diagnoser" construction, initially considering normal operation; (ii) linking the strategies implemented by means of `transitions` and `guard` with the possible observable and non-observable events that may occur from the initial state; (iii) linking the states obtained according to `input` or `output signal` of actuators and sensors states; and (iv) linking the strategies implemented by means of `transitions` and `guard` to the events. In *analysis of Petri net models sub-phase,* the purpose is the simulation and verification of the structure and dynamic behavior of the models, based on PN properties. The *refine of the Petri net models sub-phase* should then review the control system models based on these analysis and, if necessary, improve the models.

The *implementation phase* is performed by *developer actor*. The used *artifacts* are PN models, simulation data, Foundation for Intelligent Physical Agents (FIPA) templates and controllers languages, and the generated *artifact* is the specification for control system programs. The code is generated using Java Agent DEvelopment framework (JADE) [2] and its extension Workflow Agent Development Environment (WADE) [4]. JADE plus WADE are open source middleware based on FIPA standards and facilitate the reconfiguration bringing the workflow approach to internal logics, providing fault tolerance mechanisms and a way to invoke *web services*. For low-level control, there is few hardware that can be implemented based on SOA and HMAS concepts, e.g., in [17], new developments and hardware are proposed; however, their solution is proprietary. Therefore, the code generation is made following a graphical language proposed in IEC61131 [9], such as sequence flow chart (due its similarities to PN models) or using C code. The C codes are obtained using IOPT web tools which follow ANSI C syntax rules and generate the source files: (i) *net_types_h* that includes data-types for `places marking, input and output signals` and `events`; (ii) *net_main.c* that is the main execution loop (main function); (iii) *net_io.c* that is the input and output code used do read and write the values from physical hardware; (iv) *net_functions.c* that has the functions to implement all IOPT semantics and rules: transition firing, guards, events, output actions, etc.; (v) *net_exec_step.c* that has the function that executes one entire IOPT execution step, using the various functions defined in *net_functions.c*; and (vi) *makefile* that is an optional Unix project makefile. All code produced compile directly on most systems and do not need any change, except the *net_io.c* file that must be adapted to each target application.

The *operation phase* is performed by *processes actors* (i.e., operators and managers), the *used artifacts* are processes metric, alerts and incidents, and the *generated artifact* is the improvements list.

The *integration phase* manages the other phases to implement improvements.

3   Application Example

The application of the method uses as example a susbsystem of a disperse productive system called Distributing WorkStation $(D-WS)$ (Fig. 3). The devices, their control functions, commands and signals of actuation and detection are also identified in this figure. The $D-WS$ provides a cylinder body (black [*bcb*], red [*rcb*] or aluminum [*acb*]) workpiece to other subsystems which perform operations to join a cylinder body with a piston (black [*bp*] or aluminum [*ap*]), a spring [*s*] and a cover [*co*] workpieces and obtaining the final products. The [*bcb*], [*rcb*] and [*acb*] workpieces are stored in the "stacking magazine" buffer, and a double-acting piston [1A] pushes one workpiece (*wp*) out (one at a time) to the

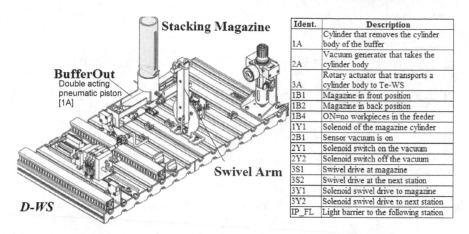

Ident.	Description
1A	Cylinder that removes the cylinder body of the buffer
2A	Vacuum generator that takes the cylinder body
3A	Rotary actuator that transports a cylinder body to Te-WS
1B1	Magazine in front position
1B2	Magazine in back position
1B4	ON=no workpieces in the feeder
1Y1	Solenoid of the magazine cylinder
2B1	Sensor vacuum is on
2Y1	Solenoid switch on the vacuum
2Y2	Solenoid switch off the vacuum
3S1	Swivel drive at magazine
3S2	Swivel drive at the next station
3Y1	Solenoid swivel drive to magazine
3Y2	Solenoid swivel drive to next station
IP_FL	Light barrier to the following station

Fig. 3. A Distributing Workstation $(D-WS)$ and its devices.

"buffer out". Then, a swivel arm gets a *wp* in magazine via a suction gripper vacuum to move it to the transfer point of the another subsystem, the Testing WorkStation $(Te-WS)$. The PFS of the *production plan* of the manufacturing system, refinement of *intermediate product PrH-[rcb]* and sub-refinement of *TH-[request provides wp of D-WS to Te-WS]* are in Fig. 4.

Figure 5 has the PFS of the processes of customers to select *suppliers*. A *customer* looking for *suppliers* to contract supplying of the *products* at an acceptable *price* and delivery time (or deadline). If more than one *supplier* provides an *offer*, then the *TH-[customer order]* accepts one based on some criteria such as the lowest *price*.

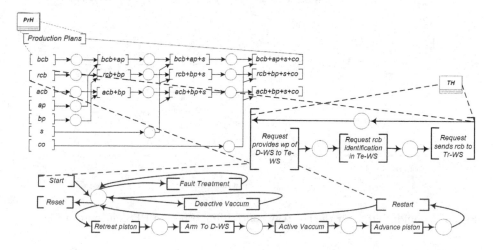

Fig. 4. PFS models that represent a production plan, workflows and a control strategy.

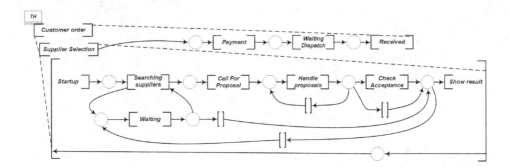

Fig. 5. Refinement of the model *TH-[customer order]* (see above and right in Fig. 1).

Figure 6 details in IOPT the control strategy of *TH-[request provides wp of D-WS to Te-WS]* (see on right and bellow in Fig. 4). Each `transition` has "Guard (G) expressions" according to code listed in Fig. 3. For instance, the "Arm-ToDWS" `transition` has associated the "G: 1B1=1 AND 1B2=0" that means "magazine is front position" and the "1B1 sensor" is sending signal on. When the "ArmToDWS" fires a `token` is put in "ArmInDWS" `place` sending a `output signal` "3Y1="1 that in turn modifies the state of this solenoid. This IOPT has also `input events`: (i) "*StartOn*" of "*StartDWS*" `transitions` to initiate the $D - WS$, (ii) "*ResetOn*" to reset the $D - WS$, and (iii) *FaultTreatment* to solve fault occurrence.

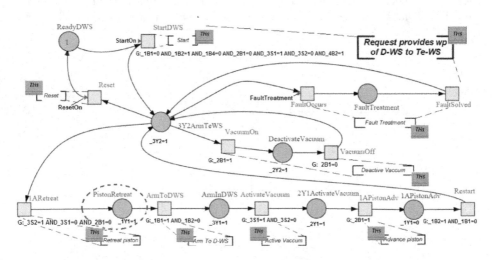

Fig. 6. Detail in IOPT for the strategy control illustrated in PFS on right of Fig. 4.

Figure 7 presents *OpHs* models of the devices listed on right in Fig. 3. In this example, the movement sensors [1B1] and [1B2] are located in the course limits of [1A]. The [1A] has two normal states which are the advanced state

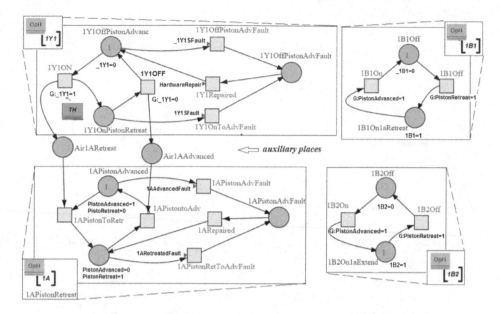

Fig. 7. PN models de control objects which are linked using IOPT elements.

(1Y1OffPistonAdvanc) or retreated (1Y1OnPistonRetreat) and one fault state (1Y1OffPistonAdvFault) which represents a situation that the piston is advanced stuck. The IOPT technique allows relating conditions for change among states (represented by G:) and for representation of the environment influence. In this case, there are two input events one (1Y1SFault) that represents a situation for change of normal to the fault state; and another (HardwareRepair) that represents the repair of the device. Thus, OpH models are linked by IOPT elements and **auxiliary places** related to the dependence of the other holon. For instance, for the **firing** of the **transition** (1APistonToRetr) which retreats [1A], the command action (which is represented by G:1Y1=1 in this Fig. 7) must be send by *TH-[request provides wp of D-WS to Te-WS]* (see in Fig. 6).

Figure 8 presents an example of *diagnoser* for the command of [1A] retreating (represented by *TH-[Diagnostic for 1ARetreating]*). The models of the *TH* responsible by the reconfiguration control strategy and the *dignoser* evolve together. The possible states are diagnosed (see highlighted blue dashed line). Signals commands of control strategy (represented by G:) and the **input** and **output signals** of the control objects are linked in these models. For instance, the "Piston Retreated" control strategy (**place** in Fig. 6) is linked to **transition** "1APistonRetreated" of "diagnoser" through the **guard** "G: PistonRetreated"; while the **transition** "InitDiagFor1A" in *TH-[Diagnostic for 1ARetreating]* has **guard** "G:Diagn1ARetreat" linking to *TH-[Diagnostic for D-WS]*.

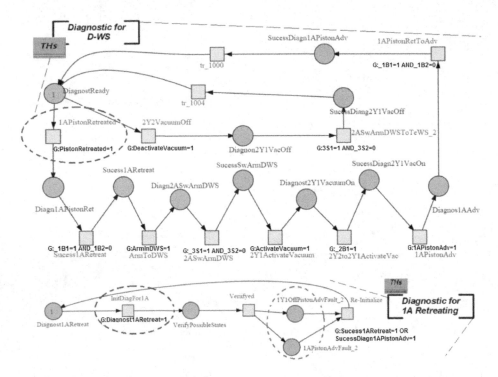

Fig. 8. "Diagnoser" for $D-WS$ linked to control strategy and signals of control objects.

The JAVA codes are generated using JADE plus WADE platform and a snippet for the negotiation among customers and suppliers illustrated in Fig. 5 is as follows:

```
private void defineTransitions() {
          registerTransition(new Transition(), STARTUP_ACTIVITY,
                  SEARCHINGSUPPLIERS_ACTIVITY);
          registerTransition(new Transition(),SEARCHINGSUPPLIERS_ACTIVITY,
                  CALLFORPROPOSAL_ACTIVITY);
          registerTransition(new Transition(), CALLFORPROPOSAL_ACTIVITY,
                  HANDLEPROPOSALS_ACTIVITY);
          registerTransition(new Transition(), HANDLEPROPOSALS_ACTIVITY,
                  HANDLEPROPOSALS_ACTIVITY);
          registerTransition(new Transition (ALLPROPOSALSRECEIVED_CONDITION,
                  this), HANDLEPROPOSALS_ACTIVITY, CHECKACCEPTANCE_ACTIVITY);
          registerTransition(new Transition (NOSUPPLIERAVAILABLE_CONDITION, this
                  ), SEARCHINGSUPPLIERS_ACTIVITY, WAITING_ACTIVITY);
          registerTransition(new Transition(), WAITING_ACTIVITY,
                  SEARCHINGSUPPLIERS_ACTIVITY);
          registerTransition(new Transition(SUPPLIERCONTRACTED_CONDITION, this),
                  CHECKACCEPTANCE_ACTIVITY, SHOWRESULT_ACTIVITY);
          registerTransition(new Transition(DEADLINEEXPIRED_CONDITION, this),
                  WAITING_ACTIVITY, SHOWRESULT_ACTIVITY);
          registerTransition(new Transition(DEADLINEEXPIRED_CONDITION, this),
                  HANDLEPROPOSALS_ACTIVITY, SHOWRESULT_ACTIVITY);
          registerTransition(new Transition(), CHECKACCEPTANCE_ACTIVITY,
                  WAITING_ACTIVITY);   }
```

Based on model in Fig. 6, the IOPT web tool generated the files to control D-WS and a snippet of the file net_exec_step.c for the **transition** StartDWS is:

```
/* Transition 394 - StartDWS */
int t_394_enabled( empty_NetMarking* prev,
                   empty_NetMarking* avail )
{    return ( avail->p_185 >= 1 );   }
int t_394_events( empty_InputSignalEvents* events )
{    return ( events->StartOn );    }
int t_394_guards( empty_NetMarking* marking,
                  empty_InputSignals* inputs,
                  empty_PlaceOutputSignals* place_out,
                  empty_EventOutputSignals* ev_out )
{    return ( ev_out->_1B1 == 0 && ev_out->_1B2 == 1 && ev_out->_1B4 == 0 &&
     ev_out->_2B1 == 0 && ev_out->_3S1 == 1 && ev_out->_3S2 == 0 && inputs->_4B2
     == 1 );     }
void t_394_remove_marks( empty_NetMarking* marking )
{    marking->p_185--;   }
void t_394_add_marks( empty_NetMarking* marking )
{    marking->p_11++;    }
void t_394_generate_output_events( empty_OutputSignalEvents* ev_out )
```

4   Conclusions

This paper proposes a method that combines Service-Oriented Architecture (SOA) with Holonic and Multi-Agent System (HMAS) techniques to model and implement a Reconfigurable and Distributed Manufacturing Control System (RDMCS). The method presents solutions such as, services orchestration using holarchy composition to represent control levels and utilization of tools to facilitate the implementation of agents that request web services. The approach is bottom–up and top–down through use of extensions of Petri Net (PN): the Input Output Place Transition (IOPT) for functional description and Production Flow Schema (PFS) for conceptual representation. The PFS models are also integrated with an ontology to ensure a suitable semantic for reuse and communication. Furthermore, the method facilitates the reconfiguration, ensuring a flexibility of design because the models can be oriented on process, product or machine. An application is presented to illustrate the proposed design method. Beyond facilitating the modeling, the resultant RDMCS presented operational advantages such as, better and more efficient control solution to use manufacturing resources. This proposal can be tailored to other systems, innovating the development of a RDMCS based on HMAS and SOA concepts.

Acknowledgments. Our thanks to the agencies CNPq, CAPES and FAPESP.

References

1. Béhé, F., Galland, S., Gaud, N., Nicolle, C., Koukam, A.: An ontology-based meta-model for multiagent-based simulations. Simulation Modelling Practice and Theory **40**, 64–85 (2014)

2. Bellifemine, F., Poggi, A., Rimassa, G.: JADE-A FIPA-compliant agent framework. In: Proc. of PAAM 4th International Conference on Practical Application of Intelligent Agents and Multi-Agent Technology, vol. 99, pp. 97–108 (1999)
3. Botti, V., Boggino, A.G.: ANEMONA: A multi-agent methodology for Holonic Manufacturing Systems. Springer (2008)
4. Caire, G., Gotta, D., Banzi, M.: WADE: a software platform to develop mission critical applications exploiting agents and workflows. In: Proceedings of the 7th International Joint Conference on Autonomous Agents and Multiagent Systems: Industrial Track. International Foundation for Autonomous Agents and Multiagent Systems, pp. 29–36 (2008)
5. Cândido, G., Barata, J.: A multiagent control system for shop floor assembly. In: Mařík, V., Vyatkin, V., Colombo, A.W. (eds.) HoloMAS 2007. LNCS (LNAI), vol. 4659, pp. 293–302. Springer, Heidelberg (2007)
6. Colombo, A.W.: Development and Implementation of Hierarchical Control Structures of Flexible Production Systems Using High Level Petri Nets. Meisenbach Verlag (1998)
7. Gomes, L., Barros, J., Costa, A., Nunes, R.: The input-output place-transition Petri net class and associated tools. In: 2007 5th IEEE International Conference on Industrial Informatics, INDIN 2007, pp. 27–32. IEEE (2007)
8. Hasegawa, K., Miyagi, P.E., Santos Filho, D.J., Takahashi, K., Ma, L., Sugisawa, M.: On resource arc for Petri net modelling of complex resource sharing system. Journal of Intelligent and Robotic Systems 26(3–4), 423–437 (1999)
9. John, K.H., Tiegelkamp, M.: IEC 61131–3: programming industrial automation systems: concepts and programming languages, requirements for programming systems, decision-making aids. Springer Science & Business Media (2010)
10. Kolberg, D., Zühlke, D.: Lean automation enabled by industry 4.0 technologies. In: Information Control Problems in Manufacturing, vol. 15, pp. 1919–1924 (2015)
11. Leitão, P., Colombo, A.W., Restivo, F.: An approach to the formal specification of holonic control systems. In: Mařík, V., McFarlane, D.C., Valckenaers, P. (eds.) HoloMAS 2003. LNCS (LNAI), vol. 2744, pp. 59–70. Springer, Heidelberg (2003)
12. Murata, T.: Petri nets: Properties, analysis and applications. Proceedings of IEEE 77(4), 541–580 (1989)
13. Quintanilla, F.G., Cardin, O., L'Anton, A., Castagna, P.: Implementation of a process orchestration model in a service oriented holonic manufacturing system. Information Control Problems in Manufacturing 15, 1167–1172 (2015)
14. Sampath, M., Sengupta, R., Lafortune, S., Sinnamohideen, K., Teneketzis, D.C.: Failure diagnosis using discrete-event models. IEEE Transactions on Control Systems Technology 4(2), 105–124 (1996)
15. da Silva, R.M., Junqueira, F., dos Santos Filho, D.J., Miyagi, P.E.: A method to design a manufacturing control system considering flexible reconfiguration. In: 2014 12th IEEE International Conference on Industrial Informatics (INDIN), pp. 82–87, July 2014
16. da Silva, R.M., Watanabe, E.H., Blos, M.F., Junqueira, F., Santos Filho, D.J., Miyagi, P.E.: Modeling of mechanisms for reconfigurable and distributed manufacturing control system. In: Camarinha-Matos, L.M., Baldissera, T.A., Di Orio, G., Marques, F. (eds.) DoCEIS 2015. IFIP AICT, vol. 450, pp. 93–100. Springer, Heidelberg (2015)
17. Vrba, P., Tichý, P., Mařík, V., Hall, K.H., Staron, R.J., Maturana, F.P., Kadera, P.: Rockwell automation's holonic and multiagent control systems compendium. IEEE Transactions on Systems, Man, and Cybernetics, Part C: Applications and Reviews 41(1), 14–30 (2011)

The Designing Process for a HMES Used for the Management of Radiopharmaceuticals Production

Andrei-Octavian Silisteanu

Faculty of Automatic Control and Computer Science, University Politehnica of Bucharest,
1-7 Polizu, 011061 Bucharest, Romania
andrei.silisteanu@nipne.ro
National Institute for Physics and Nuclear Engineering "Horia Hulubei",
30 Reactorului St., Magurele, Ilfov, Romania
andrei.silisteanu@nipne.ro

Abstract. This paper discusses the design, implementation and validation of a management system for radiopharmaceuticals production based on a reference Holonic Manufacturing System (HMES) architecture. Starting from the PROSA reference architecture our main goal is to design an integrated platform for resources management, production scheduling, manufacturing process control and data traceability and storage. All these operations have to be performed and monitored according to latest nuclear safety standards and environment regulations. The paper shortly presents the particularities of radio-isotopes pharmaceutical production inside a specific nuclear facility and proposes a HMES system design that could be easily adapted for any type of facility, since the manufacturing workflow and the production's environment conditions are similar.

Keywords: Holonic manufacturing · Semi-heterarhical control · Radiopharmaceuticals production · NetLogo simulation

1   Introduction

Radiopharmaceuticals are an established tool for key investigations in numerous disciplines of the life sciences and for diagnosis and treatment of many life threatening diseases. Produced using a cyclotron and dedicated radiochemistry equipment and laboratories, those products are used for positron emission tomography (PET) and single photon emission computed tomography (SPECT).

The main challenges of the radiopharmaceutical facilities are to manufacture valid nuclear medicine products in the shortest time possible and in a safely manner for the employees and surrounding environment. They are specialized in producing a small set of products in small volumes, according to the demand of hospitals and PET centres. Even having a specific chemical structure, radioactivity and usage, each product follows the same production path: radio-isotopes are produced in a particle accelerator (cyclotron), transferred after into technology isolators for chemical synthesis and vial dispensing, passing through quality check laboratory for conformity tests and in

V. Mařík et al. (Eds.): HoloMAS 2015, LNAI 9266, pp. 47–58, 2015.
DOI: 10.1007/978-3-319-22867-9_5

the last stage, final products are packed and transported to the clients in shielded containers. A typical radiopharmaceutical product workflow is presented in Fig. 1.

The preparation of radiopharmaceuticals requires a safe, clean and aseptic workplace. Special environment conditions must be fulfilled continuously during the manufacturing process. These conditions could be divided in two main categories: radioprotection safety conditions (radioactivity doses, pressure cascades and air change cycles) and environment manufacturing conditions (temperature, humidity and pressure, number of particles) as defined by GMP[1], guide or recommended by IAEA[2] in their technical reports [1].

The automation of manufacturing processes and environmental monitoring is present only at local level: every equipment has its own PC running dedicated control software forming a couple of "automation islands" [2]. Data sharing between islands and with the entire manufacturing system represents a difficult task due to the different standards and automation platforms involved.

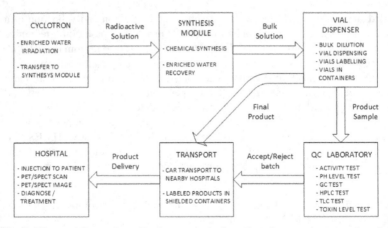

Fig. 1. The workflow of a radiopharmaceutical product from cyclotron to hospital

The process data or the test results are locally stored or printed. Therefore comes the need for an integrated software solution for managing the internal logistic of the production and the big amount of process and environmental data. For the Quality Control (QC) Laboratory, the software must provide Laboratory Information Management System (LIMS) functionality [3]. A LIMS will provide the effective monitoring and recording at the batch level, creating records that trace the path of the products as they are passing from production stages to packaging. While most of laboratory work has often been done externally from the LIMS, instrument-to-LIMS interfaces are now being developed by manufacturers. Such interfaces allow raw data to be imported directly to the LIMS, which then can store, process, and report all the information for analysis [4].

---

[1] GMP : Good Manufacturing Practice.
[2] IAEA: International Atomic Energy Agency.

A successful attempt has been made in automating the entire radiopharmaceutical production process using a PLC controlled system [5]. However, the tested architecture has the following drawbacks: the manufacturing process is product specific, no supervisory system for perturbation or failures is present and QC routine check of the final product is missing. Our proposed software architecture intends to cover all the production's stages and aspects as required by GMP.

The application of holonic concepts to manufacturing is motivated by the inability of existing manufacturing systems to deal with evolution of products within an existing production facility and to maintain a satisfactory performance outside normal operating conditions [6]. The term holon was chosen for capturing the dualistic capabilities of autonomy and cooperativeness within a single entity. The concept was found suitable to encompass the entities, physical as well as abstract, in manufacturing control and management [7]. The strengths of a holonic organization are represented by the efficiency in the uses of resources, the high reactivity due to decentralization, and the adaptability to change in their existing environment.

The reference architecture for manufacturing, PROSA is built around three types of basic holons: product, resource and order control: recipes or process plans, resource handling and internal logistics [8].

The remainder of the paper is structured as follows: section 2 the radiopharmaceutical manufacturing process and the building block of the software application; section 3 details the structure of the HMES system and section 4 details its functionality; section 5 contains the simulation of the manufacturing process. Conclusions and future challenges are presented in section 6.

2   Radiopharmaceuticals Manufacturing Process and Core Components of the Management System

The radiopharmaceutical manufacturing process has a typical flow-shop structure and starts when a client's order is received and the entire facility (machines and human personnel) is ready for operation. The first step of production is represented by the enriched water irradiation using a cyclotron. The radioactive water is then transferred inside a technology isolator, where a chemical synthesis module mixes chemical reagents from a cassette to obtain the product bulk solution. Next, the vial dispenser is calculating the required product quantity and activity for each vial, according to client's order. A sample from the product batch is sent to QC laboratory and after running a series of test methods on analytical instruments, the laboratory confirms the product's dispatch to hospitals or rejected the entire product batch for non-conformities. Since radiopharmaceuticals are based on short-lives radioisotopes (between 109 min. and 360 min. half-time[3]) an important goal of every facility is to ensure that the production timeline is strictly respected. The products must reach the hospitals in the right time and with the specific requested activity. Orders for different

---

[3] Half-time: the time period after the number of element's atoms and activity is reduced to half its value.

types of products are executed in separate production batches to avoid the risks of cross-contamination [9].

The production process must be supervised by an environment monitoring system as all the production stages are environment dependent. The air quality in the production area and the radioactivity levels must be continuously monitored together with physical environment parameters. After production, the recorded logs must be stored for reports and for further batch audits. Alarm and action limits are defined for each environment parameter and provide a useful tool in taking real-time corrective action or critical decisions (production stop or delay) in case of perturbations.

Aiming for multidisciplinary information and application integration, we propose a production management system based on the following core components:

- A *web based application* to access the database information and confirm, reject or postpone in real-time a client order for a specific product. A graphical user interface will provide access over internet and non-proprietary OS based access to stock list and facility resources needed for manufacturing the requested product.

- A *production scheduler* based on time constraints imposed by radioactive decay of the radionuclides contained in products and personnel, machines or other resources availability. The scheduler will calculate if a new order can be done in the required time or planned orders parameters can be adjusted to obtain the new demanded products from the same batch.

- A *process monitor module*, enabling the facility's supervisor to have an overall view of the production area and its environment. This module will bring real-time information about the manufacturing stages of the products, production room environment and radiological monitoring system. Collecting all the data from radiation detectors in a live chart, this module will provide the supervisor the exact location of the product at any time. Warnings can be received in case of machines or operations failures, permitting corrective actions to be taken in useful time.

- A *product tracking module*, will gather all the information about the raw materials the product is made from or single-use materials (cassettes, gloves, needles) that came in contact with product during manufacturing process. If non-conformities or microbiologic contamination are detected during quality check tests the tracking module can search its labels barcode database to provide the product component list.

- A *data storage module* in a Historian Database will provide a useful tool for process data analysis, process optimization and for generating complete production reports. Production batch records must be stored for at least 2 years (according to GMP) and must be available all the time for inspectors and audit procedures. Gathering different data in various formats from independent machines and storing them in a common format will be the main advantage provided by this module.

A centralized management system represents the optimal solution for data exchange and access. In the production scheduling process, shorter production times are obtained as high level planning algorithms are used [10].

3   The Proposed HMES Architecture

Starting from PROSA basic holons defined in [11], we will introduce the design of a HMES management system, defining its architecture, types of holons, modules of implementation and functionality.

The disturbances that could frequently affect the manufacturing process (machines breakdown or running out of vital resources, improper environment conditions in the production area, product contaminations or high levels of radioactivity) must be taken in consideration both in the scheduling and in the production process.

The proposed system has a 3 layers architecture as represented on Fig. 2. At scheduling level, a web-based MES software will provide the link between the client orders and the production database. For every order received, the application will interrogate the database to find which resources, raw matters and human operators are available for executing the order in the requested timeframe. The estimated time for order delivery will be calculated by analysing the previously production process parameters stored in the database. If the orders can be completed in time, a confirmation will be sent to the client, and all the orders information will be passed to the management level, where basic PROSA holons and specific holons like Environment Holon, Time Holon or Operational Holon are structuring the data for the automation level. At this level, a PLC sends commands for the physical resources and reads data from them. A SCADA controller will read the environment parameters from the sensor network and provide information to the Environment Holon. In the same time, the recorded process data from PLC and from SCADA system are transferred to production database for storage, analysis and reports.

A customizable open-source MES application will provide the graphic interface for accessing the product models, available production resources and human resources, and the stock of raw matters and supplies involved in the manufacturing process. A product model contains the product recipe (raw matters, chemical reagents and the sequence of operations performed by resources, product physical and chemical specifications).

The Production Database is storing the production data, environment data and the process historian. Production data are composed by product models, resources list, raw material stocks, suppliers list, employees working program, process time list and delivery time list.

Environment data are represented by an environment model with a GMP defined set of rules for environment parameters (air quality, temperature pressure, humidity).

Product Holon (PH) is storing the information about a product type. Any type of products that can be manufactured by the nuclear facility and the resource setup is defined in the PH. This holon is in fact a theoretical description of a physic product, but not directly associated with it like the Resource Holon.[12]

Production Scheduler is in charge with scheduling of the entire production process (from the first stage of production until customer's products delivery). The scheduler is gathering all the needed information from the Product Holon, Resource Holon, Time Holon and Opera Holon and launch and track the execution of the Order Holon.

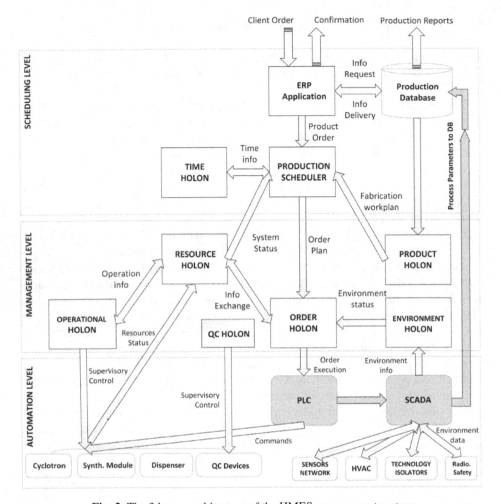

Fig. 2. The 3 layers architecture of the HMES management system

Resource Holon (RH) is storing the information about manufacturing resources (cyclotron, technology isolators, synthesis module and quality control devices).

During the manufacturing process, the RH is providing resources working status and load information. In a nuclear facility we encounter two main types of resources: fully automated and human operated resources.

Operational Holon (OPH) is storing the information about the human operators. It possessed the same level of knowledge as a trained operator for a specific resource. Its role is not only to assist the human operator in taking a decision (like Staff Holon in PROSA), but to replace him when needed. Actions like setting up a resource for work or a visual inspection of a product test can be easily implemented by hardware-software modules.

Time Holon (TH) is storing the information about the delivery times for each client. It contains a predefined schedule for the working days, and stores values for the transport times according to car traffic at different hours. Production Scheduler must take in consideration these values to avoid losing to much product activity on the on the way to hospitals. If a product could be manufactured on time by the production line but it can't be delivered on time to customers the order will be rescheduled.

Order Holon (OH) is storing all the necessary information to produce one certain type of product. This holon is created only when a product order is entered into the system. The OH allocates all the resources needed for the product manufacturing and it holds the status of the unfinished product for every production stages.

Environment Holon (EH) is storing the information about the production environment. This holon is comparing the data received from the SCADA system with the Environment Model stored in the Production Database and notifies the Order Holon if environment condition are proper for radiopharmaceutical production. If perturbations occur during the production process, the Order Holon will decide if the product has been compromised and it may cancel the entire batch execution.

Quality Holon (QH) is storing the information about the quality tests that must be performed for each product type, the test machines required to perform test operation and the analytical methods they will use for testing the product samples.

PLC is a programmable logic controller connected to all the manufacturing resources on the shop-floor line. PLC inputs receive instructions for order execution from the Order Holon and its outputs are sending control commands to the connected manufacturing resources. Status and operating parameters of the resources are read and transferred into Product Database for storage and reports.

SCADA system is in charge with environmental parameters monitoring. The system is connected to HVAC and technology isolators own measuring devices and also to the radiological monitoring system. This system is providing real-time data for the Environment Holon, warning the human operators if alarms level or action levels are reached and transferring the entire environment data intro production database for storage and reports.

4   HMES Functionality for Environment and Scheduling

Since the production process is strongly dependent both on facility's environment and technical isolator's internal environment, alarm levels and action levels are defined for each parameter stored in the environment model. Alarm level warns the SCADA system and the human operators (or Operational Holon) that one or more parameters are not in the desire range and requires investigative actions. Action level alarms require immediate corrective actions from the HMES. If the system is unable to restore the environment conditions in a given period of time, the production is delayed, but in the case of critical parameters[4] deviations an entire product batch is lost. Several methods of controlling the environment by adjusting the HVAC parameters in real time have been proposed and developed in [13] and [14].

---

[4] Critical parameters: number of particles < 0,5 and 5 μm (inside technology isolators) and radioactivity levels.

The launching of a product order by the proposed HMS is taking place in the following steps represented in Fig. 4. Step 1: An order for a specific product is received by the Production Scheduler. Step 2: Product Holon is contacted to check the product recipe. Step 3: Product Holon checks that all the raw materials and supplies are available and provide the resources list necessary for production. Step 4: Production Scheduler contacts the Resource Holon. Step 5: Resource Holon confirms the requested resources are available for work and they are able to perform the requested operations.

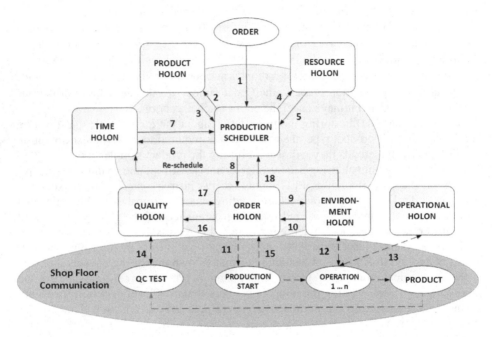

Fig. 3. The interaction between HMES holons for scheduling and order launching

It a resource is not available, it could be replaced by a backup resource. If human operators are not available, Operational Holon will perform their tasks. Step 6: Production Scheduler consults the Time Holon to check the order can be delivered in the required time. Step 7: Time Holon confirms the order can be done in the required time, otherwise the order is cancelled or re-scheduled. Step 8: Order Holon is created for the current product order. Step 9: Environment Holon is contacted before production start to check if all the required environment conditions are met. Step 10: Environment Holon confirms the environment is proper for production, otherwise delays the production start until all the parameters are according to Environment Model stored in the database. In this case Time Holon will be consulted to see if the order will fit on delivery time with this delay. Step 11: Production is initiated in the shop-floor level. Step 12: During operations executions, some resources are production environment changes (radiation levels, airflows). Environment Holon will track the changes and will analyse if they exceed the values from the environment model. If the parameters can't be restored to the desired values in a required time, the production will be stopped. Step13: During production, some resources require human operators and dedicated control software. In case one operator isn't available to execute an operation or it may be too dangerous for him (radiation level), the Operational Holon can communicate with the control software and execute the operator's tasks. Step 14: The final product has been obtained in the last stage of the shop-floor. A product sample is sent to QC laboratory for conformity tests. Quality Holon will assign test devices and analytical methods for the product sample analysis. Step 15: Order Holon is being informed that the product has ended. Step 16: Quality Holon is contacted to confirm the product conformity tests. Step17: Quality Holon confirms all tests were successful; otherwise production is cancelled until the unconformity problem is identified and solved. Step 18: Scheduler is informed that the order has been completed.

5   Simulation of the Proposed HMES Using NetLogo

A HMES model for controlling the radiopharmaceutical production was developed in NetLogo. NetLogo world is, basically, composed by two types of agents, the stationary agents (patches) and the mobile agents (turtles). The patches are arranged in a grid way, so they can form the world in over that the turtles move around [15]. In the proposed architecture, the dot shaped turtle (the product) is passing the production line from the cyclotron to the transport car, and after that, to the hospital. The cyclotron, the two synthesis modules and the dispenser are examples of Resource Holons while the Quality Holon is represented by the analytical instruments performing product quality test (from 1 to 5). The Resources Holons are represented by white and grey patches. Product Holon is created with a process plan containing the details and sequence of operations that must be fulfilled. During its lifecycle the Product Holon will interact with the Resource Holon in order to guarantee a good product execution.

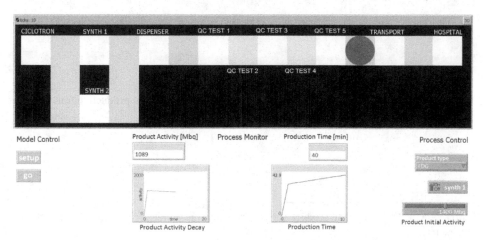

Fig. 4. NetLogo simulation of a radiopharmaceutical production line

Execution times for each resources and QC devices involved in production are stored and can be modified in the software program. Taking these values from the real experimental facility [16] the total production time and the final product activity can be calculated and compared for each type of product. The process control interface let users choose the product type and the product initial activity. Using radioactive decay law[5], the model can calculate the final product activity the hospital will receive. An on/off switch simulates the out-of-order state for the main automated synthesis module (SYNTH1). In this case, the production line will be switched to backup synthesis module (SYNTH2). An area to visualize the results was included, considering the graphical representation of the product activity and the production time.

Three scenarios were simulated for production of 18F-FDG[6]: production using automated synthesis module, production using the manual operated backup module, and a simulated failure in the Class A[7] dispenser environment (which induce additional 20 minutes recovery time delay). The results are shown in Fig. 5.

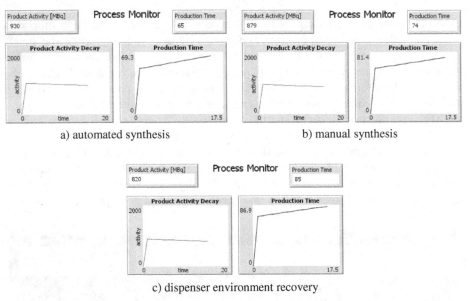

a) automated synthesis   b) manual synthesis

c) dispenser environment recovery

Fig. 5. Simulated results for the final product activity (MBq[8]) and total production time (min.)

---

[5] $A(t) = A_0 \, e^{-\lambda t}$ The final product activity depends on initial activity, time and λ decay constant.

[6] FDG is the commonly used radiopharmaceutical product.

[7] Class A : environment where the number of 0.5 µm particles/m³ are less than 3500.

[8] MBq : megabecquerel. One becquerel represents one disintegration per second.

6   Conclusions and Future Challenges

In this paper it has been presented a Holonic architecture for managing the radio-pharmaceutical production process. The main advantages that results from the use of holonic concepts are the centralized storage of various types of data and the implementation of the manufacturing process with autonomous and cooperative entities. The resulting system is a modular and flexible one and can be easily adapted for any other types of radiopharmaceutical facilities as a LIMS system with extended functionality. The real-time scheduling and the continuous environment monitoring represent key aspects in obtaining good quality products while minimizing the operator's exposure to radiation.

To assets the proposed holonic system design a simulation model has been implemented using NetLogo environment. Results obtained for different simulated scenarios are compared to reveal the importance of every minute for products based on short-life radionuclides. The current model could be updated with any types of radionuclide specification and machines operations timing, providing a useful tool for production scheduling. Simulated results can be also used to study if the real existing system is able to produce and deliver new radiopharmaceutical products.

Future research includes the implementation of all types of holons described in this paper. The work will focus on Environment Holon interaction with production holons using an environment model and on production's scheduling optimization using genetic algorithms.

Acknowledgment. For this research paper Andrei-Octavian Silisteanu acknowledges the support of the Sectorial Operational Program Human Resources Development (SOP HRD), financed by the European Social Fund and the Romanian Government under the contract number POSDRU/159/1.5/S/134398/ .

References

1. International Atomic Energy Agency: Cyclotron Produced Radionuclides: Guidance on Facility Design and Production of [18F] Fluorodeoxyglucose (FDG). IAEA Radioisotopes and Radiopharmaceuticals Series No. 3, Vienna (2012)
2. Stark, J.: Product Lifecycle Management 21st Century Paradigm for Product Realization 2nd edn. Decision Engineering. Springer (2011)
3. Tagger, B.: An Introduction and Guide to Successfully Implementing a LIMS (Laboratory Information Management System) (2011). http://www.cs.ucl.ac.uk/staff/B.Tagger/LimsPaper.pdf
4. Pavlis, R.: Trends in instrument-to-LIMS interfacing. Scientific Computing World (May/June 2004)
5. Medema, J., Luurtsema G., Keizer, H., Tjilkema, S., Elsinga, P.H., Franssen, E.J.F., Paans, A.M.J., Vaalburg, W.: Fully Automated and Unattended [18F]Fluoride and [18F]FDG Production using PLC Controlled Systems. European Cyclotron Progress Meeting 31 (1997)
6. Giret, A., Botti, V.: Holons and agents. Journal of Intelligent Manufacturing, 645–659. Kluwer Academic Publishers (2004)

7. Lind, M., Roulet-Dubonnet, O., Nyen, P.A., Gellein, L.T., Lien, T., Skavhaug, A.: Holonic Manufacturing Paint Shop. In: Mařík, V., Strasser, T., Zoitl, A. (eds.) HoloMAS 2009. LNCS, vol. 5696, pp. 203–214. Springer, Heidelberg (2009)
8. Germain, B., Valckenaers, P., Van Brussel, H., Hadeli K., Bochmann, O., Zamfirescu, C., Verstraete P.: Multi-Agent Manufacturing Control: An Industrial Case Study In: Monostori, L., Kadar, B., Morel, G. (eds.) Intelligent Manufacturing Systems, pp. 207–212. Pergamon Press, Elsevier (2003)
9. Mathia, E.: Pharmaceutical product cross-contamination: industrial and clinical pharmacy practice. Dar Es Salaam Medical Students' Journal 19(2), 17–19 (2012)
10. Raileanu, S., Parlea, M., Borangiu, T., Stocklosa, O.: A JADE Environment for Product Driven Automation of Holonic Manufacturing. In: Borangiu, T., Thomas, A., Trentesaux, D. (eds.) Service Orientation in Holonic and Multi-Agent Manufacturing Control. SCI, vol. 402, pp. 265–278. Springer, Heidelberg (2012)
11. Verstraete, P., Germain, B., Hadeli, K., Valckenaers, P., Van Brussel, H.: On applying the PROSA reference architecture in multi-agent manufacturing control applications. Multiagent Systems and Software Architecture, Proceedings of the Special Track at Net.ObjectDays, Germany (2006)
12. Borangiu, T., Raileanu, S., Rosu A., Parlea M.: Holonic Robot Control for Job Shop Assembly by Dynamic Simulation. In: Guedes, L.A. (ed.) Programmable Logic Controller. InTech (2010). http://www.intechopen.com/books/programmable-logic-controller/holonicrobot-control-for-job-shop-assembly-by-dynamic-simulation
13. Hadjiski, M., Sgurev, V., Boishina, V.: Multi agent intelligent control of centralized HVAC systems. In: Energy Saving Control, vol. 1(pt. 1), pp. 195–200. IFAC Workshop on Energy Saving Control in Plants and Buildings (2006)
14. Treado, S., Delgoshaei, P.: Agent-Based Approaches for Adaptive Building HVAC System Control. In: International High Performance Buildings Conference, Paper 26 (2010)
15. Barbosa, J., Leitao, P.: Simulation of multi-agent manufacturing systems using Agent-Based Modelling platforms. In: 9th IEEE International Conference on Industrial Informatics, pp. 477–482 (2011)
16. Ursu, I., Craciun, L., Niculae, D., Zamfir, N.V.: The Radiopharmaceuticals Research Center (CCR) of IFIN-HH at start. Romanian Journal of Physics 58, 1327–1336, Bucharest (2013)

Behavioural Validation of the ADACOR^2 Self-organized Holonic Multi-agent Manufacturing System

José Barbosa[1(✉),3], Paulo Leitão[1,2], Emmanuel Adam[3], and Damien Trentesaux[3]

[1] Polytechnic Institute of Bragança, Campus Sta. Apolónia, Apartado 1134, 5301-857
Bragança, Portugal
{jbarbosa,pleitao}@ipb.pt
[2] LIACC - Artificial Intelligence and Computer Science Laboratory,
R. Campo Alegre 102, 4169-007 Porto, Portugal
pleitao@ipb.pt
[3] LAMIH UMR CNRS 8201, UVHC, Le mont Houy, 59313 Valenciennes cedex 9, France
{emmanuel.adam,damien.trentesaux}@univ-valenciennes.fr

Abstract. Global economy is driving manufacturing companies into a paradigm revolution. Highly customizable products at lower prices and with higher quality are among the most imposed influence factors. To respond properly to these external and internal constraints, such as work absence and machine failures, companies must be in a constant adaptation phase. Several manufacturing control architectures have been proposed throughout the years displaying more or less success to adapt into different manufacturing situations. These architectures follow different design paradigms but recently the decentralization and distribution of the processing power into a set of cooperating and collaborative entities is becoming the trend. Despite of the effort spent, there is still the need to empower those architectures with evolutionary capabilities and self-organization mechanisms to enable the constant adaption to disturbances. This paper presents a behavioural mechanism embed in the ADACOR^2 holons. A validation procedure for this mechanism is also presented and results extracted. This validation is achieved through the use of a benchmark and results are compared with classical hierarchical and heterarchical architectures as also with the ADACOR.

Keywords: Behavioural self-organization · Multi-agent systems · Reconfigurable manufacturing control

1 Introduction

The current panorama of the world economy is pushing the manufacturing companies to adopt more adaptive and responsive control architectures. Product customization, higher quality and shorter life-cycles are on the epicentre of the requirements imposed to manufacturing companies [1]. Situations of worker absence, resource breakdown and product demand fluctuation are also, at an internal level, a daily concern that require an increase of responsiveness and adaptation from the manufacturing control point of view. A proper manufacturing control architecture is mandatory, required to

© Springer International Publishing Switzerland 2015
V. Mařík et al. (Eds.): HoloMAS 2015, LNAI 9266, pp. 59–70, 2015.
DOI: 10.1007/978-3-319-22867-9_6

present responsiveness to the imposed disturbances, either at an internal or external level, guaranteeing the highest possible performance level of operation.

Traditionally, manufacturing control architectures relied on hierarchical organization as the mean to design those control systems. This type of organization has the advantage of collecting the information and place the processing and decisional capacity at central nodes that have a wider view of the system state and that are able to achieve high levels of performance optimization. At the other side, a considerable drawback can also be pointed out, related with the fact that the information processing time is high, decreasing dramatically the system responsiveness.

More recently, there's the growing trend of promoting the decentralization of the decision entities, bringing them closer to where they are really needed. This paradigm is also aligned with new research trends, such as the Cyber Physical System [2] and the Industrial Internet [3] paradigms.

Manufacturing control architectures have been proposed throughout the years that already use the decentralization concepts. Notably in the holonic paradigm, two reference architectures can be pointed out, namely the PROSA [4] reference architecture and the ADACOR (ADAptive holonic COntrol aRchitecture for distributed manufacturing systems) [5].

Despite the aforementioned, this new generation of manufacturing control architectures still need to further explore evolutionary theories and bio-inspired mechanisms, such as self-organization. To this part, there are already some propositions, namely the PROSA+ANTS [6] and the P2000+ [7]. The first, extends the PROSA reference architecture with inspiration from the ants food foraging that is used as forecast technique, while on the second one, a buffer type self-organization mechanism is used as the system regulation mechanism.

This paper briefly presents the ADACOR^2 manufacturing control architecture that proposes to enhance its predecessor by acting at two levels: micro level, named behavioural self-organization, and at a macro level, named structural self-organization. The assessment and evaluation of the behavioural component is drawn, starting by depicting a mechanism used during this process and analysing important Key Performance Indicators (KPI).

The rest of the paper is organized as follows: Section 2 makes a brief description of the ADACOR^2 self-organized holonic multi-agent system architecture while Section 3 describes a magnetic based self-organization mechanism used during the validation process. Section 4 describes the validation procedure and results of the behavioural self-organization vector. At last, Section 5 rounds up the paper with the conclusions.

2   A Self-organized Manufacturing Control Architecture

ADACOR^2 sets foundation of the well-known holonic manufacturing control architecture, named ADACOR. Therefore, ADACOR^2 makes use of the same set of holons as it have been defined in ADACOR, namely on the Supervisor Holon (SH), Product Holon (PH), Task Holon (TH) and Operational Holon (OH).

Briefly, the SH is responsible to introduce optimized schedules into its holarchy, the PH possesses the knowledge to produce the product that it's responsible for, whereas the TH has the responsibility to manage a product instance that is being produced, taking manufacturing decisions concerning that product. Finally, the OH maps the resources available at the shop-floor, managing its internal agenda, either negating directly with the TH or accepting the schedules from the SH.

Precisely at this last point, ADACOR proposed a binary configuration, where when the system is operation under a well-defined situation, the SH introduces optimization issuing an optimized schedule into lower level holons balancing into a more heterarchical organization where THs negotiate directly with the OHs, increasing the responsiveness of the system. This binary state is ADACOR's most strong point, allowing the combination of optimization with responsiveness, but it's also a weak point since it limits the system into two predefined configurations.

ADACOR^2 makes use of evolutionary theories and self-organization principles to enable the ADACOR architecture to evolve smoothly as possible and as drastic as necessary, unbounding the system from the two predefined configurations [8].

In ADACOR^2, the evolution towards the system re-configuration is supported in two distinct manners:

- A micro-level self-organization, which is related to the self-organization of the behaviour of individual holons, provoking the emergence of a new global behaviour, and in this way a system adaptation. To achieve this, holons have built-in a set of different behaviours and use embedded learning and discover mechanisms to detect new opportunities to evolve and the proper way to re-configure their behaviours [9].
- A macro-level self-organization, which is related to the re-organization of the interactions among the holons, provoking a new global behaviour based on a new society of holons [10]. To achieve this, holons also possess a set of mechanisms that can be used to detect better structural organization and mechanisms to proceed to its implementation.

The need to act at these two different levels is justified by having different disturbance groups, which impact the system in different levels. Having this in mind, ADACOR^2 is enriched with different mechanisms as ways to overcome these constraints levels. The low impact perturbations, being more limited in time and space, can be addressed locally using low impact measures as opposite to high impact perturbation where a deep and long term change in the system can be necessary. Behavioural self-organization is then applied into the micro-level of the system while the structural self-organization is acting on the macro-level allowing the system to evolve into a new configuration (see Figure 1).

Considering that the system is working with a given configuration, C_i, it can either evolve by applying one and/or two of the considered self-organization mechanisms. When a self-organization procedure is applied to either overcome a disturbance or to improve the current holon/system performance, it is said that the system evolves into a new configuration, C_{i+1}, since the current system state has changed.

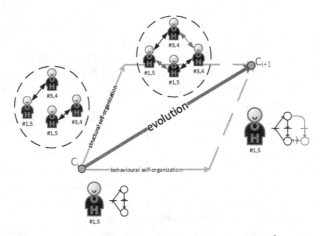

Fig. 1. Evolutionary components in ADACOR[2]

The behavioural self-organization is observed at micro level, where each individual holon may change its internal behaviour according to the external conditions, resulting in a smooth evolution. The second component, named structural self-organization, is observed at the macro level and drives system to a drastic evolution by changing the relations between the holons. In this way, the system can either evolve using behavioural self-organization and/or structural self-organization, to face the external or internal disturbances.

The holons internal organization must also be re-designed to accommodate these self-organization components and to include a nervousness controller. This controller becomes necessary in this self-organized architectures since entities (and the system) might display instability features due to the entities constant will of adaptation [11].

3   A Behavioural Self-organized Mechanism

Having in mind the two self-organization components, there is still the need to develop and embed into the holons such mechanisms. This section presents, in a simplified manner, one of the used mechanisms that enable the holons, namely the THs, to adapt dynamically their behaviour.

The concept of a Potential Field (PF) is a technique that gets inspiration from the magnetism phenomenon, particularly from the inherent attraction and repulsion forces. This phenomenon can be the inspiration to design dynamic and reactive techniques. These concepts have already been used in several application areas such as in game development [12] robots motion planning [13] and even in manufacturing control [14].

Since this approach is reactive, where the emitted force (or field) is changed as soon a given condition changes, it is a good candidate to be used as a behaviour technique for very reactive environments. In such way, an algorithm based on this concept was developed and deployed in ADACOR^2 holons.

Each OH emits a set of PFs based on the offered services, as shown in Figure 2. Briefly, Figure 2 is built by 3 OHs, mapping resources, namely OH$_1$ and OH$_2$ offer the service *yellow* (non-negative values) while OH$_3$ offers *red* and *purple*. The PF must be propagated accordingly with the transportation routes that are mapped in the figure by the thick straight arrow, e.g., it is possible to route from OH$_1$ to OH$_2$. In such way, OH$_2$ back-propagates the *yellow* PF value to OH$_1$, which then calculates its value reflected on it. The value on the final OH is calculated considering the distance to the emitting source OH, i.e. has farther the OH, the lower the PF is. Notice also that in this case, a propagation of the OH$_2$ PF value is also relayed back since it is possible to convey from OH$_3$ to OH$_1$.

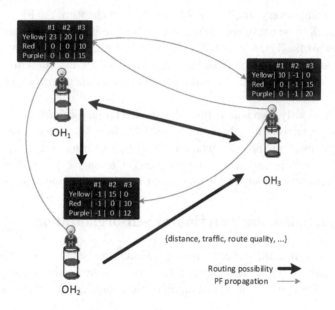

Fig. 2. Potential Field concept

The PF values are stored in the OHs using a blackboard system [15], represented as the black rectangles in Figure 2, being accessible to the holons that need to use them, e.g., THs searching for a processing resource. Additionally, the back-propagation of the PF value ends when the calculated value on the OH is lower than a pre-defined threshold. On the other side, the holons that require the execution of a given service, e.g., a TH that needs a processing task, will check in the current OH for the attractive fields of the next desired service. The selection of the OH that will perform the necessary service is selected by simply, chose the highest emitting field for the service.

Several resource parameters can be used to calculate the strength of each PF, namely the resource workload, the service processing times, the service quality and a scheduled maintenance.

$$OH_i^{PF_{pf}} = \sum W_P \times P_P$$

where,

- W_P is the weight given to parameter P.
- P_P is the value of the parameter P.

In this way, every time a given considered parameter changes, the correspondent OH is responsible to re-calculate the strength of the PF, and to propagate it to its adjacent nodes (i.e. to its adjacent OHs).

Having this information spread over a set of OHs, the THs must then select the most appropriate OH. In this decisional phase, the TH will follow the maximum emitting PF value.

Although being a very simple, reliable and fast mechanism, the PF approach has a major drawback to be considered and that is related to its myopia. Note that from the point of view of the TH, it is only worthy to select the next processing task since if more tasks are allocated, the allocation assumptions for the subsequent tasks will dynamically change and are not therefore guaranteed in the processing execution moment.

As seen previously, two holons from the architecture are considered in the development of this mechanism, namely the OH and TH. These holons have well defined and independent roles in the process, where the OH is responsible for the generation and spread of the system conditions, whereas the TH is only concerned on monitoring and taking decisional actions, abstracting itself from the underlying process.

4   Validation of the Behavioural Self-organization

This section describes the use case used to validate the behavioural self-organization vector, particularly the system organization, the resources skills and the products catalogue. Additionally, the tests assumptions and results are also described.

4.1   The AIP-PRIMECA Cell Description

The FMS, depicted in Figure 3, is composed by 7 machines connected using a conveyor system. The rack conveyor system allows the parts needing processing operations to reach the desired machine using a transport shuttle.

Each machine (from M_1 to M_7) offers a set of skills, needing a defined amount of time to complete the processing task, and the shuttles need to convey for different transportation times depending on the start and destination nodes [16].

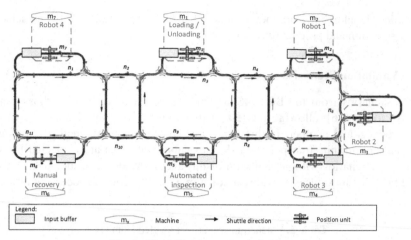

Fig. 3. The AIP-PRIMECA cell layout

The system offers a catalogue of products, namely the BELT, AIP and LATE, that are composed by the appropriated set of sub-products, particularly the letters b, e, l, t, a, i and p. A visual perspective of the sub-products is given in Figure 4.

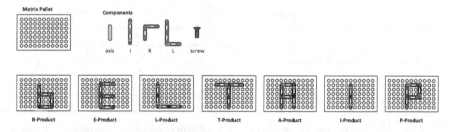

Fig. 4. Sub-products representation

To realize each sub-product, an assembly process must be followed, see Table 1. As an example, to produce the sub-product i, the assembly base plate must be loaded into the shuttle, followed by two axis components, one I and one Screw, followed by an inspection and ending with an unloading procedure.

Table 1. Products processing sequence

Oper	B	E	L	T	A	I	P
#1	Loading	Loading	Loading	Loading	Loading	Loading	Loading
#2	Axis	Axis	Axis	Axis	Axis	Axis	Axis
#3	Axis	Axis	Axis	Axis	Axis	Axis	Axis
#4	Axis	Axis	Axis	Rcomp	Axis	Icomp	Rcomp
#5	Rcomp	Rcomp	Icomp	Lcomp	Rcomp	Screw	Lcomp
#6	Rcomp	Rcomp	Icomp	Inspection	Lcomp	Inspection	Inspection
#7	Icomp	Lcomp	Screw	Unloading	Icomp	Unloading	Unloading
#8	Screw	Inspection	Screw		Screw		
#9	Inspection	Unloading	Inspection		Inspection		
#10	Unloading		Unloading		Unloading		

The decisional choices are then concerned with the appropriate machine selection, routing selection and product release order.

4.2   Validation Scenarios

Several scenarios from the Bench4Star benchmark are used, namely those ranging from A0 to E0 [16], allowing the test of different batch combinations, varying the batch products and number. In this work, all the scenarios have real transportations times and non-infinite transportation shuttles (note that these are neglected for some scenarios). Scenarios without and with disturbances are also considered, namely the #PS12 [16] that introduces a 60s breakdown in M_2 at the end of processing of every 4 jobs.

Table 2. Production scenarios (adapted from [16])

	Number of shuttles	Transportation times	Order #	Products		
				BELT	AIP	LATE
A0	10	Real	#1	1	-	-
			#2	-	1	-
B0	10	Real	#1	-	2	-
C0	4	Real	#1	1	-	-
			#2	-	1	-
D0	10	Real	#1	1	-	-
			#2	2	1	-
E0	10	Real	#1	2	1	-
			#2	-	2	1
			#3	-	-	2

Four manufacturing control architectures are compared in both situations, namely a fully hierarchical architecture, where a high level entity is always providing optimized schedule, a heterarchical architecture where entities are completely autonomous, and finally the ADACOR and ADACOR[2] approaches. Particularly, in the ADACOR[2] tests, the entities are allowed to switch between two different behaviours, namely between a market-based, following a Contract Net Protocol approach, and the Potential Field [9].

4.3   Behavioural Self-organization Assessment

In order to provide a proper validation, each of the aforementioned architectures were simulated, considering each production scenarios, 30 times. Several KPIs, e.g., the C_{max}, throughput and predictability, were extracted, providing a number of results that, after analysed, allow the assessment and validation of the control architectures. With the simulation results, statistical analysis was performed, namely average values and standard deviation were made.

One of the most used KPI in manufacturing control is the C_{max} that is a direct measure of the total time needed for the manufacturing control to produce a given amount of products. In such, and for simplicity reasons, this KPI will be used for the assessment of the behavioural part.

The first batch of simulations were conducted for scenarios where all parameters are well known and controlled, i.e. a system without disturbances. Experimental results for all the non-disturbance situations are shown in Figure 5.

As it can be seen, the hierarchical approach alongside with ADACOR and ADACOR² present the most optimized solution. This is explained by the fact that in these approaches, the SH is constantly introducing optimization schedules to the OHs, since everything is predictable and under control. The heterarchical approach presents the worst results since the THs are directly interacting with the OHs and in this way, myopic phenomena may appear.

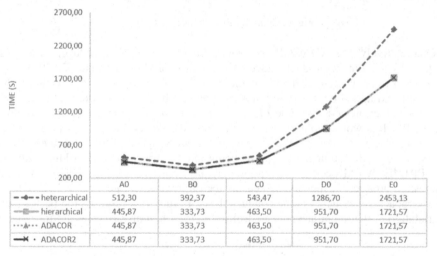

	A0	B0	C0	D0	E0
heterarchical	512,30	392,37	543,47	1286,70	2453,13
hierarchical	445,87	333,73	463,50	951,70	1721,57
ADACOR	445,87	333,73	463,50	951,70	1721,57
ADACOR2	445,87	333,73	463,50	951,70	1721,57

Fig. 5. Cmax for non-disturbance scenarios

A system without disturbances is not realistic and not expected nowadays and so any manufacturing control architecture must be tested within these disturbance working conditions in order to assess its viability. In this way, the #PS12 scenario, as defined in [16], is used. This disturbance scenario introduces a 60s malfunction in M_2 at every 4th processing operation. The experimental results for the C_{max} KPI are shown in Figure 6.

After analysing the graph, it is possible to observe that under these conditions, ADACOR² is the one that achieves a better performance, allowing to produce the same amount of work in less time, i.e. providing a lower C_{max}. Additionally, and as already shown in [5] the ADACOR control architecture surpasses the hierarchical and heterarchical control solutions.

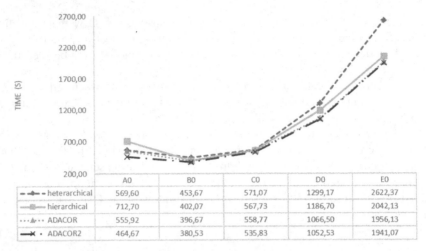

Fig. 6. Cmax for disturbance scenarios

Quantitatively, the ADACOR[2] control architecture is able to reduce, on average, the C_{max} by 91s for the production scenario A0, 23s for C0 and 15s for E0. The apparent margin improvement decrease, as the batch size increases, seems counterproductive and is explained by the behavioural parameter adjustment. It is expected that with a proper selection and fine-tune of the selected behaviour parameters will improve these KPIs. It is worthy to note that a parameter adjustment was not performed during the simulation tests, despite the change of the working conditions for the different scenarios, e.g., the number of shuttles being able to transport the. Additionally, the AIP-PRIMECA FMS cell configuration may have harder freedom limits when a high congestion production appears, decreasing the improvement rate.

An impact assessment can be conducted, see Figure 7, foreseeing the performance degradation of the manufacturing control strategies when disturbances are introduced.

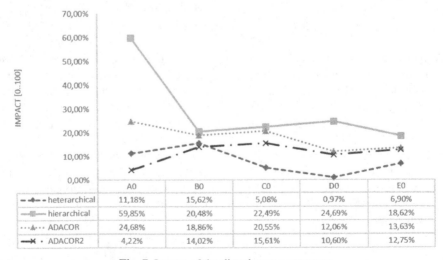

Fig. 7. Impact of the disturbance occurrence

Expectably, the heterarchical approach is the one that suffers less impact due to the disturbance introduction. As commonly known, in completely heterarchical structures, the entities react locally to the disturbances, making them more responsiveness. On the opposite side, the hierarchical approach, due to the higher amount of time that the superior entity needs to re-compute an optimal plan, has the worst performance impact. ADACOR and ADACOR^2 suffer impact levels between those bounds and have good impact performance indexes. ADACOR^2 has a gain over ADACOR, meaning that the dynamic selection of behaviour, in reaction to disturbances, helped to a decrease of the overall system impact.

Globally, and as it is possible to conclude, the ADACOR^2 manufacturing control architecture is the one that best perform under the full range of production scenarios.

5   Conclusions

The current manufacturing world is demanding for innovative control architectures that are able to constantly adapt to the daily constraints. To achieve this, holonic principles implemented using agent technology is a good candidate to address those constraints. Despite of the good results, there is still the need to further enhance those architectures, particularly allowing them to evolve alongside with the disturbances.

The ADACOR^2 manufacturing architecture combines the holonic design principles, it uses the agent based technology and empowers this combination with bio-inspired mechanism, namely self-organization principles. In fact, ADACOR^2 proposes to act at two distinct levels as the way to address different disturbances that may appear.

This paper addresses the behavioural vector, acting at the holons internal level, and assess and validates this approach by means of use of a benchmark. Results have shown that using these principles, ADACOR^2 is able to achieve better results than a hierarchical, heterarchical and the ADACOR control architecture.

Future work, related to this, will be devoted to the development of different behavioural mechanisms and the test in different production system configurations.

References

1. ElMaraghy, H., AlGeddawy, T., Azab, A., ElMaraghy, W.: Change in Manufacturing – Research and Industrial Challenges. In: Enabling Manufacturing Competitiveness and Economic Sustainability, pp. 2–9 (2012)
2. Lee, E.A., Seshia, S.A.: Introduction to embedded systems: a cyber physical systems approach, 1. ed., print. 1.08. Lulu: LeeSeshia.org (2012)
3. Evans, P.C., Annunziata, M.: Industrial Internet: Pushing the Boundaries of Minds and Machines (2012). Whitepaper, General Electric, http://www.ge.com/docs/chapters/Industrial_Internet.pdf
4. Brussel, H.V., Wyns, J., Valckenaers, P., Bongaerts, L., Peeters, P.: Reference Architecture for Holonic Manufacturing Systems: PROSA. In: Computers in Industry, pp. 255–274 (1998)

5. Leitão, P., Restivo, F.: ADACOR: A Holonic Architecture for Agile and Adaptive Manufacturing Control. Computers in Industry **57**(2), 121–130 (2006)
6. Valckenaers, H.P., Kollingbaum, M., Van Brussel, H.: Multi-agent Coordination and Control using Stimergy. Computers in Industry **53**, 75–96 (2004)
7. Bussmann, S., Schild, K.: Self-Organizing Manufacturing Control: An Industrial Application of Agent Technology. In: Proceedings of the Fourth International Conference on MultiAgent Systems (ICMAS-2000), Washington, DC, USA, pp. 87–94 (2000)
8. Barbosa, J., Leitão, P., Adam, E., Trentesaux, D.: Dynamic self-organization in holonic multi-agent manufacturing systems: The ADACOR evolution. Computers in Industry **66**, 99–111 (2015)
9. Barbosa, J., Leitao, P., Adam, E., Trentesaux, D.: Self-Organized Holonic Multi-agent Manufacturing System: The Behavioural Perspective. In: IEEE International Conference on Systems, Man, and Cybernetics, pp. 3829–3834 (2013)
10. Barbosa, J., Leitão, P., Adam, E., Trentesaux, D.: Structural Self-organized Holonic Multi-Agent Manufacturing Systems. In: Mařík, V., Lastra, J.L., Skobelev, P. (eds.) HoloMAS 2013. LNCS, vol. 8062, pp. 59–70. Springer, Heidelberg (2013)
11. Barbosa, J., Leitão, P., Adam, E., Trentesaux, D.: Nervousness in Dynamic Self-organized Holonic Multi-agent Systems. In: Highlights on Pratical Applications of Agents and Multi-Agent Systems, pp. 9–17 (2012)
12. Hagelbäck, J., Johansson, S.J.: A Multiagent Potential Field-Based Bot for Real-Time Strategy Games. International Journal of Computer Games Technology **2009**, 1–10 (2009)
13. Dolgov, D., Thrun, S., Montemerlo, M., Diebel, J.: Path Planning for Autonomous Vehicles in Unknown Semi-structured Environments. The International Journal of Robotics Research **29**(5), 485–501 (2010)
14. Zbib, N., Pach, C., Sallez, Y., Trentesaux, D.: Heterarchical production control in manufacturing systems using the potential fields concept. Journal of Intelligent Manufacturing (2010)
15. Engelmore, R., Morgan, A.J. (eds.) Blackboard systems. Addison-Wesley, Wokingham, England; Reading, Mass (1988)
16. Trentesaux, D., Pach, C., Bekrar, A., Sallez, Y., Berger, T., Bonte, T., Leitão, P., Barbosa, J.: Benchmarking flexible job-shop scheduling and control systems. Control Engineering Practice **21**(9), 1204–1225 (2013)

Digital Factories and Manufacturing Control Systems

A Service-Oriented Architecture Implementation in the Digital Factory of the University

Jeffrey Wermann[1(✉)], Eduardo Cardoso Moraes[2,3], and Armando Walter Colombo[1]

[1] Institut I^{2}AR, University of Applied Sciences Emden/Leer, Emden, Germany
{jeffrey.wermann,armando}@hs-emden-leer.de
[2] PEI/UFBA, Federal University of Bahia, Salvador, Brazil
eduardo.moraes@ifal.edu.br
[3] Federal Institute of Alagoas, Maceio, Brazil

Abstract. In reaction to the changing requirements for modern manufacturing systems, which lead to an increasing demand for flexibility and reconfigurability, different technologies had been developed in the past to meet these requirements. In today's competitive dynamic market, the successful integration of new architectures and technologies in manufacturing processes is inevitable for all organizations. One promising approach is to map the concepts of "Service-Oriented Architecture" into the automation area. In order to test and evaluate the capabilities of this architecture and its related technologies, the University of Applied Sciences Emden/Leer has been building its "Digital Factory" following this approach. This paper will provide an overview about how the SOA concept has been implemented at the "Digital Factory" and what is going to be realized in the future.

Keywords: Service-Oriented architecture · SOA in automation · DPWS · Control systems

1 Introduction

In today's competitive dynamic market, the successful integration of new architectures and technologies in manufacturing processes is inevitable for all organizations. The aim of these new evolving architectures and technologies is to move some of the manufacturing processes' decisions down in the organizational hierarchy, in order to reduce the time required for the decision making process and to be able to adapt rapidly to the market's and customer's fast changing requirements. High competition, globalization, business process outsourcing, rising regulatory environments and demanding consumers are forcing enterprises to transform the way they provide their business and services. These forces are transforming the companies to produce with higher quality at lower costs and they need to change rapidly to attend to these requirements to survive.

As described above, the society demands more and more personalized products with high quality. It also requires a high level of automation and computerization.

© Springer International Publishing Switzerland 2015
V. Mařík et al. (Eds.): HoloMAS 2015, LNAI 9266, pp. 73–83, 2015.
DOI: 10.1007/978-3-319-22867-9_7

Automation is rising in importance in industrial environments, especially in developed countries where labor is more expensive, and the quality expectations are higher. Since the individuality of the products increases, the costs for such production facilities are becoming too high. Also the storage organization is getting more complicated.

These changes impact in lower time-to market and shorter product life cycles. To keep improving their process the companies are investing in computer integrated manufacturing to control all areas and testing new paradigms to amend their process. The most of current production methodology is based on centralized databases where the users insert values using proprietary values and protocols. Interested parties must then connect cyclically the same database in order to extract relevant information to be used for the entire enterprise architecture [3]. To acquire the level of real-time information in the complete product life cycle, it is necessary to use gateways capable of dialog with different networks and protocols. The complete interoperability provided by default standards and its acceptance by the market is still on the way.

But some good initiatives are being created and tested. Flexible manufacturing systems is an approach focused on changes in work orders, production schedules, new design of factories and tools to provide efficient changes in factories.

To reach that level of customization, the integration between diverse areas intra and inter enterprise is necessary. It is available through a set of components: software, hardware, peopleware and the best methodologies efficiently applied. The progress in information technology is transforming the industrial workplace, more specifically the automation area. But there still exists a gap caused by the limited, or not real-time capable communication infrastructure between manufacturing elements, generating barriers for the adoption of flexible, intelligent production systems with a high degree of reconfigurability and interoperability.

The following report will describe and make research in a Service Oriented Architecture system which has been developed at the University of Applied Sciences Emden/Leer. It will provide an overview on how this topic is researched and is putting a strong emphasis on the practical implementation of a SOA based system at the laboratories of the University of Applied Sciences Emden/Leer by describing the equipment and technologies used, as well as the first results.

1.1 Paper Structure

This paper will be structured as follows: Chapter 2 will talk about the state of the art of SOA in Automation. this chapter will describe some outstanding technologies in the manufacturing area. Chapter 3 introduces the Digital Factory at the University of Applied Sciences Emden/Leer. Chapter 4 details the SOA implementation in the Digital Factory and the chapter 5 discusses the achievements and outlooks.

2 State of the Art: SOA in Automation

As described in the last chapter the progress in information technology is transforming the companies and especially industrial ones.

The global manufacturing sector represents 25% of world GDP with over twenty million enterprises, and 28% of world employment [6]. Manufacturing is still a key economic driver world-wide.

According to Evans Data Corp.'s Web Services Development Survey [6], the percentage of working Service-Oriented Architectures has almost doubled. Web Services are also expected to have a 58% increase in implementation within the few upcoming years. The implementation of cloud based computing services allows the enterprise to save more money, which in turn means having more profits. According to a recent Gartner report the global revenue from cloud computing will exceed $180 billion by 2015 (Figure 1). These revenues include the shift to cloud-based computing services, and the planning behind this shift.

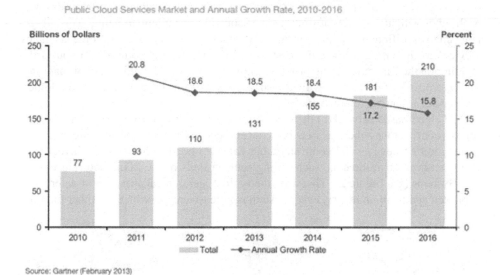

Fig. 1. Cloud computing Market growth forecast (Source Forbes [9]).

As shown in Figure 1, the investments in cloud services are rising and the total market of cloud-based systems is expected to grow from $76.9B in 2010 to $210B in 2016. The Figure 1 analyses the cloud services market size and annual growth rates, which demonstrates the high interest of the companies in investing in this technology.

The term Service Oriented Manufacturing rises with the fast evolution of computers in all business fields, especially the manufacturing sector, which in turn introduced Computer Aided Manufacturing as a technology that integrates advanced computing capabilities in processes to facilitate and automate manufacturing.

There is not a consensus in academy and there are many definitions of the SOA concept, but for the purposes of this paper, the following has been adopted: "A service-oriented architecture is a set of architectural tenets for building autonomous yet interoperable systems." [5]

Service-Oriented Architecture offers a possibility to provide the required system-wide visibility and device interoperability in complex collaborative automation systems which are subject to frequent changes. SOA is based on the Web Service technology and its acceptance is growing in the world of industrial automation and is already used as a platform for controlling and surveillance. They have been proven in business system situations, and initial analysis suggests that SOA could meet the technical and business level requirements for future automation systems [1]. SOA is essentially an architectural paradigm that defines instruments to publish, find and bind services. SOA is characterized by message-based communication, loose coupling and open standards. These features make it particularly applicable for a universal multi-vendor environment where interoperability is critical [2].

Different service requestors (clients) are able to invoke and search for the requested service in different Manufacturing service clouds, exchange information with each other without interaction from a super controller or a human being. This advantage enables different manufacturing elements to assemble and combine as many services as they need to have the best virtual manufacturing solutions or routes depending on their manufacturing task (system intelligence). This life cycle of manufacturing processes takes place with the support of advanced computing technologies, and service-oriented architectures [4].

The cloud-based network of different services in manufacturing areas is also sometimes referred to as the "service bus". Members of this service bus are not only manufacturing devices and controllers, but can also be all other systems involved in manufacturing environments, such as engineering tools or the Manufacturing Execution Systems (see Figure 2). This way, the typical hierarchical structure of enterprises is broken apart and, in theory, every system is able to interact with each other directly.

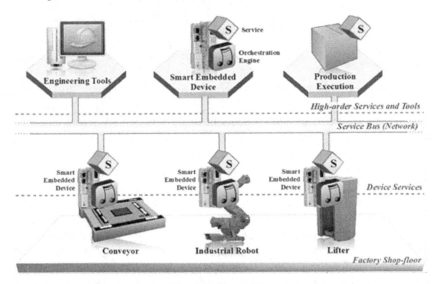

Fig. 2. Service Bus connecting different components

A successful implementation of Service Oriented Manufacturing and the service discovery methods result in:

- Installation time/cost reduction: due to the ease of reconfiguration and setup of devices.
- Interoperability (compatibility) and reduced complexity for technology suppliers: as the devices communicate with each other regarding to the service provided by each, not by the internal specifications of each device.
- Cost reduction: through increased utilization of machines and services reuse.
- Reduction of waste and energy for enhanced manufacturing and production efficiency via increased production speeds, raw material consistency and more precise tooling accuracy.

To implement these SOA approach we will discuss three dominant technologies:

2.1   DPWS

DPWS is a standard that defines the minimum requirements that allow secure web-services messaging, discovery, description and the implementation of WS-Discovery in resources constrained devices. DPWS is regarded as the USB-technology for Ethernet [5]. DPWS is built on the core web-services standards (SOAP, WS-discovery, WS-Addressing...etc). Figure 3 shows the structure of the DPWS standard with its related protocols.

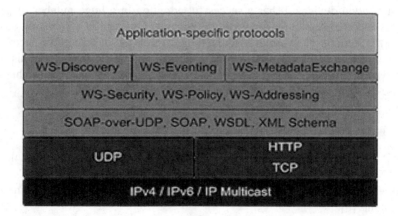

Fig. 3. DPWS Structure

The DPWS technology defines:

- The hosting services: Directly related to the device, which is important for the discovery process.
- The hosted services: functional services that depend on the hosting device for discovery.

- Discovery Services: allow network devices to advertise themselves and discover other devices.
- Metadata exchange services: allow accessing the hosted data and their metadata.
- Publish/Subscribe eventing services: allow the subscription to asynchronous messages transmitted by other services.

The purpose of the Devices Profile for Web-Services (DPWS) is to offer:

- A lightweight dynamic discovery protocol to locate web services that composes with other Web service specifications.
- A binding of SOAP to UDP (User Datagram Protocol), including message patterns, addressing requirements, and security considerations.
- A profile of Web Service protocols consisting of a minimal set of implementation constraints to enable secure Web service messaging, discovery, description, and eventing on resource-constrained. [5]

2.2   OPC UA

Another initiative to standardize a unique specification for devices to allow and ensure security of Web Services is the Object Linking and Embedding for Process Control Unified Architecture (OPC-UA). OPC UA is a Service-oriented Architecture, in which services are protocol independent and provide the basis for OPC UA functionality.

The Classical OPC is an interface to interconnect devices, providing rules for communication devices. It has a successful adoption in a huge number of products, and it is used today as a unified interface between automation systems in various levels of the automation pyramid. Although the success of classical OPC, some limitations were found like some areas where manufacturers would like to use this standard but it was not possible to use it because OPC is depending on COM technology or because of the boundaries for remote access with the usage of DCOM [6].

2.3   gSOAP

gSOAP is a mature and fast open source Web services development toolkit that facilitates development of Web services in C/C++ by offering both XML to C/C++ as well as C/C++ to XML language bindings. It supports many platforms, including embedded systems [8].

gSOAP fully automates the XML serialization process. By using these bindings, SOAP/XML interoperability is achieved with a simple API relieving the user from the burden of WSDL and SOAP details, thus enabling him or her to concentrate on the application-essential logic, and thus, being freed from worrying about the internals of Web service functionality. The end result is a self-contained, full-featured Web Service implementation that is both lightweight and portable.

The gSOAP toolkit runs on most systems such as Linux, BSD Unix, HPUX, Solaris, Irix, AIX, Mac OS X, Cygwin and Windows [8].

3   The Digital Factory at the University of Emden/Leer

To be able to demonstrate and evaluate the capabilities of the SOA paradigm in an industrial environment, a test bed, called the "Digital Factory", has been built by the research team of the institute I²AR at the university in Emden. Starting as a simple conveyor belt system many years ago, it evolved to a small factory, consisting of many different industrial devices and machines, which is able to offer a big set of functionalities. This factory, shown in Figure 4, is used both for research as well as for teaching students the implemented technologies, such as the previously described Web Service technologies.

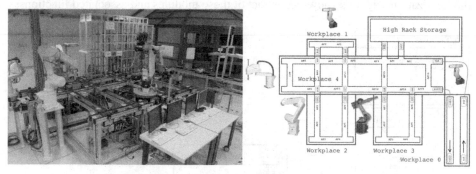

Fig. 4. The Digital Factory and its schematic view

The system allows the transportation of specific platforms, on which different material can be attached. As the system has been built for educational purposes, it was decided to have a small industrial-like process, but which uses LEGO bricks instead of real material, in order to reduce material cost and consumption. These bricks are used to build different structures, but using real industrial equipment, such as PLCs, industrial robots and different kinds of sensors and actuators.

By design, the system is following a highly modular approach, where the factory is divided into six different modules:

- Workplace 0: is the in- and output conveyor for the system, where the raw material is able to get into the factory and the finished product will be delivered to. It includes a measurement station, where the incoming material can be weighed and checked with a camera system.
- Workplace 1-3: are the main workstations of the factory. In each of these modules, a U-shaped conveyor system is used to transport the platforms to an industrial robot. Each workstation is equipped with a different robot (e.g. a KUKA KR6 or a Mitsubishi RV-12) and different tools for the robot. Therefore, the workstations have some shared operations, but also some operations, which only can be done by this specific module.
- Workplace 4: is the main conveyor belt system, which connects all the different modules. The layout of this system allows a high flexibility in the path finding for the different platforms.

- High Rack Storage: This module is a storage system, which allows storing up to 100 platforms. A Cartesian robot is used to pick up items from the main conveyor system and placing them in one of the storage places and vice versa.

4   SOA Implementation in the Digital Factory

The physical layout that was described in chapter 3 has been used to implement a Webservice-based SOA in the Digital Factory. To achieve this, first the different functions that could be exposed as Services were detected. Then, the system has been split into different functional modules, loosely based on the already existing physical modularization. Figure 5 shows an extract of these modules and associated functions:

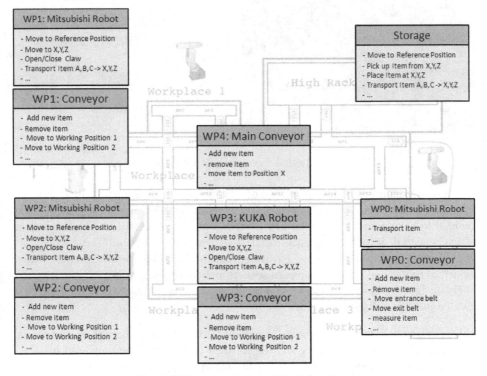

Fig. 5. Different modules and their functions

Each of the above mentioned functions (and more) were then implemented as a Web Services, using the DPWS standard. DPWS was chosen over OPC-UA, as the Digital Factory is also used to demonstrate the results of the EU FP7 project IMC-AESOP [11]. During this project and its predecessor FP6 SOCRADES, a big focus has been put into the DPWS standard, implementing it . The "Inico S1000" Smart RTU was used for this implementation. It allows real-time control of automation processes, as well as web-based monitoring and integration into Enterprise systems. It includes a full implementation of the DPWS standard and is therefore able to provide control and monitoring functionalities, which have been implemented in IEC 61131-3 Structured Text (ST) as Web Services. These services can be easily detected through the discovery mechanisms, that have been defined by DPWS and the services can be accessed via the SOAP protocol.

For more complex applications, where the capabilities of the Inico S1000 devices were too limited, the DPWS interfaces were developed ourselves using the WS4D-gSOAP framework. Examples for this are the control mechanisms for the robots, as they can't be controlled via simple digital or analog in- and outputs. Instead, a communication to the robot control system (e.g. KRC for the KUKA robot) needs to be established, which allows sending commands to the robot control system. As the robot controllers usually communicate in their own protocol, which is not compliant to the DPWS standard, an additional IPC has been used, to act as a gateway. The IPC is able to publish the robot's functions as DPWS-compliant Web Services and will translate every incoming Web Service request into the according message for the robot control to trigger the execution of the command.

Following the DPWS standard, all the implemented devices with their services can easily be detected over the laboratory's network. As it has been seen during the implementation process, (from a functional point of view) new devices and services can be added without any problems. Common DPWS compliant tools, like the DPWS Explorer will immediately be able to detect new services as soon as they are added to the system. The same way, these services can then be dynamically added to the control flow of the factory, following the current need of the industry regarding technologies to enable plug-and-produce mechanisms.

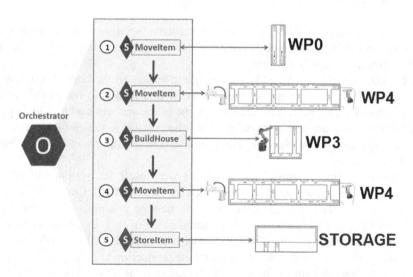

Fig. 6. Orchestration of Services of the Digital Factory

With this basic structure, each module is able to perform some basic operations. But to really be able to run a whole production process, another control layer needs to use these basic services to establish an intelligent production work flow. To do this, the orchestration capabilities of the SOA paradigm have been used. Multiple low level services can be used and put in a logic order to generate a new functionality. For example, the building of a whole LEGO house (or any other structure) can be accomplished, by using the different transport services of the system, to take a platform with bricks from the entrance to one of the robots (see Figure 6).

For this transportation, services of three different modules are used. Afterwards, the robot's services will be used to build the structure, before bringing the platform to the storage and storing it inside.

The same way the orchestration is using the basic services, the orchestrated work flow can be used as a Service itself, as it publishes its functionality as well. This can now be used in higher level systems, such as the MES to execute different processes. But the SOA structure also allows breaking up typical hierarchical structures, so that even the basic services might be accessible by higher level systems. This can for example be useful for SCADA systems to get data directly from the process.

The results also show the migration of a system that was originally built in a traditional way into a SOA. The SOA can be seen on the one hand in the representation of functionalities as services, but also in the above mentioned break of hierarchical structures, where the newly generated services can now be used by different components on all levels. The results show that using these web technologies, different devices are able to interact with each other easily and new services can be added and removed dynamically, therefore setting the base for plug-and-produce mechanisms.

5   Outlook

With the previously described basic setup for a manufacturing system which follows the SOA concept by using Web Service technologies, many things will be able to be implemented and tested in the future.

A SCADA system will be added to be able to access all the control functions and to be able to monitor the status of the system. A first idea is to use mobile devices, such as tablet PCs, to get remote access to some of the services and provide a graphical interface to interact with the system. It will be possible to create own plans for the structures that should be built by using simple configuration tools (e.g. LDraw or BlockCAD).

Parallel to the improvement of the control system itself, the system will also need to be connected to higher level systems, such as MES or ERP. Currently, neither of these is implemented, but each is necessary to be able to simulate a manufacturing system, that is close to "real-life" implementations. For this, it will be beneficial to use established software to showcase how the SOA approach allows easy connection between existing state-of-the-art systems and the production system.

After the whole system has been implemented, several benchmarks can be done to evaluate the capabilities of SOA based manufacturing systems. It will be possible to see the advantages and disadvantages of such a structure. An important topic that needs to be taken into consideration when evaluating the results is the real-time behavior. As the solution is based on web technologies, which derive from a world where the real-time constraints are softer than in an industrial area, this will need to be tested. Furthermore, the security needs to be looked into. By flattening the hierarchies inside a production system by connecting every device into a system-wide service cloud using the same protocols, it is necessary to prove, that this solution provides enough security mechanisms to prevent the misuse of certain parts of the system.

References

1. Colombo, A.W., Jammes, F., Smit, H., Harrison, R., Martinez Lastra, J.L., Delamer, I.M.: Service-Oriented Architectures for Collaborative Automation. In: IEEE (2005)
2. Colombo, A.W., et al.: Industrial Cloud-Based Cyber-Physical Systems, The IMC-AESOP approach. Springer (2014)
3. Moraes, E.C., Lepikson, H.A.: Potential impact for energy consumption with Service Oriented. Advanced Materials Research, vols. 1030–1032 (2014). DOI:www.scientific.net/amr.1030-1032.1925
4. Tao, F., Zhang, L., Venkatesh, V.C., Luo, Y., Cheng, Y.: Cloud manufacturing: a computing and service-oriented manufacturing model. Proceedings of the Institution of Mechanical Engineers, Part B: Journal of Engineering Manufacture **225**, 1969–1976 (2011). doi:10.1177/0954405411405575(10)
5. Driscoll, D., Mensch, A.: Microsoft: OASIS Devices Profile for Web Services (DPWS) Version 1.1. (retrieved February 27, 2014) from OASIS Standard (July 1, 2009). http://docs.oasis-open.org/ws-dd/ns/dpws/2009/01
6. Mahnke, W., Leitner, S.-H., Damm, M.: OPC unified architecture. Springer, Heidelberg (2009). ISBN 9783540688990
7. OPC Foundation (2014): What is OPC? - OPC Foundation. https://opcfoundation.org/about/what-is-opc/ (checked on September 30, 2014)
8. Engelen, R.: An XML Web Services Development Environment for Embedded Devices. http://www.cs.fsu.edu/~engelen/cases03.html (checked on November 3, 2014)
9. Gartner, C.L.: Predicts Infrastructure Services Will Accelerate Cloud Computing Growth Forbes Website (accessed in November 19, 2014). http://www.forbes.com/sites/louiscolumbus/2013/02/19/gartner-predicts-infrastructure-services-will-accelerate-cloud-computing-growth/
10. Cardoso Moraes, E., Augusto Lepikson, H.: Service-Oriented Framework for Oil Fields Automation. Applied Mechanics and Materials **496**, 1438–1441 (2014)
11. Colombo, A.W., Bangemann, T., Karnouskos, S., Delsing, S., Stluka, P., Harrison, R., et al.: Industrial Cloud-Based Cyber-Physical Systems, ed. Springer (2014)

A Volatile Knowledge Approach to Improve the Autonomy of Holons: Application to a Flexible Job Shop Manufacturing System

Emmanuel Adam[✉]

UVHC, LAMIH Lab., UMR CNRS 8201, 59313 Valenciennes, France
emmanuel.adam@univ-valenciennes.fr

Abstract. It is well known now that MAS are particularly adapted to deal with distributed and dynamic environment. The management of business workflow, or data flow, flexible job shop manufacturing systems is typically a good application field for them. This kind of application requires flexibility to face with changes on the network. In the context of FMS, where products and resources entities can be seen as active, and subject to events, a volatile knowledge concept has been defined. We illustrate our proposition on an emulator of the flexible assembly cell in our university.

Keywords: Volatile knowledge · Flexible job shop manufacturing systems · Multiagent system

1 Introduction

To be competitive, manufacturing industries have to adapt to changing conditions imposed by the market. The greater variety of products, the possible large fluctuations in demand, the shorter lifecycle of products expressed by a higher dynamics of new products, and the increased customer expectations in terms of quality and delivery time are challenges that manufacturing companies have to deal with to remain competitive. In recent decades, scientific developments in the field of production have defined new architectures including the heterarchical/non-hierarchical ones that play a prominent role in FMS.

Several bio-inspired approaches have been proposed, and are still proposed. Some are based on stigmergy, such as for example, the Ant colony optimization (ACO) [5], the Firefly Algorithm [13], ... Other are based on Particle Swarm Optimization (PSO) [7], such as Bee Based Algorithms [10] (Bee Colony Optimization, Honey Bee Colony Algorithm, ...), Shuffled Frog Algorithm [12], Roach Infestation Optimization (RIO) [6] ...

In this paper we try, to avoid the use of a shared environment, and of a control layer (we have already proposed approaches using Potential Fields, and a holonic architecture [1]) for the management of dynamic and mobile entities that evolve on a uni-directional routing graph, and that can be concurrent (such as conveyors of a flexible job shop manufacturing system).

© Springer International Publishing Switzerland 2015
V. Mařík et al. (Eds.): HoloMAS 2015, LNAI 9266, pp. 84–95, 2015.
DOI: 10.1007/978-3-319-22867-9_8

Our objective is to propose a solution implementable only on the mobile and decisional entities, without the necessity to computerize all the elements of the graph (i.e. the nodes, the edges, . . .) and using an acceptable number of messages exchanged between these entities.

We took inspiration from the stigmergy to propose the notion of volatile knowledge. In stigmergic approaches, an information (like 'presence of a resource') is put in several locations of the environment with a value more or less important relatively to the distance between the location and the position of the resource. These values are 'evaporated' by a mechanism that reduces them regularly [1].

Similarly, in the concept of volatile knowledge, each knowledge of an agent is qualified by a confidence level that the agent degrades regularly; and a knowledge is removed if it has a too low level of confidence. Thus, rather than depositing pheromones that degrade themselves in a shared environment, the agents (the shuttles) communicate between them knowledge whom they degrade the confidence levels. The advantage of this solution over existing bio-inspired approaches is that the control is totally distributed among the 'intelligent' (mobile and/or decisional) devices: there is no need to use a centralized and common layer that would manage the signals deposited by the agents in the environment. Another advantage is that the solution is directly implemented inside the active devices; it is not a centralized solution computed by a main controller that assigns the tasks to the mobile agents.

Such a forgetting of information has already been used in order to improve the learning times in Reinforcement Learning [14]. In fact the notion of forgetting has been studied since years in the context of classical logic (it also known as variable elimination) [9]. In this paper, we focus essentially on the forgetting of observations.

This paper presents the notion of volatile knowledge dedicated to the management of a flexible job shop manufacturing system. An experimentation of this concept using a benchmark dedicated to manufacturing cell management is then presented (in the third section).

2 Volatile Knowledge for Flexible Assembly Cells Management

In [2] and [8], we have proposed our concept of volatile knowledge adapted to the management of communication between autonomous vehicles that evolve on a uni-directional routing graph (a road being composed of two opposite uni-directional lines). We apply in this paper this concept to the management of a flexible job shop manufacturing system, this new application lead us to improve the previous model of volatile knowledge.

---

[1] For example, if $f(t)$ is the 'force' of the information (its value) on a location at the date t, at date $(t + 1)$, the 'force' will be $f(t + 1) = \gamma \times f(t)$, with $\gamma \in [0, 1]$ being the degradation coefficient of the value. N.B. A mechanism of diffusion is also used in stigmergic approaches, but we do not use it in the concept of volatile knowledge.

We consider a flexible assembly cell, as described in [11]; it is composed of autonomous shuttles that receive orders to build products. A product is composed of different parts, and needs to be deposit on a shuttle, removed once it is complete and checked. These tasks (add a component, deposit, check, remove) are done by workstation distributed in the cell. Each workstation is able to provides one or more services, and they cannot been shared at the same time. Also, the paths between the workstation are uni directional. The shuttles try to find the best workstations to create the products; namely, the shortest sequence of workstations that provides the desired services. To do that, the shuttles can decide at each crosspoint which path they will use.

In our approach, a shuttle informs the other shuttles about its intention (the next workstation its plan to go), and about event (like fault/repairing of a workstation). So, two types of knowledge are used: reservation of a workstation, fault/repairing of a workstation.

Of course, we use 'as usually' a holonic architecture but we try to give the most autonomy as possible to the holons at the base of the holarchy. In the work presented in this paper, we use only two levels, the top level being constituted of one holon that just transmits product orders to the lower holons and that just traces the position and states of lower holons. Indeed, the lower holons being myopes, each of them has only a local and partial view of the system (the holons and the environment); to allow to a human operator to control the system, it is necessary to have a global access to this one.

2.1   Elements of Volatile Knowledge Model

A knowledge is a partial view of the environment or of the other agents, namely for a given object o of the environment (the traffic network for example); it is (generally) an incomplete copy of it, so a representation of o with missing attributes and methods.

We define a knowledge κ_o^a (cf. def. 1) on an object o for an agent a with: o_a', a partial view of o from a; $date_{\kappa_o^a}$, the date when the knowledge has been created or updated (by a or by another agent if the knowledge has been received); $builderAgent_{\kappa_o^a}$, the 'builder' of the knowledge (name of the agent that has created/updated the knowledge from its perception); $senderAgent_{\kappa_o^a}$, the 'sender' of the knowledge (name of the agent that could have sent the knowledge to a); $conf_{\kappa_o^a} \in [0, 1]$ the confidence that a has on κ_o^a; $deg_{\kappa_o^a} \in [0, 1]$ the percentage of confidence degradation applied at each 'step'; $threshold_{\kappa_o^a} \in [0, 1[$ the threshold under which the knowledge is no more considered (and has to be removed); $shareable_{\kappa_o^a}$, the fact that the knowledge is shareable or not by a.

$$\kappa_o^a = \begin{pmatrix} o_a', date_{\kappa_o^a}, builderAgent_{\kappa_o^a}, senderAgent_{\kappa_o^a}, \\ conf_{\kappa_o^a}, deg_{\kappa_o^a}, threshold_{\kappa_o^a}, shareable_{\kappa_o^a}, aggregation_{\kappa_o^a} \end{pmatrix} \quad (1)$$

Confidence and Volatility. In a dynamic environment, it is necessary to allow an automatic update, a cleaning of the outdated or invalidated beliefs.

In our model, at each step, each passage in the life cycle of an agent (perception-cognition-action) or at each 'tick' given by a simulator, the confidence on a knowledge is degraded: $conf_{\kappa_o^a} \leftarrow conf_{\kappa_o^a} \times (1 - deg_{\kappa_o^a})$.

A knowledge κ_o^a can be either perennial ($deg_{\kappa_o^a} = 0$) or volatile ($deg_{\kappa_o^a} > 0$) (we note $\overline{\kappa_o^a}$ a perennial knowledge). For an agent a, the first knowledge about an object given to it (by the creator of a, human or not), $\overline{\kappa_{o_0}^a}$, is considered as perennial (for example, a shuttle agent (mobile agent) starts with the manufacturing cell map, knowing the length of the roads between the resources; i.e. the weights of the edges). All the other knowledge relative to the same object, $\kappa_{o_i}^a$, will be considered by a as volatile .

Initially, $conf_{\overline{\kappa_{o_0}^a}} = 1$, but when volatile knowledge about o are added, this confidence is degraded; we propose that: $conf_{\overline{\kappa_{o_0}^a}} = (1 - \max\limits_{i=1..n}(conf_{\kappa_{o_i}^a}))$. If more than one knowledge exists relatively to the same object, it is necessary to normalize the confidence values.

Confidence Evolution. All the knowledge, except the perennial knowledge, decreases at each step its confidence: $conf_{\kappa_o^a} \leftarrow conf_{\kappa_o^a} \times (1 - deg_{\kappa_o^a})$

The degradation coefficient is dependent on the knowledge nature (perennial or volatile) as well as of the knowledge object.

For example, a knowledge relative to a rail/road load would have a greater degradation coefficient than a knowledge relative to a fault on a workstation.

And a knowledge relative to the workstation occupancy should be stored in the knowledge only as long as this occupancy is true.

When the knowledge confidence goes under its threshold ρ [2], the knowledge is removed from the list of current knowledge and is added in a list of 'doubtful' knowledge. So, if no event occurs about an object o, finally only the perennial knowledge (the first known value about the object) will subsist in the agent memory.

When an agent perceives or receives an information similar to one in its knowledge list, the confidence is updated, and the degradation coefficient is adapted to reflect the actual confidence evolution.

This principle of knowledge management is dedicated to agents evolving in a dynamic environment subject to modifications; it allows an agent to take into account different observations about the same object, in order to take a decision.

2.2 Aggregation of Knowledge

Consequently to our model of knowledge, at a given time different knowledge about the same object co-exist in the beliefs of an agent a. We have defined three methods of knowledge selection or aggregation; the two first are common for mobile entities that evolve on a graph; the third one is dedicated to mobile entities that use resources in a flexible assembly cell.

---

[2] The threshold ρ is fixed *a priori* , and is shared by all the knowledge for a given agent. For a binary agent, $\rho = 1$: as soon as a doubt exists on a knowledge, it is removed.

Frequent changes of state: When an object is subject to frequent change of a state (like the load of a road/rail); the agent a uses a fitness proportionate selection (i.e. roulette wheel selection) to choose which knowledge, which value of an object, that will be taken into account to evaluate a strategy. Indeed, it is not envisageable for a mobile agent to be fully trustful with the last information sent by another agent. In the example of the Figure 1 the agent selects the knowledge $\kappa_{r_2}^a$ and plan its next actions considering that the speed limit on the rail is $0.65 m/sec$.

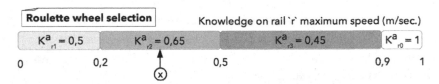

Fig. 1. Example of roulette wheel selection of a knowledge.

Rare but important changes of state : When the knowledge is relative to an important change of state of an object o, that happens rarely, but has a huge impact on the system performance (for example, a workstation failure); the agent a selects the surest knowledge (that is generally the most recent knowledge about o). In the example presented in Figure 2 the agent selects the knowledge $\kappa_{r_3}^a$, which is the the more probable, and it schedules its next tasks by considering that the workstation 'w' has a failure.

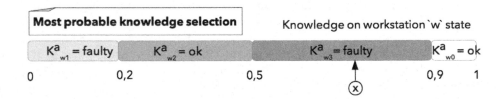

Fig. 2. Example of selection of the most probable knowledge.

Use of a resource: This third type of knowledge corresponds relatively to reservation of a resource. When a mobile agent 'a' plans to use a resource for a given duration, it sends this information to the other agents, with a degradation coefficient computed so that the knowledge will be forgotten by the agents when it ('a') will leave the resource. The knowledge relative to the use or the future use of a resource, are added up by agents to compute how much time it will effectively cost to use the resource.

For example, in the Figure 3, the agent knows that the duration for a process on the workstation 'w' is $10sec$. (it is its first and so perennial knowledge about 'w', $\overline{\kappa}_{fw_0}^a$), and that three other agents are using or have planed to use 'w' (respectively for 20, 40 and 30*sec.*). If *nbProcessings* is the number of processings that the agent has to make on 'w', the total duration for using 'w' is the sum $20 + 40 + 30 + nbProcessings \times 10$.

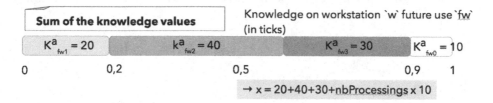

Fig. 3. Example of sum of knowledge.

3 Applications of Volatile Knowledge: Flexible Job Shop Problem

We have applied our model on different applications, such as traffic road simulation and management of autonomous vehicles. In this paper, we give a brief description of the instantiation of our model to the flexible manufacturing cells management. In order to evaluate the volatile knowledge approach proposed in this paper, we use a case study inspired from the benchmark proposed in [11]. This benchmark consider jobs to be processed on different machines. Each job has its own production sequence composed of some elementary manufacturing operations that can be executed on one or more machines. Most of the flexible job shop problems are proved to be NP-hard [4] and the flexibility increases greatly the complexity of the problem because it requires an additional level of decisions (i.e., the selection of machines on which the jobs should be processed) [3]. So it is important to benefit of reactive, distributed and fast solution.

3.1 AIP: a Real Flexible Manufacturing Cell

The benchmark is based on a real flexible manufacturing cell located in our University. Seven machines are connected using a transportation system, which is a one-direction monorail system with rotating transfer gates at routing nodes. Thus, this transportation system can be considered as a directed, strongly-connected graph, where shuttles move to build the products.

The Figure 4 is a screen copy of our simulator that represents the AIP manufacturing cell; nodes $n_1, \ldots, n_{11}$ are decisional nodes where a shuttle can decide the next node to reach; the orientation of the small nodes can not be changed.

The machines $M_1, \ldots, M_7$ are also nodes, where the shuttles can stop to do some processing on the product they have to build. There are eight different processings proposed by the machines: load a plate, put an axis, put a component that represents a 'r', or an 'L' or an 'I', put a screw, inspection of the product, and unloading of the plate where the product has been fixed. Some machine can do several processing (for example, machine M_2 can either put an axis, a 'r' component or an 'L' component). On Fig. 4 can be seen the time units needed to make a particular job (except for machines M_6 and M_7 that are not used in the case studies used in this article).

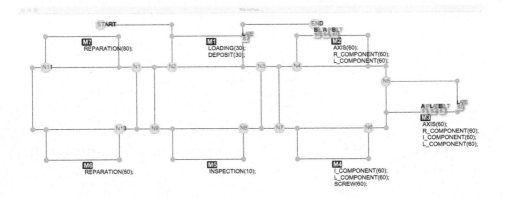

Fig. 4. Schema of the flexible assembly cell.

Building a product consists of combining elements to represent letters ('A', 'b', 'E', 'I', 'L', 'T' and 'P' in the AIP). Each product starts by a plate loading and conclude with an inspection and a plate unloading. The Figure 5 shows the components and the different jobs created from these ones (a view of the real AIP is presented in [11]).

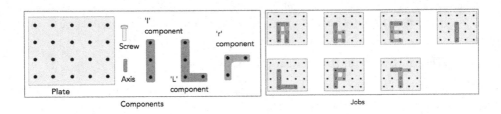

Fig. 5. Schema of the components and jobs used in the AIP cell.

Each processing necessitates 60 'ticks', except the Inspection that costs 10 'ticks' and a loading or a deposit that cost each 30 'ticks'. So, for example, except the move time along the rails, to build a letter 'A' costs $30+7\times60+10+30 = 490$ 'ticks'.

3.2   Experimentations

In order to implement the concept of volatile knowledge, a simulator has been developed with the JADE platform [3]. The map of the AIP has been drawn with the JOSM tool [4] and is used as an oriented graph. The Figure 4 is a screen copy of the simulator. The shuttles are the grey boxes named $s_1, \ldots, s_8$ on top of whom are written the products they have to build. At each time a shuttle has to create a new product, it creates the list of the different strategies (the list of different resources/machines sequence) that allows the agent to create it (to make the list of jobs). Each strategy is then evaluated according to the length of the path it describes, and to the estimated time required to do the described jobs. The agent chooses the shortest strategy after each job, or when it receives a knowledge relative to a modification of the AIP components (state of a rail, of a resource).

Scenario Without Fault. Several scenarios have been evaluated, we focus here on the scenario 'I0#3' from the benchmark. In this scenario, eight shuttles (s_1, ..., s_8) are 'launched' sequentially; s_1, s_4, s_7 have to build each a sequence of products 'b,E,L,T', s_2, s_5 are each dedicated to a sequence 'A,I,P', and shuttles s_3, s_6, s_8 have to make each a set of products 'L,A,T,E'.

The scenario 'I0#3' has then been evaluated: (a) without any cooperation and communication between the shuttles; (b) with communication of local information about a resource only when arriving on this resource; (c) with communication to the others of the next objective (so the next future use of a resource); (d) with 'full cooperation', that-is-to-say with communication of next objectives and of informations about resources.

Of course the results shows that the full cooperation improve the makespan; of 10% with the best politic. Indeed, an agent can use different politics to take into account the message sent by the others. It can decides to recompute the utilities of its strategies to build its product: (i) when it reaches a resource; (ii) when it leaves a resource; (iii) when it joins a point; (iv) as soon as it receives an information.

This last politic (iv) results in a important nervousness: the agent can 'changes its mind' during its way to reach a station, and as the rails are mono directional, the decision to go to another resource and to make a loop in the manufacturing cell to reach a resource leads to some traffic jam, that imply a degradation of the strategies performance.

A similar problem occurs when the politic (i) is used; when an agent reach a resource, it computes the new utilities of its strategies according to the new information it receives since the last resource, and can decide to bypass the reached resource for another one that seems better to it.

---

[3] A Java Agent DEvelopment framework, cf. http://jade.tilab.com/

[4] JOSM tool (https://josm.openstreetmap.de) is an extensible editor of OSM maps (OpenStreetMaps : http://www.openstreetmap.org/) that aims to create a free map of the world.

The second politic (ii) seems intuitively the best that it is actually; an agent computes the next best path to the next best resource when it leaves a resource after having completed one or some processings.

The politic (iii) allows to an agent to recompute the utilities of its strategies and the next place to go only when it arrives on a point. This is a good compromise between a nervousness and a stable behaviour; the agent can benefit of the messages sent by the other without showed a kind of chaotic behaviour.

The Figure 6 presents some results from the experimentation; it describes the time (in number of 'ticks') needed by a shuttle to build a product. So it is important to notice the highest point on each line: it gives the makespan, the date of creation of the last product. Here, we can see that the politic (ii) and (iii) are the best and that they have relatively similar results.

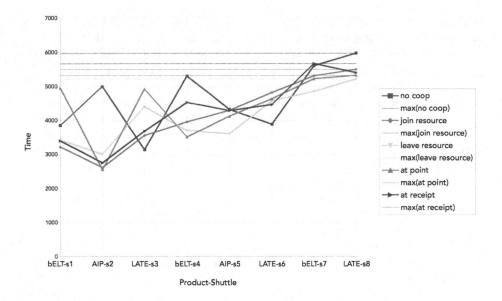

Fig. 6. Comparison of the different adaptation politics

To study now the economic aspect, we can compare the total time spent by the shuttle on the cell, and the time spent by each shuttle to wait for a resource without moving. The Figure 7 presents (relatively to the use of no cooperative agents): the percentage of reduction of time spent by the shuttles on the cell, where the politic (ii) have the best result; the percentage of reduction of the makespan, where the politics (ii) and (iii) allow a reduction of approximatively 10%. In this figure, we can see that the time spent by the shuttles without move with the politic of adaptation (iii) is close to the time spent by no cooperative agents; and that the politics (i) and (iv) present the more nervous behaviour and so the cases where the shuttles use more energy to move.

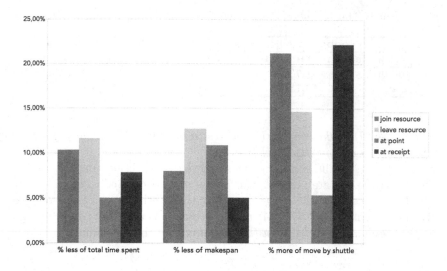

Fig. 7. Comparison of the adaptation politics regarding the green aspect

Thus, with cooperation, the conflicts concerning resources occupancy are avoided, or at least limited: a shuttle selects the workstation corresponding to its next task that has the lowest occupancy rate (at the date it planned to use it).

Dynamic Scenario. The use a holonic approach or a distributed multiagent approach appears necessary only when a system is too complex to be deal with a single entity, or when the system and the environment are subject to dynamic external events or perturbations.

So the main objective of our proposal is to enable to the shuttle to adapt to dynamic and probable events such as rush orders, breakdowns, order cancellation. In [11], fifteen scenarios of events that occur in dynamic production system have been detailed. In this paper, we use the dynamic scenario '#PS4': "At a given time, the machine processing time increases for all its operations in a given time window." So a shuttle has to avoid the use of this machine (resource) if it is possible and if it is more beneficial to use another machine (resource).

In our scenario, the machine M_3 is modified from $step = 1000$ to $step = 2000$, all of its processing times increase from 60 $ticks$ to 300 $ticks$. Table 1 describes the new number of steps for the scenario 'I0#3' after adding a fault on the machine M_2. Without cooperation, with the fault, the total time is $\approx$ 50% greater than in normal case. With cooperation, the total time with the perturbation is $\approx$ 30% more important than in normal case (with cooperation), if the degradation coefficient linked to knowledge about perturbation is too high. With a smaller degradation coefficient, the information about the incident stays longer in the agents memory, avoiding them to try uselessly to go back to the faulty machine; thus the total time with perturbation is only $\approx$ 20% greater than

Table 1. Time (in nb of steps) following a fault on the machine M_2

.	No cooperation	Cooperation	Coop. low degradation
.	**Malus/no fault**	Malus/no fault	**Malus/no fault**
total	**51,7%**	37%	**22%**
max	**49,7%**	31%	**26,6%**

in normal case. *Thus the cooperation allows to minimize the impact of a fault of 50% relatively to an egocentric behaviour.*

In this paper, we have not use the knowledge selection method linked to 'frequent changes of state'; indeed, this one is more dedicated to modification of rail/road load due to traffic congestion, but this method can be use to resolve the dynamic scenario '#PS7': *"At a given time, a part of the conveyor system is due for maintenance in a given time window."* of the benchmark.

4   Conclusion

In order to add a new reactive approach to our low-level holon, and in order to allow the propagation of knowledge between mobile agents in a dynamic environment, without modifying the environment by the add of electronic devices, a model of volatile knowledge has been presented.

This model, simple and so fast, allows representing different types of knowledge used to manage flexible assembly cells. It also allows to propagate knowledge about perturbations, and to return to normal situation, in a distributed way without coordinator. It could be considered as a stygmergic approach that does not use a shared environment. Thus, our proposal can be applied in most of the assembly cells where the shuttles, or the products, are 'intelligent' enough to manage and communicate information with the other products.

One of the main issue that we have, is relative to the fact that in the evaluations presented in this paper, we make the assumption that all the agents are cooperative, and no defective; they cannot send wrong knowledge (if a sensor has a dysfunction). So one of our main perspective is to introduce the notion of confidence that depends of the sender.

Another perspective that we have is to include the human operator in the loop, as our shuttle are fully autonomous and evolve in a non computerized environment, the interactions and cooperation with human operator seem more easy to define.

Acknowledgments. This research was financed by the International Campus on Safety and Inter-modality in Transportation, the Nord/Pas-de-Calais Region, the French Regional Delegation for Research and Technology, and the French National Centre for Scientific Research. We are grateful for the support of these institutions.

References

1. Adam, E., Berger, T., Sallez, Y., Trentesaux, D.: An Open-Control Concept for a Holonic Multiagent System. In: Mařík, V., Strasser, T., Zoitl, A. (eds.) HoloMAS 2009. LNCS, vol. 5696, pp. 145–154. Springer, Heidelberg (2009)
2. Adam, E., Grislin, E., Mandiau, R.: Autonomous Agents in Dynamic Environment: A Necessary Volatility of the Knowledge. In: Bajo Perez, J., et al. (eds.) Trends in Practical Applications of Heterogeneous Multi-agent Systems. The PAAMS Collection. AISC, vol. 293, pp. 103–110. Springer, Heidelberg (2014)
3. Brandimarte, P.: Routing and scheduling in a flexible job shop by tabu search. Ann. Oper. Res. **41**(1–4), 157–183 (1993)
4. Conway, R., Maxwell, W., Miller, L.: Theory of scheduling. Dover Books on Computer Science, Dover Publications (Reprint edn.) (2003)
5. Dorigo, M., Blum, C.: Ant colony optimization theory: A survey. Theor. Comput. Sci. **344**(2–3), 243–278 (2005)
6. Havens, T., Spain, C., Salmon, N., Keller, J.: Roach infestation optimization. In: Swarm Intelligence Symposium, SIS 2008, pp. 1–7. IEEE (September 2008)
7. Kennedy, J., Eberhart, R.: Particle swarm optimization. In: Neural Networks, vol. 4, pp. 1942–1948. IEEE (November 1995)
8. Ketenci, U., Adam, E., Grislin, E., Mandiau, R.: Volatile knowledge for mobile agents : application to autonomous vehicles management. In: 11th European Workshop on Multi-Agent Systems (EUMAS 2013), Toulouse, France (2013) (short paper)
9. Lin, F., Reiter, R.: Forget it! In: Proceedings of the AAAI Fall Symposium on Relevance, pp. 154–159 (1994)
10. Teodorović, D.: Bee Colony Optimization (BCO). In: Lim, C.P., Jain, L.C., Dehuri, S. (eds.) Innovations in Swarm Intelligence. SCI, vol. 248, pp. 39–60. Springer, Heidelberg (2009)
11. Trentesaux, D., Pach, C., Bekrar, A., Sallez, Y., Berger, T., Bonte, T., Leitão, P., Barbosa, J.: Benchmarking flexible job-shop scheduling and control systems. Control Engineering Practice **21**(9), 1204–1225 (2013)
12. Vakil Baghmisheh, M., Madani, K., Navarbaf, A.: A discrete shuffled frog optimization algorithm. Artificial Intelligence Review **36**(4), 267–284 (2011)
13. Yang, X.S., He, X.: Firefly algorithm: recent advances and applications. International Journal of Swarm Intelligence **1**(1), 36–50 (2013)
14. Yen, G.G., Hickey, T.W.: Reinforcement learning algorithms for robotic navigation in dynamic environments. ISA Transactions **43**(2), 217–230 (2004)

Invariant-Based Production Control Reviewed: Mixing Hierarchical and Heterarchical Control in Flexible Job Shop Environments

Henning Blunck[✉] and Julia Bendul

School of Mathematics and Logistics, Jacobs University Bremen gGmbH,
28759 Bremen, Germany
{h.blunck,j.bendul}@jacobs-university.de

Abstract. We are interested in the interplay of hierarchical and heterarchical control to reduce myopic behavior in a setting where central planning establishes relaxed schedules and distributed control is applied to make remaining decisions at runtime. We therefore pick up an idea introduced by Bongaerts et al. [4] to generate *invariants*, relaxed schedules, as constraints on distributed production control.

We apply this concept to the Flexible Job Shop Scheduling Problem (FJSSP), represented as disjunct graphs, introduce a measure to quantify the "tightness" of invariants, constrains the set of local decision heuristics that can be applied in such setting and present a simulation implementation, based on standard problem instances and optimization models with initial results. They validate the proposed measure and highlighting the need for further investigation of the interplay between problem structure and achieved performance.

Keywords: Production control · Invariants · Scheduling · Distributed decision making

1 Introduction

Responding to increasing complexity in dynamics in manufacturing systems, the distribution of control capacity and authority has been investigated as an alternative control scheme for production planning and control (PPC) systems [11]. While "first-generation" distributed PPC systems allowed for no coordination between decision making entities, subsequent extensions of the concept gradually increasingly promoted the idea of mixing centralized and distributed decision making in the control hierarchy [11,27].

This raises the question of finding the optimal "mix" of hierarchical and distributed control approaches as a function of the controlled system, order characteristics and decision preferences. The idea of using relaxed schedules (invariants) as a vehicle to mix both control paradigms has been proposed in [4], but so far not been experimentally investigated (c.f. Sec. 2.1) as a vehicle to establish semi-hierarchical control systems.

© Springer International Publishing Switzerland 2015
V. Mařík et al. (Eds.): HoloMAS 2015, LNAI 9266, pp. 96–107, 2015.
DOI: 10.1007/978-3-319-22867-9_9

The remainder of this article is structured as follows: Section 2 reviews the relevant concepts and previous findings. Section 3 describes the approach to invariant creation and implementation used in this contribution. First results are presented in Section 4 and the findings as well as ideas for future research are briefly discussed in Section 5.

2   Definitions and Literature Review

2.1   Balancing Hierarchical and Heterarchical Control

It is commonly believed that the optimal control architecture is a function of the system to be controlled and the decision preferences applied. As a rule of thumb, (highly) hierarchical systems allow long term optimality in calm planning environments and low flexibility production systems while (highly) heterarchical systems enable short term optimization in turbulent environments and controlled systems that allow alternative process paths [11,19,27].

Both Philipp et al. [20] and Zambrano Rey et al. [29] hypothesize that the system performance, when plotted as a function of control heterarchy, follows a curved shape with a global optimum attained for a mixture of hierarchical and heterarchical control, where the advantages of better responsiveness and short term optimization of distributed control systems can be harvested, while minimizing the amount of myopia induced by distributed decision making. The identification and reduction of myopia in distributed control settings has lately received increased attention from the works of Zambrano Rey et al. [29,30].

Reasons for myopic decision making include

- the decomposition of the original planning problem [21, Ch.2]
- selfish actors (known in Game-Theory as *Cost of Anarchy* [12]),
- decision making based on local information only [c.f.e.g. 17,24,27], and
- time-constraints on decision making [30].

Existing simulation studies on the combination of hierarchical and distributed production control differ in their approach: Scholz-Reiter et al. [25] constrained the set of parallel worksystems where scheduling decisions are made locally. Mönch and Drießel [18] change the information and planning horizon. Mediating agents are proposed and investigated e.g. in [6,8]. In [29], supervisor agents are given enhanced decision making time and computing power to perform simulation-optimization to attain better scheduling decisions. Grundstein et al. [14] investigate the combination of central scheduling and autonomous production control by investigating the interdependend between order release method, local decision making heuristic, and production performance, without finding conclusive relationships.

To the best of our knowledge, we are the first to quantitatively investigate the idea of an invariant-based mixing of hierarchical and heterarchical control, as proposed in [4]. The proposed model extends the idea of [25] in that scheduling decisions can be removed at any point in the schedule (not necessarily spatially confined to particular worksystems) and is different to the other contributions mentioned above in that elements of hierarchical and heterarchical coordination are not working simultaneously but subsequently, constituting a constructional distributed decision making system [24, Ch.1.1].

2.2   The Flexible Job Shop Scheduling Problem

The Flexible Job Shop Scheduling Problem (FJSSP) extends the classical Job Shop Scheduling problem by relaxing the a priori assignment of operations to worksystems [5]. The FJSSP is particularly interesting for the sequential application of hierarchical and heterarchical control, since it combines the allocation (assigning operations to machines) and sequencing (determining a sequence of operations on each machine) sub-problems, that are often dealt with separately in hierarchical production planning systems [10]. It is prone to gain attention with the rise of flexible manufacturing systems (FMS).

Out of the large number of test-instances published for the FJSSP. We use here a total of 393 test-instances from [1,2,5,9,13,16]. As elaborated in [2], the test-instances are not only different in size (number of jobs, operations and machines) and level of machine flexibility, but arose from different considerations and with different analysis intentions in mind. For a first analysis, the test-instances by Hurink et al. [16] and Dauzère-Pérès and Paulli [9] were both generated from JSP instances by gradually increasing operation flexibility [2] (c.f. table footnotes). We hence distinguish 11 problem groups for our analysis.

Table 1. Test-Instances used in this publication. Notes summarized from [2].

Source	# Instances	Notes
Brandimarte [5]	10	medium degree of machine-flexibility
Hurink et al. [16]	66 · 4	4 series with increasing processing flexibility[a], processing times independent of machine
Dauzère-Pérès and Paulli [9]	6 · 3	6 different setups, each with 3 levels of machine flexibility.[b] Slightly different processing times across machines
Chambers and Barnes [1]	21	obtained from JSP problems by replicating machines acc. to different heuristics
Behnke and Geiger [2]	60	"Similar" machines are grouped into workcenters
Fattahi et al. [13]	20	Randomly generated, medium-sized problems

[a] EDATA: Few operations with ≥ 1 possible machine, RDATA: Most operations assignable to > 1 machine, and VDATA: All operations with > 1 possible machines.

[b] Probability of a machine being assignable to a given operation set to $0.1, 0.3, 0.5$ respectively.

3   Model

3.1   Background: Flexible Job-Shop Scheduling on Graphs

Disjunct (or mixed) graphs were introduced as a representation of scheduling problems by [23] and are widely used to represent scheduling problems [3].

Let $G(V, A, E)$ be a mixed graph, consisting of the set of nodes (V), and sets of undirected (E) and directed (A) edges. We denote by $\tilde{G} = (V, A)$ the *directed* subgraph of G, composed of the same node set, but only the directed edges. A directed edge $A \rightarrow B$ indicates a precedence relationship $A \prec B$ in that operation B cannot be started until A has finished (Finish-Start Constraint). The set of directed edges in a scheduling graph can naturally be subdivided into a set of technical and environmental constraints A_T (that are constraints on the planning process) and scheduling decisions A_S [4].

While the classical disjunct graph formulation assumes a solved assignment problem (operations are assigned to one worksystem each), it can be extended to represent a more complex situations [c.f. 10], by assigning a processing time matrix P to every operation, indicating if and in which time, an operation can be processed at a given worksystem. If in the initial graph, an undirected edge exists between any two operations that can be processed on the same worksystem [10]. A FJSSP then is solved feasibly if and only if (1) every operation has been assigned to one worksystem, (2) there exists a directed path $\in \tilde{G}$ between any two operations assigned to the same worksystem and (3) $\tilde{G}$ is acyclic [5,10].

The term invariant in natural and computer sciences describes a statement or property whose value is unaltered during an applied transformation. For the domain of FJS-scheduling, a schedule-invariant is understood as a subset of all assignment and sequencing decisions (directed edges $\in A_S$, c.f. [4]) that have to be observed (remain unchanged) during production control transformation of the scheduling graph.

3.2   General Setup

Our simulation model is based on a graph as described in Sec. 3.1 that represents the test-instances introduced in Sec. 2.2.

The model is executed as follows: After representing the scheduling problem as a graph (Fig. 1a), we start by applying a centrally computed solution (Section 3.3) to the problem graph (Fig. 1b), which we then relax (Sec. 3.5) to an invariant by removing scheduling decisions (Fig. 1c). The invariant is handed over to a controller, defined by the agent class assigned to operations and worksystems respectively (c.f. Sec. 3.6) that then makes the resulting decisions at runtime, based on local information (Fig. 1d). The controller assigns agents to the operations (nodes in the graph) and worksystems and initiates the simulation. Once an operation starts processing, an actual processing time is calculated following a truncated[1] Normal distribution with the planned processing time μ as expected

---

[1] We do not allow negative processing times. However, even with the highest standard deviations investigated here, such event has a probability of $\approx 0.1\%$.

value and a standard deviation of $CV \cdot \mu$. While other performance measures are possible, we focus on minimizing the makespan (maximum Lateness $L_{max}(\sigma)$) in this contribution. Since the schedule is *left-justified*, i.e. operations start as early as possible without changing operation sequence, not as late as possible, the results will not minimize e.g. Work in Process (WIP). We measure ratio of the CP-solution and the makespan attained including process time variability and distributed control as the *relative Performance* of the semi-hierarchical control structure (c.f. Sec. 4).

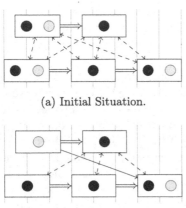

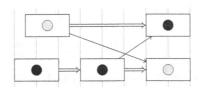

(a) Initial Situation.

(b) Central Schedule applied, redundant information removed, no open conflicts.

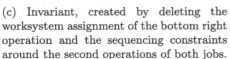

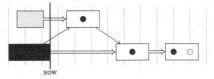

(c) Invariant, created by deleting the worksystem assignment of the bottom right operation and the sequencing constraints around the second operations of both jobs.

(d) Snapshot of the distributed production control solving the sequencing problem based on FIFO as actual processing times are realized.

Fig. 1. Stylized visualization of the approach taken here. Scheduling problem with two machines, two jobs and a total of five operations. Rectangles represent operations and their planned processing times. Circles represent assignable worksystems. Filled operations are already underway and actual processing times ($\sim \mathcal{N}(\mu, CV \cdot \mu)$) are known. Solid arcs represent precedence constraints introduced during scheduling. Double arrows indicate technical precedence constraints. Dashed edges represent still open sequencing decisions between operations.

3.3   Implementation of Hierarchical Planning

To emulate a hierarchically derived production schedule, we use the Constraint Programming FJSSP model, shipped with the popular optimization suite IBM CPLEX Studio 12.6. The model has (with minor adjustments) been used to find optimal solutions to some previously unsolved problem-instances[2] [2,22]. So we may assume both broad availability and competitive performance of the model and solver.

---

[2] The same we use here, c.f. Sec. 2.2.

Each problem instance was computed for a maximum of 20 minutes on a UNIX-machine with an Intel Xeon quad-core processor, 2.8 GHz and 3 GB of RAM and the best (shortest makespan) solution attained in this time was considered the hierarchical production schedule for this instance.

3.4 Removing Redundant Scheduling Decisions

Removing redundant edges from the scheduling graph has been considered important before for the application of various scheduling heuristics [5], but is gains even higher importance in the context of invariant-based scheduling: To effectively measure and compare the degree to which the original schedule was relaxed, it is necessary to remove redundant information from the mixed graph, so that any further relaxation does in fact open feasible decision alternatives. To this end, we replace a an arc $a \in A_S$ with an undirected edge[3], if and only if there exist a directed path between start- and end-node of a in $\tilde{G} \setminus \{a\}$[10].

3.5 Invariant Creation and Assessment

For this initial investigation we define two schedule-relaxation-heuristics, each of which is applied to $\alpha \in [0, 1]$ of all operations (we call α the schedule removal degree).[4] We investigate two simple relaxation heuristics:

Removing the sequencing information. By keeping machine assignments proposed by the initial scheduling but removing the sequencing decisions (removing the added directed edges from the graph) for α of all operations. For $\alpha = 1$, we have created the related JSP problem, thus a natural hierarchical decomposition found in the FJSSP [5, Ch.3] and also currently present in many hierarchical PPC systems.

Resetting Operations. We entirely reset (delete scheduled constraints and worksystem-assignment) for α of all operations. For $\alpha = 1$, we attain the original FJSSP problem.

In addition to measures suggested e.g. in [7], we propose to measure the degree of freedom preserved by an invariant as the share of schedulable (i.e. not technologically constrained) edges in the graph for which the invariant does not prescribe an orientation (i.e. there does not exist a directed path between the two ends of the undirected edge) and the operations could still be assigned to the same worksystem (i.e. a precedence decision might become necessary).

Note that in a disjunct graph representation as described in Sec. 3.1 with removed redundant edges (Sec. 3.4), also the relaxation of machine assignments will lead to such conflicting edges.

---

[3] Note that we do not delete technological constraints from $\tilde{G}$.

[4] This is a first attempt to create invariants of different "tightness" but not the only way to attain them. Relaxation heuristics do not need to be node-based.

3.6 Distributed Production Controller

As stated before, the FJSSP is particular in that any valid production schedule has to solve both the assignment and sequencing subproblems. In the research on dispatching rule based FJS-scheduling, a "shortest queue length" heuristic seems to be commonly applied to solve the assignment problem [c.f. 26].

A QLE-control can be implemented in a mixed-graph by giving the operation agent the authority to choose a worksystem (by querying all possible worksystems for the current queue length, i.e. the expected finishing time of the last operation) and assigning itself to worksystem i where $i := \arg\min_{i \in W}\{q_i + p_i\}$ where W is the set of possible worksystems, q_i is the queue length of worksystem i and p_i is the processing time of the operation on worksystem i. The worksystem agents of the chosen worksystem forms an precedence constraint from the last entry in their queue to the newly assigned operation (i.e. implements a FIFO strategy).

Building upon which, we define two controllers which implement two different sequencing heuristics:

A _FIFO_-Controller processes the operations at the worksystems in the sequence of assignment (i.e. in the sequence in which their respective last predecessor was finished).

A _LRPT-Controller_ sequences operations by decreasing remaining workcontent (LRPT: Longest Remaining Processing Time). Where ≥ 1 worksystem is possible, the average processing time over all possible worksystems is assumed in this contribution, expressing no prior belief concerning the upcoming assignment decision.

3.7 Distributed Control Heuristics that Guarantee Valid Schedules

The FIFO- and LRPT- Production controller (Sec. 3.6) implement a decision logic on the side of the operations and worksystems respectively that is based on local information.

However, to avoid forming a directed cycle (and hence an invalid schedule) global information about the existence of paths is required.[5] It is hence easy to imagine a situation in which an agent decides to form a precedence constraint, closing a directed cycle on the graph (c.f. Fig. 2), a problem particular to invariant-based scheduling problems.[6]

Following [15], we can investigate the dynamic on the graph, the observable result of the interplay of worksystem and operation agents, as the combination of (1) a _neighborhood assessment strategy_, applied by an entity to make a decision within its decision space (forming edges, committing to worksystems, ...) and

---

[5] With such information, a node would not be allowed to form a precedence constraint $A \prec B$ if there exist a path $B, \ldots, A$ in the graph.

[6] The problem could only be averted by updating the entire graph after every scheduling decision (i.e. converting edges into arcs, if there exists a directed path). This however would require central coordination and high computational effort.

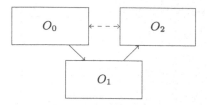

Fig. 2. Stylized invariant-based scheduling problem with two scheduling decisions imposed by the invariant (solid, directed arcs) and a remaining scheduling decision (dashed edge). Given their limited information horizon, Operations O_0 and O_2 are not aware of the path existing between them. A decision by either of the two, to form a precedence relationship $O_2 \prec O_0$ would now form a directed cycle and hence an invalid schedule.

(2) a *temporal organization strategy*, which defines in which order entities take decisions. Using this notation, we can outline a set of constraints that guarantee valid schedules, given a valid invariant.[7]

Theorem 1. *A dynamic Ω is guaranteed to create a valid, non-preemptive schedule on a mixed graph representing any valid invariant, if the temporal organization strategy only allows an operation O to form scheduling decisions*

1. *once all immediate predecessors (in-neighbors in $\tilde{G}$) have been completed and*
2. *if the end of the directed edge points at an operation on which processing has not started yet.*

Proof. Condition (1) guarantees through transitive closure that all (not just the immediate) predecessors of an operation O (i.e. operations from which a directed path to O exists) have been completed, before O can form a scheduling constraint. Condition (2) then guarantees that no such new constraint can close a directed cycle in $\tilde{G}$.   □

Note that in particular, all distributed control systems that are based on dispatching rules and hence also the two controllers investigated here (c.f. Sec. 3.6), satisfy above conditions.

4   Initial Results

4.1   Validation of Invariant Assessment Measure

Fig. 3 shows the measure of invariant tightness discussed in Sec. 3.5. The proposed measure for invariant flexibility shows to serve two important purposes: (1) It does in fact measure the existence of decision alternatives (it grows with α) and (2) it distinguished the problem sets, highlighting the different degree sequencing and assignment decisions are present in the problem.

---

[7] Note that the conditions outlined here are sufficient, but not necessary and other conditions might be found.

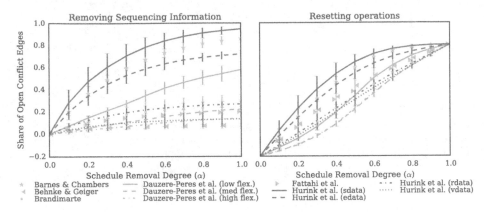

Fig. 3. Share of open conflicts (c.f. Sec. 3.5) for both investigated relaxation heuristics. Over all instance groups

4.2 Impact on Performance

We measure the relative performance of the combination of an invariant and a controller as the ratio of the makespan calculated in Sec. 3.3 and the makespan attained with this configuration. Over all instance-sets, relaxation heuristics and removal degrees, the LRPT-Controller outperforms the FIFO-controller.[8]

Non-surprisingly, test-instances with high machine flexibility fare significantly better when given decision alternatives at runtime (eventually outperforming pure hierarchical planning). Notably, a mix of hierarchical and distributed control (as considered optimal in [20,29], c.f. Sec. 2.1) consistently fares worse then pure approaches with worst relative performance figures attained for *alpha* between 0.25 and 0.5.

We believe that this result comes courtesy of the random schedule relaxation policies applied here. With only some, probably incoherent, operations free to make autonomous decisions, any deviation from the previously determined schedule causes more harm than good because the disturbance created by the local decision making of one operation does lead to the emergence of new sub-schedules but fails to integrate with the framework still imposed around it. A successful schedule, given stochastic processing times, does not seem to be accessible through simple, undirected neighborhood search from the best known solution to the deterministic problem.

The key to successful heterarchical production control then, it appears, lies not in giving autonomy to single operations (as investigated here), but rather to substructures in the scheduling graph. In particular, we should be able to replicate the results from [25], by only deleting sequencing and assignment decisions between parallel servers. A natural extension of the concept of parallel worksystems would be one of clusters of worksystems or operations, like suggested in [28]. A purely random based "neighborhood search" approach, starting from

---

[8] Which comes courtesy of our focus on total makespan.

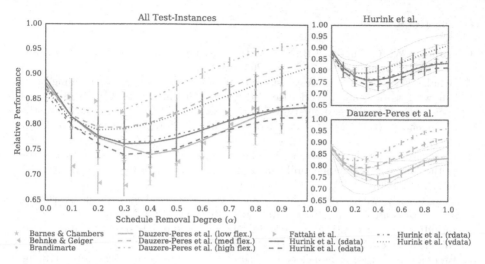

Fig. 4. Relative Performance for all (left) and instance sets with increasing flexibility [9, 16] (right). Node-Reset relaxation heuristic, LRPT-Controller, $CV = 0.3$.

the deterministic solution, is apparently not a good approach to finding a good solution for the stochastic production control problem.

5   Discussion and Future Research

We have proposed an implementation of invariant-based scheduling for flexible job shops and proposed a measure to quantify invariants. We have shown that distributed decision heuristics have to be constrained in order to generate valid schedules. Besides demonstrating the validity of our approach, our simulation experiments shows that, in order to achieve competitive performance, the process of schedule relaxation and distributed control has to consider the particularities of the scheduling problem and the subsequent distributed control approach.

Future research should hence seek to identify problem parameters in combination with relaxation and control heuristics that perform particularly well. The strict representation of the problem as a network thereby allows to use network science methods and concepts (like motifs) to be applied in defining such relaxation approaches. Ideally, this would allow future scheduling systems to intentionally relax the set of constraints such that production control can work best, establishing an anticipation relationship, found in many distributed decision making systems [24, Ch.1.3], but not in today's PPC systems.

References

1. Barnes, J.W., Chambers, J.B.: Solving the job shop scheduling problem with tabu search. IIE Transactions **27**(2), 257–263 (1995)
2. Behnke, D., Geiger, M.J.: Test instances for the flexible job shop scheduling problem with work centers. Tech. Rep. 12–01-01, Helmut-Schmidt Universität der Bundeswehr Hamburg, Lehrstuhl für Betriebswirtschaftslehre, insbes. Logistik-Management (May 2012), http://edoc.sub.uni-hamburg.de/hsu/volltexte/2012/2982/
3. Błażewicz, J., Pesch, E., Sterna, M.: The disjunctive graph machine representation of the job shop scheduling problem. European Journal of Operational Research **127**(2), 317–331 (2000)
4. Bongaerts, L., Monostori, L., McFarlane, D., Kádár, B.: Hierarchy in distributed shop floor control. Computers in Industry **43**(2), 123–137 (2000)
5. Brandimarte, P.: Routing and scheduling in a flexible job shop by tabu search. Annals of Operations Research **41**(3), 157–183 (1993)
6. Brennan, R.W.: Performance comparison and analysis of reactive and planning-based control architectures for manufacturing. Robotics and Computer-Integrated Manufacturing **16**(2–3), 191–200 (2000)
7. Brennan, R.W., Norrie, D.H.: Metrics for evaluating distributed manufacturing control systems. Computers in Industry **51**(2), 225–235 (2003). virtual Enterprise Management
8. Cavalieri, S., Garetti, M., Macchi, M., Taisch, M.: An experimental benchmarking of two multi-agent architectures for production scheduling and control. Computers in Industry **43**(2), 139–152 (2000)
9. Dauzère-Pérès, S., Paulli, J.: An integrated approach for modeling and solving the general multiprocessor job-shop scheduling problem using tabu search. Annals of Operations Research **70**(1–4), 281–306 (1997)
10. Dauzère-Pérès, S., Roux, W., Lasserre, J.: Multi-resource shop scheduling with resource flexibility. European Journal of Operational Research **107**(2), 289–305 (1998)
11. Dilts, D., Boyd, N., Whorms, H.: The evolution of control architectures for automated manufacturing systems. Journal of Manufacturing Systems **10**(1), 79–93 (1991)
12. Dubey, P.: Inefficiency of nash equilibria. Mathematics of Operations Research **11**(1), 1–8 (1986)
13. Fattahi, P., Saidi Mehrabad, M., Jolai, F.: Mathematical modeling and heuristic approaches to flexible job shop scheduling problems. Journal of Intelligent Manufacturing **18**(3), 331–342 (2007)
14. Grundstein, S., Schukraft, S., Scholz-Reiter, B., Freitag, M.: Coupling order release methods with autonomous control methods – an assessment of potentials by literature review and discrete event simulation. International Journal of Production Management and Engineering **3**(1), 43 (2015)
15. Hadzhiev, B., Windt, K., Bergholz, W., Hütt, M.T.: A model of graph coloring dynamics with attention waves and strategic waiting. Advances in Complex Systems **12**(6), 549–564 (2009)
16. Hurink, J., Jurisch, B., Thole, M.: Tabu search for the job-shop scheduling problem with multi-purpose machines. Operations-Research-Spektrum 15(4), 205–215 (1994)

17. Lin, G.Y.J., Solberg, J.J.: Effectiveness of flexible routing control. International Journal of Flexible Manufacturing Systems **3**(3–4), 189–211 (1991)
18. Mönch, L., Drießel, R.: A distributed shifting bottleneck heuristic for complex job shops. Computers & Industrial Engineering **49**(3), 363–380 (2005)
19. Ouelhadj, D., Petrovic, S.: A survey of dynamic scheduling in manufacturing systems. Journal of Scheduling **12**(4), 417–431 (2009)
20. Philipp, T., Böse, F., Windt, K.: Evaluation of autonomously controlled logistic processes. In: Proceedings of 5th CIRP International Seminar on Intelligent Computation in Manufacturing Engineering, Ischia, Italy, pp. 347–352 (2006)
21. Pochet, Y., Wolsey, L.A.: Production Planning by Mixed Integer Programming. Springer Series in Operations Research and Financial Engineering. Springer, New York (2006)
22. Puget, J.F.: Solving flexible job shop scheduling problems (November 2013). https://www.ibm.com/developerworks/community/blogs/jfp/entry/solving_flexible_job_shop_scheduling_problems?lang=en (accessed: March 10, 2015)
23. Roy, B., Sussmann, B.: Les problèmes d'ordonnancement avec contraintes disjonctives. Note DS 9 (1964)
24. Schneeweiß, C.: Distributed decision making, 2 edn. Springer (2003)
25. Scholz-Reiter, B., Görges, M., Philipp, T.: Autonomously controlled production systems - influence of autonomous control level on logistic performance. CIRP Annals - Manufacturing Technology **58**(1), 395–398 (2009)
26. Tay, J.C., Ho, N.B.: Evolving dispatching rules using genetic programming for solving multi-objective flexible job-shop problems. Computers & Industrial Engineering **54**(3), 453–473 (2008)
27. Trentesaux, D.: Distributed control of production systems. Engineering Applications of Artificial Intelligence **22**(7), 971–978 (2009). distributed Control of Production Systems
28. Vrabič, R., Husejnagić, D., Butala, P.: Discovering autonomous structures within complex networks of work systems. CIRP Annals - Manufacturing Technology **61**(1), 423–426 (2012)
29. Zambrano Rey, G., Bonte, T., Prabhu, V., Trentesaux, D.: Reducing myopic behavior in fms control: A semi-heterarchical simulationoptimization approach. Simulation Modelling Practice and Theory **46**, 53–75 (2014). simulation-Optimization of Complex Systems: Methods and Applications
30. Zambrano Rey, G., Pach, C., Aissani, N., Bekrar, A., Berger, T., Trentesaux, D.: The control of myopic behavior in semi-heterarchical production systems: A holonic framework. Engineering Applications of Artificial Intelligence **26**(2), 800–817 (2013)

An Approach for Characterizing the Operating Modes in Dynamic Hybrid Control Architectures

Jose Fernando Jimenez[1,2(✉)], Abdelghani Bekrar[1],
Damien Trentesaux[1], and Paulo Leitão[3,4]

[1] LAMIH UMR CNRS 8201, University of Valenciennes and Hainaut Cambrésis UVHC,
59313, Le Mont Houy, France
j-jimenez@javeriana.edu.co,
{abdelghani.bekrar,damien.trentesaux}@univ-valenciennes.fr
[2] Pontificia Universidad Javeriana, Bogotá, Colombia
[3] Polytechnic Institute of Bragança, Bragança, Portugal
p.leitao@ipb.pt
[4] LIACC - Artificial Intelligence and Computer Science Laboratory, Porto, Portugal

Abstract. Nowadays, manufacturing control system faces the challenge of featuring optimal and reactive mechanisms to respond to volatile environments. In automation domain, hybrid control architectures solve these requirements as it allows coupling predictive/proactive and reactive techniques in manufacturing operations. However, to include dynamic coupling features, it is necessary to characterize the possible new operating modes and visualize its potential when a switching is needed. This paper presents an approach to characterize the operating modes of dynamic hybrid control architectures to support the dynamic switching process. The results, obtained through a simulation in a multi agent platform of flexible manufacturing systems, showed the interest of our approach in terms of including the characterization of operating modes as decisional criteria towards a system switching.

Keywords: Operating modes · Switching · Dynamic · Hybrid control architectures · Semi-heterarchical · Reconfiguration

1 Introduction

Manufacturing enterprises face the challenge of deploying efficient and agile operations in a demand-driven market [1]. In this sense, hybrid control architectures provide the optimality and reactivity needed to enhance the planning and scheduling in the manufacturing process. These architectures exploit the advantages of coupling predictive and reactive decision-making while mitigate possible drawbacks [3]. But, despite the effort introducing combined solutions in the manufacturing control system, a static configuration in the architecture limits the possibility of featuring a real efficient and agile behavior. For this reason, it is crucial to include dynamic features in these architectures to respond to the exigencies of the high-demanding market.

© Springer International Publishing Switzerland 2015
V. Mařík et al. (Eds.): HoloMAS 2015, LNAI 9266, pp. 108–119, 2015.
DOI: 10.1007/978-3-319-22867-9_10

Recently, researchers have included dynamic features in hybrid architectures [4, 5, 6]. These architectures, named in this paper as *dynamic hybrid control architectures* (D-HCA), are intended to feature a continuous change of configuration of the control system's architecture. In this switching process, the D-HCA switches from one operating mode to another one by changing the structure and/behavior of the system. An *operating mode* is defined as a specific parameterization (definition of all parameters) that characterizes the functioning settings of the whole control system. The advantage of switching between operating modes (eg., from a predictive mode to a reactive one) aims to search for a better behavior or to respond to a degraded behavior (disturbance). In this context, D-HCA contributes to improve the control process in terms of flexibility and adaptability for achieving the optimality and reactivity required.

Despite this, one of the major limitations of D-HCA is the absence of a clear characterization of the operating modes. This lack of characterization makes it difficult to evaluate the benefits of a new possible operating mode and, consequently, makes it difficult to state if it is worth to switch or not. For these reasons, it is crucial to create a framework that characterize each of the operating modes as it identifies the specific properties that distinguish its unique capability, gives insights about the estimated result when is applied, and provides a comparison reference within different operating modes.

In this particular case, the paper proposes a general approach to characterize the operating modes in dynamic hybrid control architectures. It also aims to assess its characteristics and to validate the use of this assessment as decisional criteria towards a switching event. Our motivation for conceiving a general approach responds to the possibility of applying this approach not only to manufacturing, but also to supply chains or service systems (i.e., hospital) among others. The paper is organized as follows: Section 2 reviews the characteristics of the operating modes of some existing D-HCA. Then, section 3 describes a generic model characterizing the operating modes. Section 4 instantiates the general model into a case study of a flexible manufacturing system. Section 5, describes the experimental case study and illustrate the benefits of using a characterization in the operating modes. And finally, section 6 resumes the conclusions of this study and provides recommendations for further research.

2   Operating Modes in Dynamic Hybrid Control Architectures

Considering the development of control systems in manufacturing, it is examined some of the operating modes in the state-of-the-art of D-HCA to construct a general characterization of an operating mode. Table 1 provides a summary of the literature reviewed. From our point of view, it can be identified two main issues regarding the distinctiveness of the operating mode: the *operating mode characteristics,* defined as the value of attributes that serve as settings of the operating mode; and, the *operating mode objective*, defined as the theoretical goal of the operating mode according to the expected performance in the controlled system.

Table 1. Dynamic hybrid control architectures in manufacturing control systems.

D -HCA	Operating modes	Objective of Operating modes	Characteristics of Operating modes
ADACOR [5]	Structures resulted from clustering within holons	Responsiveness due a swarm reconfiguration	Stationary and transient states according swarm emergence in holons interactions
D - MAS [6]	Constructed according the explored patterns	Responsiveness due a swarm reconfiguration	Composition of intentions of mobile units
ORCA [7]	Construction of interaction of operating modes	Responsiveness due a switching in heterogenic agents	Different interaction between predictive and reactive approaches
RAILEANU et al APPROACH [8]	Predefined operating modes (Three operating modes)	Different planning goals for each operating mode	Predefined according planning goal and perturbation avoidance
ADACOR² [9]	Structures resulted from clustering within holons	Evolve smooth or drastically according current necessity	Stationary and transient according swarm emergence in holons interactions
GOVERNANCE MECHANISM [10]	Resulted from the interaction between predictive/reactive	Evaluation of a global control performance indicator	Predefined specification of the entities in structural and behavioral level

From the literature reviewed, two different cases in the identification of the operating modes appear

On one side, articles [5][6][7][9] use **self-organized** processes. Despite the fact that these approaches lack to demonstrate a clear identification of the operating mode, they explicitly show a unique distinctiveness that characterizes the corresponding system configuration. In this case, the objective of these operating modes is not an expected result. Instead, the system evolves to a better configuration in order to respond the corresponding necessities. For the D-HCA, the main advantage of this approach is that it will feature a continuous evolution in terms of allowing a straightforward synchronization. However, as disadvantage, the emergent behavior resulted from the switching process might have difficulties of reaching an optimal configuration or operating mode.

On the other side, some researchers use explicit **improving search** processes [8, 10] that feature well-defined operating modes that describe the structure and behavior characteristics of a D-HCA. These approaches define an unique composition of each operating mode and contribute to remark the distinctiveness between each of them. In this case, it is defined an expected objective in the manufacturing execution associated to each operating mode. For the D-HCA, the main advantage is that it is known exactly the control configuration before and after the switching. In fact, it can be reached an optimal mode when an effective switching process is considered. However, it might have difficulties synchronizing online the new operating mode due to the complexity of making changes in the agents' intentions.

In resume, the evolution of operating modes in the self-organized case is an efficient method to switch among these modes. In fact, these approaches benefit from the reactivity achieved in the multi-agent system whilst changing continuously to a better operating mode. Nonetheless, a consideration of predefined operating modes allows improving the switching process in order to support both efficient and reactive features. This issue motivated us to explore the characterization of operating modes as they turn to be decisional strategies within the control system. The next section introduces our approach for characterizing the operating modes.

3   An Approach to Characterize the Operating Modes Towards a Switching Process

This section describes a general characterization of the operating mode assuming a D-HCA composed of agents or holons. The proposed characterization is based on the vector used in the governance mechanisms framework presented in [10]. According to this approach, an operating mode is illustrated by a vector that describes the specific settings of the architecture in the multi-agent system (See fig. 1). This vector gathers a subset of the parameters (governance parameters).to describe the system functioning. The governance parameters are the rules of conduct that dictate the entity behavioral guidelines. The main advantages of this framework are that the vector is providing a well-defined identification of the different operating modes; it allows to evaluate the entire system functioning towards a switching process; and facilitates the change of configuration when is necessary.

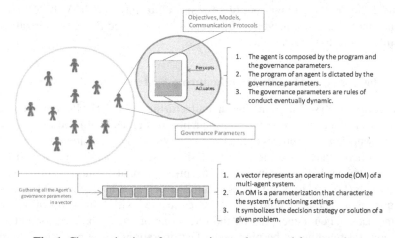

Fig. 1. Characterization of an operating mode: general framework

The characterization of an operating mode is depicted in fig. 1. An agent contains one or a set of governance parameters as an essential component that dictates the agent behavior. These parameters provide the characteristics and state the set of rules that agents apply. Moreover, in a switching process, they might change within different predefined states (finite or infinite) in order to adjust the agent behavior. An operating-mode vector is a representation of functioning settings of the system. This vector gathers all the governance parameters of the agents and symbolizes a decision strategy or solution to a given problem. At the end, the switching process becomes an optimization problem that search over a set of possible operating modes best configuration. However, due the dynamic characteristic of the multi-agent environment, it is considered a dynamic optimization problem for its characteristics.

For the characterization, it is identified for each operating mode the attributes and a general fitness. The attributes are the characteristics of the operating mode resulted from the arrangement of the vector. For instance, the values of certain parameter or the co-relation of two or more parameters are examples of this attributes. The general fitness is a unique characterization function that evaluates the quality of the operating mode. This general fitness is calculated from the attributes of the operating mode and the system state. At the end, the general fitness is the decisional criteria in a switching process.

An instantiation of this general framework on a specific flexible manufacturing system is proposed in the next section.

4   Operating Modes in D-HCA of a Flexible Manufacturing System

In this section, a D-HCA of a specific flexible manufacturing system is modeled based on the multi-agent paradigm. At first, it is introduced the flexible manufacturing system for locate the reader in this specific manufacturing problem. Then, it is presented the corresponding control system architecture (D-HCA) based on the governance mechanism framework [10]. Finally, it is defined the characterization of the operating modes towards a switching process.

4.1   The Case of a Flexible Manufacturing System

Manufacturing System: A flexible manufacturing system (FMS) corresponds to an automated production facility where production resources are linked using a transportation network and can process redundant operations. The considered case study here is a simplified model of some existing FMS system, typically, automated gear box manufacturing systems. It consists in an uni-directional manufacturing cell without recirculation (fig. 2). Jobs are released into the cell in a load station M_0 into the cell main conveyor. The main conveyor is interconnected with four workstations with one machine each. Then, depending on the intentions of each job, each job enters to the correspondent machine to be processed. The operations to be performed by the jobs are loading (O_L), process operations from 1 to 4 (O_1, O_2, O_3, O_4) and unloading (O_U). At the end, the jobs are removed at a unload station (M_5) when they had been processed. The shop floor has full flexibility as it features redundant machines (M_1, M_2, M_3, and M4) capable to perform all possible operations (O_1, O_2, O_3 and O_4). Operation O_L and O_U are performed by the load and unload stations, respectively. Remark that the identical redundancies in machine and operations are for the sake of understanding the degradation and enhancement when switching to a new operating mode is performed. Regarding the decision making in this FMS, it has been identified the following decisions: release sequence, machine sequence and operation sequence. The *release sequence* is the order that the jobs arrive to the cell and start in the shop-floor. The machine sequence is the combination of machines to be used by each job for processing. The operation sequence is the choice of operations to be processed in each machine.

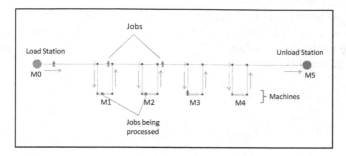

Fig. 2. Flexible manufacturing system

Case Study Scenario: The case study is composed of a data set of 8 jobs (501 to 508). Each job has the same number of operations as O_L, O_1, O_2, O_3, O_4 and O_U. The transportation times and processing times are also fixed (see table 1 and 2). The release of the products is done with a difference of 3 time units. The production order is measured by the total makespan from the time the first job is loaded until the last job starts to be unloaded.

Table 2. Transportation times between machines in time units.

	M0	M1	M2	M3	M4	M5
M0		5	7.5	10	12.5	
M1			5	7.5	10	12.5
M2				5	7.5	10
M3					5	7.5
M4						5

Table 3. Operation's processing times in time units.

	All machines	Machine 1 after perturbation
O_L	0.1	0.1
O_1	5.0	7.5
O_2	4.0	6.0
O_3	7.0	10.5
O_4	6.0	9.0
O_U	0.1	0.1

4.2 Controlling System Architecture and Governance Mechanism Entity

The proposed D-HCA is divided into a *controlling system* and a *governance mechanism entity*. While the controlling system composes the manufacturing system, the governance mechanism entity monitors and changes the mode (here, functioning settings) of the controlling system.

Controlling System Architecture: The general structure of the controlling system is divided two layers: a global and a local layer. These layers contain a unique corresponding global (GDE) and several local (LDE) decisional entities (see fig. 3) as agents representing the products in the manufacturing system. For the interaction within the real manufacturing system, physical entities (MPE) located in a physical layer - as resources or task - are represented virtually by the LDE. Each GDE and LDE contains its own objective and governance parameters. The motivation of dividing the architecture in two control layers respond to the allocation of predictive and reactive techniques featured in the D-HCA. Consequently, in this approach, it is allocated the predictive technique to the global layer, while the reactive technique is allocated to the local layer.

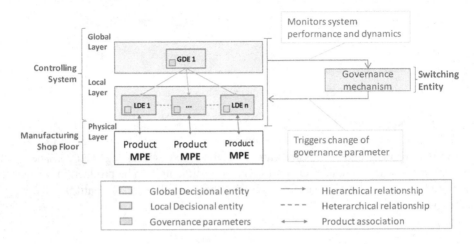

Fig. 3. D-HCA with governance mechanism entity

Governance Mechanism Entity: The governance mechanism entity is a switching mechanism responsible of the changing of the governance parameters of GDE and LDE agents. In fact, it is a control close-loop that starts with the monitoring of performance of the controlling system, continues with switching process for enhancing the system performance and it triggers finally a change in the system functioning settings.

Agent Governance Parameters: The governance parameters in the decisional entities (GDE and LDE) are defining the functioning of the predictive and reactive decision making technique. Considering that the GDE host the predictive technique, the governance parameters of the GDE could be the role of the global entity, the global searched objective, the influence within the environment or even the decision-making technique (mathematical programming or genetic algorithm), among others. On the LDE side, the governance parameters might be the roles of the local entity, the action rules and the level of communication, among many others. In this paper, the governance parameters in GDE and LDE are the roles within the manufacturing environment for each decisional point (Release, machine and operation sequence). On one side, the GDE features a *coercive or permissive* role as the coercive role imposes the global intention to the local intentions, while the permissive ignores global intentions and leaves the intention to local autonomy. On the other side, each LDE has only a *submissive* role as they follow imposed decisions over own intentions, when available. Otherwise, it will follow an own default local intentions.

Agent Objective: The objective of the decisional entities is defining the searched goal of each agent. The GDE is responsible for the global completion time performance (makespan), while the LDE are responsible for the making of its operations by the machines. The machines in this case are static and not controllable resources that are giving a service to LDE.

4.3   Operating Modes and Its Characterization

Operating Mode Definition: The vector that represents the operating mode is modeled as the combination of the global and local roles (see fig. 4). The operating mode in this study case is a vector of 27 elements: Three elements representing the governance parameters of the GDE, and other 24 elements representing the governance parameters of the 8 LDE's created. For the first three elements, these are the GDE role concerning the release, machine and operation sequence's decisions, respectively. Its values are coercive or permissive as it impose or neglect the product LDE intentions. For the next 24 elements, these are the LDE role for each LDE entity concerning also the release, machine and operation sequence's decisions. Its value is submissive as they respond depending the interrelation with the GDE entity. But, considering that the last 24 elements do not have any variability, the operating mode is shortened to just to the 3 first elements. For each element will be used the letter C for a coercive role, the letter P for permissive role and the letter S for submissive. Consequently, with the simplified representation of the operating mode and the letter codification, the operating modes resulted from the scenario are the following: CCC, CCP, CPC, CPP, PCC, PCP, PPC and PPP.

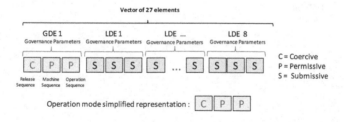

Fig. 4. Composition of the operating-mode's vector

Operating Mode Attributes: The attributes used in this paper are the values of each vector's element. This attributes characterize the operating mode as it gives information of the roles of the GDE and the interrelation with the LDE. Other attributes that can be used for characterizing these operating modes in FMS could be: Number of coercive elements in the operating mode, co-relation between two or more elements from the vector, dominance between the decisions taken, among others. However, this case just uses the value as input of the operating-mode's fitness.

Operating Mode Fitness: The fitness of the operating mode is used to summarize the behavior of the operating mode at a specific time of the manufacturing execution. Thereby, it is calculated from the operating-modes' attributes and current time of calculation. In this case, a shop-floor simulation based in a D-HCA is as a fitness function for each operating mode. The simulation calculates the makespan (output) of the manufacturing scenario according the attributes of the operating mode (input 1) and the current time (input 2). In the simulation, an emulation of the shop-floor is made controlled by a GDE and 8 LDEs. The GDE is modeled in Java with a MILP predictive technique that minimizes the makespan as the benchmark proposed in reference [11]. It aims to minimize the makespan of the data set. Also, eight LDEs are configured in an agent-based programming language called Netlogo [12] with a potential fields approach as a reactive technique [13]. They aim to minimize the shortest path and the estimated own completion time in the next resource intention. At the end, each time that a switching is needed, the operating-mode's fitness is calculated per each operating mode for giving its unique characteristic.

4.4   Dynamic Situation in the Case Study Scenario

In this case study, it is analyzed the use of different modes in the manufacturing system towards a disruption event. For this, the operating-mode vector is established in a fully coercive role strategy (CCC as Coercive, coercive, coercive) for starting execution. During a execution, a disruption occurs increasing the processing times in 50% of the machine 1. The system experiences degradation, as the job that passes over machine 1 increases its own completion time. After this disruption, the switching process changes the operating mode according a selection made according to the operating mode fitness.

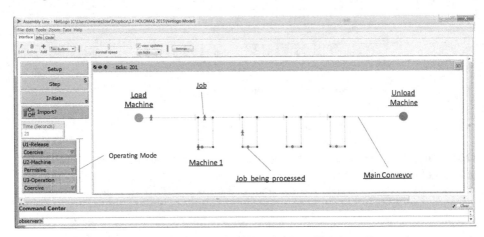

Fig. 5. NetLogo emulation of a FMS settled to a CPC Operating mode

5   Experiments and Results

In this section, it is presented the experiments performed in a simulation of the manufacturing case. The main goal of this experiment is to analyze the characteristics of the operating modes and to evaluate the possibility of using this information as criteria to activate the switching. For the emulation, the proposed D-HCA with operating modes is programmed in NetLogo (See fig. 5).

The setup of the experiments is divided in two parts. In part A, it is performed the simulation of the case study scenario without perturbations (not switching considered). This part simulates the extreme operating modes as that represent fully centralized and fully distributed architectures (CCC and PPP) throughout the whole execution. The purpose of this test is to demonstrate that the disruption is in fact degrading the execution performance. In part B, the dynamic situation of the case study scenario is considered. At first, it is settled different times of disruptions. At each, it is calculated the fitness of each operating mode according the operating-mode's attributes and current time. The purpose of this test is three folded. The experiment aims to demonstrate that there is a variability of the results of each operating mode according the characteristics of the settings and current time. The graph for the results plots the time of the perturbation versus the makespan of the data set after the disruption. To set lower bound and reference bound, one line without a slope is plotted for the coercive and permissive strategy held in part A of the experiment. The scatter dots in the graph show the makespan of the operating modes at the moment of each settled perturbation.

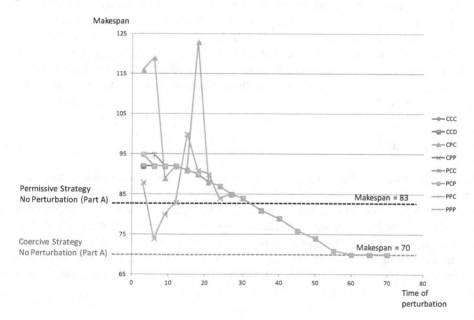

Fig. 6. Experiment results

In general terms, Fig. 6 shows the variation of fitness with the time, as well the decreasing of the makespan as the perturbation is closer to the execution end. It can be seen 3 different conclusion from the experiments performed.

At first, these experiments are a confirmation of the benefits of the fully centralized and fully distributed operating modes in control systems. For the fully centralized mode, when it is compared the total makespan without perturbation, the predictive technique accomplish the best result for the data set (70 in time units). However, when a perturbation occurs, the degradation of the makespan reaches a degradation of almost 30% in average from the initial predictive calculation. On the contrary, the fully distributed mode reaches a good performance when the disruption occurs (83 time units). In this case, the distributed strategy is better for the first half of the execution. However, in the second half, the predictive technique lift the performance even there is disruption event.

A second results, it can be seen that the switching is sensitive as it increase the time of the disruption. In this case, when the perturbation is near the beginning, the makespan is highly degraded from the lower bound. Nonetheless, while the perturbation happen closer to the execution ending, the makespan does not degrades much and even it reaches the same value as the lower bound. This trend is explained as at the beginning there still many decision making to perform in the release, machine and operation sequence. On the contrary, it get gradually closer to the lower bound as the majority of decision had been made and the system is unable to change much even it is a different setting. At the end, while the execution takes place, the flexibility of the system decreases and it become a more rigid execution.

As a final remark, it is confirmed from the results that there is variability between the operating modes. When the system features flexibility in decision making, the operating modes perform differently according its own attributes. At the end, this variability validates that a characterization of the operating modes is important in order to evaluate the strategy towards a switching process. Also, it suggests that the switching process is an optimization problem whereas it is needed to search the optimal operating mode.

6   Conclusions

The characterization of operating mode of dynamic hybrid control architecture was studied towards a switching process. The characterization is defined by the attributes and fitness of the operating mode. The fitness of the operating modes within different moments of time has a variability according the operating mode attributes. With this characterization, the switching process holds a unique criterion to evaluate the switching in the system functioning settings. The research perspective derived from this paper is continuing with the study of the characteristics of the operating modes as a way to gain insights a-priori of the expected performance.

References

1. Gunasekaran, A., Ngai, E.W.: The future of operations management: an outlook and analysis. International Journal of Production Economics **135**(2), 687–701 (2012)
2. Trentesaux, D.: Distributed control of production systems. Engineering Applications of Artificial Intelligence **22**(7), 971–978 (2009)
3. Thomas, A., El Haouzi, H., Klein, T., Belmokhtar, S., Herrera, C.: Architecture de systèmes contrôlés par le produit pour un environnement de juste à temps. Journal Européen Des Systèmes Automatisés **43**, 513–535 (2009)
4. Van Brussel, H., Wyns, J., Valckenaers, P., Bongaerts, L., Peeters, P.: Reference architecture for holonic manufacturing systems: PROSA. Computers in Industry **37**(3), 255–274 (1998)
5. Leitão, P., Restivo, F.: ADACOR: A holonic architecture for agile and adaptive manufacturing control. Computers in Industry **57**(2), 121–130 (2006)
6. Holvoet, T., Weyns, D., Valckenaers, P.: Patterns of delegate MAS. In: Third IEEE International Conference on Self-Adaptive and Self-Organizing Systems, SASO 2009, pp. 1–9. IEEE, September 2009
7. Pach, C., Berger, T., Bonte, T., Trentesaux, D.: ORCA-FMS: a dynamic architecture for the optimized and reactive control of flexible manufacturing scheduling. Computers in Industry **65**(4), 706–720 (2014)
8. Raileanu, S., Parlea, M., Borangiu, T., Stocklosa, O.: A JADE environment for product driven automation of holonic manufacturing. In: Borangiu, T., Thomas, A., Trentesaux, D. (eds.) Service Orientation in Holonic and Multi-Agent Manufacturing Control. SCI, vol. 402, pp. 265–277. Springer, Heidelberg (2012)
9. Barbosa, J.: Self-organized and evolvable holonic architecture for manufacturing control, Ph.D dissertation. Univ. of Valenciennes (UVHC), France (2015)
10. Jimenez, J.F., Bekrar, A., Trentesaux, D., Zambrano-Rey G., Leitão, P.: Governance mechanism in control architectures for flexible manufacturing systems. In: 15th Symposium Information Control Problems in Manufacturing INCOM. (2015) (accepted)
11. Trentesaux, D., Pach, C., Bekrar, A., Sallez, Y., Berger, T., Bonte, T., Leitão, P., Barbosa, J.: Benchmarking flexible job-shop scheduling and control systems. Control Engineering Practice **21**(9), 1204–1225 (2013)
12. Tisue, S., Wilensky, U.: Netlogo: A simple environment for modeling complexity. In: International Conference on Complex Systems, pp. 16–21, May 2004
13. Zbib, N., Pach, C., Sallez, Y., Trentesaux, D.: Heterarchical production control in manufacturing systems using the potential fields concept. Journal of Intelligent Manufacturing **23**(5), 1649–1670 (2012)

Interacting Holons in Evolvable Execution Systems: The NEU Protocol

Paul Valckenaers[(✉)] and Patrick A. De Mazière

Department of Healthcare and Technology, UC Leuven-Limburg, Louvain, Belgium
{Paul.Valckenaers,Patrick.DeMaziere}@ucll.be

Abstract. This paper presents an interaction protocol that allows system components to change (upgrade, customize, etc.) without requiring other components to change as well. This protocol enables system designs in which components interact through fine-grained conversations and do not need to support data exchange formats covering large chunks of information. The discussion addresses how a simple design evolves into more sophisticated versions through local adaptations and improvements. Finally, the ability to use the protocol across application domains is addressed, allowing for critical user mass to emerge.

Keywords: Holonic manufacturing systems · Holonic execution systems · Non-linear process planning · Erlang/OTP · e-Health

1 Introduction

Legacy is a major curse in information systems. Legacy implies unavoidability; too many developments break when legacy is not respected properly while replacing would require far too much effort, time and financial resources. Legacy also implies significant limitations and frustrating constraints. From today's perspective, legacy software was designed and developed with limited insight for underpowered computer hardware. As a result and with hindsight, many poor design choices have been casted in iron and concrete.

In this respect, data model lock-in is a common issue with legacy. For instance, a purchasing and logistic software, developed for the military when only men could enlist, lacks the ability to enter multiple values when ordering underwear for a soldier. This constraint resulted in a system that only provided full attire for women with a C-cup (i.e. the single available field was used already to indicate size).

Data model lock-in, rendering the software unable to distinguish relevant features in its world-of-interest, presents itself in various manifestations and places. For instance, a finite capacity planner may have 8-hour time buckets in which multiple shorter operations will fit. When this planner reveals to be overly optimistic for one shift (e.g. several operations need the last hour within the 8 hour shift), its data model only allows to increase operation times for all shifts, not exclusively for the shift that has a problem.

© Springer International Publishing Switzerland 2015
V. Mařík et al. (Eds.): HoloMAS 2015, LNAI 9266, pp. 120–129, 2015.
DOI: 10.1007/978-3-319-22867-9_11

Such facts-of-life prompted an ERP veteran consultant to state "keep these legacy technologies away from your core business". She was implying that, when legacy data models entail oversimplications affecting your core business, it rapidly may get you out-of-business. Hence, to avoid creating tomorrow's legacy software and systems, we need to design software systems that are able to evolve. This paper presents a key mechanism to achieve this in holonic executions systems.

2   NEU Protocol

This section introduces the NEU interaction[1] protocol from [1]. The protocol originates from research on a HMES[2], which is PROSA-based and uses a delegate multi-agent system to generate short-term forecasts for resource loads and product routings [2]. In the NEU protocol, the main interacting software processes are the order holon and its product holon. Resource holons have a supporting role in the discussion.

The product holon is responsible for the technical aspects (process plans) and reflects a product type in the world-of-interest. The order holon is responsible for the logistical aspects (product routing and initiating processing steps) and reflects the product instance (actually its instantiation). Both holons remain agnostic about the concerns of the other, which is key for the overall system's ability to evolve.

The discussion below uses Erlang[3] pseudo-code to denote the program behavior. Identifiers starting with a capital are variables. Identifiers starting with a lowercase character are constants (also called an enum); they are used as tags in the messages exchanged by the processes in the sample code. In Erlang, the ! operator sends the message after this exclamation sign to the addressee before this sign. Tuples are enclosed by curly brackets and lists by square brackets.

2.1   NEU Protocol Initialization

When a production order becomes known to the HMES, an order holon (OH) is created by the *factory cockpit*. OH receives a reference PH_ADR to its product holon (PH) at creation. The first action of OH is to acquire a representation of its state from PH. OH executes:

```
PH_ADR ! {init_order_state, OH_ADR}
```

PH generates OH_State, which contains all information concerning production progress made by OH. At this initial stage, OH_State reflects that nothing has been done so far. PH sends OH_State to OH:

```
OH_ADR ! {order_state, OH_State}
```

---

[1]   Next-Execute-Update protocol.
[2]   Holonic Manufacturing Execution System.
[3]   For more information on Erlang see: www.erlang.org and www.learnyousomeerlang.com.

Note that PH can remain agnostic about the instances of its product type that are being produced. Indeed, OH will pass OH_ADR to PH with every request/message. Conversely, OH remains agnostic about the structure and content of OH_State. OH is the repository but systematically delegates any information processing involving OH_State to PH.

After this simple exchange of information, both OH and PH mirror the relevant aspects of their world-of-interest. They now enter into the main phase of their life cycle.

2.2   NEU Protocol Execution

The order holon is responsible for the creation of its product instance (i.e. execution of the production steps). The product holon knows (all possible) sequences of production steps that result in a suitable product instance. Thus, the order holon OH takes the initiative but delegates technical matters to PH. OH requests PH to compute which operations are the candidate next production steps:

```
PH_ADR ! {nxtOps, OH_State, OH_ADR}
```

PH analyses OH_State and computes a list of valid next operations. This list comprises state-changing operations (e.g. drill a hole or perform a test) as well as auxiliary operations (i.e. transportation or storage). Note that PH remains agnostic about productivity-related issues; it strictly looks at technological aspects (i.e. feasibility, validity). PH delivers a list of possible next operations to OH:

```
OH_ADR ! {nxtOpList,[Op₁, Op₂, … ]}
```

OH searches, finds and selects a resource holon (RH) that is capable of executing an operation Op_x from the list provided by PH. Order holons are cooperating with resource holons and staff holons to explore the available options and optimize the routing and processing for their product instantiation tasks. This aspect is out of scope for this paper and the interested reader is referred to [3][4][5][6].

When RH finishes executing Op_x, it informs OH about the outcome:

```
OH_ADR ! {done, Op_x, Res}
```

In order to remain agnostic about the technological aspects, OH request an update of OH_State from PH:

```
PH_ADR ! {update, OH_State_old, Op_x, Res, OH_ADR}
```

PH computes the new state for OH and sends:

```
OH_ADR ! {order_state, OH_State_new}
```

From here on, the interaction pattern repeats the phase two interactions. Note that OH does not select/execute a second production step from the list of candidate operations. As OH_State has changed, OH ignores whether this old list is still valid.

The interaction protocol derives its acronym NEU from this phase:

— <u>N</u>ext   (get the candidate operations list and select the next operation),
— <u>E</u>xecute (execute the selected operation and obtain the result),
— <u>U</u>pdate (update the order state).

2.3 NEU Protocol Finalization

When the list of possible next operations contains a finalize operation, the order holon may select it and perform any wrapping up duties (e.g. archive the trace data).

3 Evolving HMES

Starting from a simple implementation using the NEU interaction protocol, this section evolves toward and discusses more sophisticated versions, revealing how non-involved parties remain unchanged and don't notice much except for an eventual enlargement of their solution space.

3.1 Simple Product Holon

A naïve product holon implementation supports a single sequence of operations for its process plan. When the factory cockpit is used to introduce a new product type, a product holon is created with a list of processing steps as the definition of the process plan or recipe. The factory cockpit executes:

```
spawn(product_holon, start,[OP₁, OP₂, OP₃, …])
```

where spawn creates a new computing process that invokes the start function of the product_holon module:

```
start(OpList) -> …
     where OpList = [OP₁, OP₂, OP₃, …].
```

This start function takes this list of operation identifiers – OpList – as the definition of its process plan, defining a single sequence of production steps to be executed. This simple order holon implements the interaction pattern as follows:

- When an order holon requests an initial OH_State, the order holon returns this OpList:

```
receive
  {init_order_state, OH_ADR} ->
                      OH_ADR ! {order_state, OpList};
  …
end
```

- When an order holon passes its OH_State and asks for a list of candidate next operations, it returns a list containing only the first operation of this list:

```
receive
   ... ;
   {nxtOps, [NextOp | _ ], OH_ADR} ->
                      OH_ADR ! {nxtOpList,[NextOp]};
   ...
end
```

- When an order holon passes OH_State together with the operation that has been performed with its result, the product holon returns the list without the first element as the new OH_State:

```
receive
   ... ;
   {update,[ _ | NewState], _ , _ , OH_ADR}->
                      OH_ADR ! {order_state, NewState}
end
```

Erlang pattern matching assigns the first element of OH_State to NextOp, where OH_State initially equals the OpList passed to the start function by the factory cockpit. Likewise, this pattern matching assigns OH_State to NewState after removing OH_State's first element.

3.2   Test and Repair Product Holon

The simple product holon, discussed above, is extended with the ability to handle repair operations whenever the result of a test operation demand this. The factory cockpit again starts a computing process using the start function of the product holon module but with a richer process plan as its parameter.

The process plan is a list of tuples where each tuple specifies the operation, the repair operation (to be executed when the processing result is fail) and the number of times a repair may be attempted. The test operations specify this number to be non-zero. Failed tests decrement this number before each repair attempt. Repair operation failures trigger an abort.

```
-module(product_holon).

start(OpList) ->
 %% initiate the PH process.
   spawn( product_holon, loop, [OpList]).

loop(OpList) ->
%% This is the product holon software process
%% executing (its part of) the NEU protocol.
 receive
    %% a new order holons request an "initial state".
    {init_order_state, OH_ADR} ->
```

```erlang
        OH_ADR ! {order_state, OpList};

%% The first operation in OH_State is only candidate.
{nxtOps, [{NextOp, _ , _ } | _ ], OH_ADR} ->
        OH_ADR ! {nxtOpList,[ NextOp ]};

%% Maximum number of repair attempts performed.
{update,[{ _ , _ , 0} | _ ], _ , fail, OH_ADR}->
        OH_ADR ! {order_state, [ { abort, abort, 0 } ]};

%% Success; moving to the next operation.
{update,[ _ | NewState], _ , ok,  OH_ADR}->
        OH_ADR ! {order_state, NewState};

%% Add Repair operation to the front of the list,
%% and reduce the repair count for Op by one.
{update,[{Op, Repair, No}| S ], _ , fail, OH_ADR}->
        OH_ADR ! {order_state, [ {Repair, abort, 0},
                                {Op, Repair, No - 1} | S ]};

%% Switching to a new product holon.
%% function F in module M becomes the new loop for PH.
 {upgrade, M, F, Args} -> apply(M, F, [OpList | Args])
end,
%% get ready for the next OH request:
product_holon:loop(OpList).
```

Note that the order holon is unable to perceive that its simple product holon has been replaced by a product holon knowledgeable about repairs and testing. Note that the Erlang pseudo-code above actually executes. For real-world application, it needs refactoring to make it more robust and maintenance-friendly. It also may need supervision and monitoring to recover from crashes (automatically). But the pseudo-code above already implements the intended behavior for the product holon.

3.3   Discussion

The above evolution from a simple product holon into a test-and-repair product holon can be continued while the order holons never need to adapt. For instance, it is possible to introduce process plans based on:

— Dynamic precedence graphs, which are precedence graphs in which the result of the operation determines which outgoing edges are activated [7]. These edges cannot be deactivated and there are no inhibiting edges, which enabled the research prototype to use a highly efficient and decentralized implementation (using bitsets) at the expense of some expressiveness limitations. E.g. it is possible to express mutually exclusive alternatives but not unbounded test-and-repair loops.

— Petri-Nets and AND/OR graphs, properly contained into some safe subclass, deliver non-linear process plans enjoying a well-known and expressive modeling mechanism [8][9].
— Erlang code, enjoying the full expressiveness and productivity of a modern programming language. Erlang pattern matching represents possibilities and opportunities.

The order holons are only able to notice that the contents of lists of candidate operations is different. However, as long as the order holons are able to manage lists of candidates – and e.g. do not assume there will be only one candidate operation – they may cooperate with any product holon. Conversely, product holons cannot even perceive what order holons do with their information. Order holons can evolve and become better at utilizing the available resources without the need for product holon adaptation.

Stronger, the lightweight ant agents from the delegate multi-agent systems [2], used for exploring possible routings for order holons or propagating order intentions to the resource holons (to generate short-term forecasts), are able to execute the NEU protocol with the product holons, and the product holons will not notice that their order state information is fictitious. Note that the resource holons support a what-if mode generating the (expected) operation results for such fictitious states.

4   NEU Protocol Enhancement for e-Health

Our holonic execution systems research results, originally targeting manufacturing execution (HMES), have been translated and applied to various application domains, including:

- HLES, holonic logistic execution systems
- Distributed HMES, coordinating networked production in supply networks
- ITTS, intelligent traffic and transportation systems
- Open air engineering, coordination of harvesting operations
- Smart grid, demand response management and coordination
- Robotics, coordination of a fleet of autonomous wheelchairs

However, it was the translation and application to healthcare that revealed the need to enhance the NEU protocol. Unsurprisingly, when this requirement from e-health emerged, an ad hoc implementation of this enhancement existed already. Indeed, during a proof-of-concept development, in which delegate multi-agent systems generated short-term forecasts in a real-world industrial production setting, a similar demand to add more discretion, discussed below, to the basic NEU protocol emerged.

4.1   Validity / Accuracy versus Efficiency / Effort

When the product holon PH generates a list of candidate operations and the order holon OH selects one of the candidates for execution, there is a trade-off when addressing healthcare operations. When a holonic execution system is involved in real-world medical interventions, there must be no mistakes and all decisions must be "signed off" by a properly authorized person.

In these situations, the product holon[4] consults this authorized person about the decision to be made. At most, the holon software provides advice and/or volunteers supporting information. This human involvement ensures and delivers the required accuracy and validity for the information in the list. However, it is (very) expensive to involve human expertise in the decision making all the time.

When this holonic execution system is generating short-term forecasts, e.g. to keep patients informed about waiting times, human involvement must be kept to a minimum. Likewise, exploring ant agents, investigating many possible ways to deliver care, cannot afford to involve humans every time they consult the product holon. Here, the product holon must generate this list automatically. At most, humans may need to provide input once, and the software remembers and repeats the input until an expiration date is reached. This will be combined with a reminder date (before the expiration date) and the possibility to revoke or change the input.

Clearly, the enhanced NEU protocol needs to distinguish between requests that are for real – which have to be valid and accurate – and requests that are fictitious – used for planning and coordination before a final real-world commitment is made. Similar enhancements will be needed elsewhere in the holonic execution system, but the NEU protocol is not involved (e.g. in the selection of a resource and the operation from the list of candidates).

4.2   Qualified Requests

To answer the needs of a holonic healthcare execution system, where our research is targeting integrated care and multi-disease, the requests from order holons to product holons have to provide additional information. They have to indicate whether – as a priority – effort has to be kept low or whether there can be no compromise regarding validity and accuracy. Therefore, the messages contain an additional tag *(enum)* indicating what is required:

```
PH_ADR ! {nxtOps, unsigned, OH_State, OH_ADR}
PH_ADR ! {nxtOps, signed,   OH_State, OH_ADR}
```

and

```
PH_ADR ! {update, unsigned, OH_State_old, Op_x, Res, OH_ADR}
PH_ADR ! {update, signed,   OH_State_old, Op_x, Res, OH_ADR}
```

Note that the pattern matching in Erlang makes it trivial to handle the respective cases with different code, keeping the software manageable. Furthermore, distinguishing the two modes – signed and unsigned – provides additional degrees of freedom for their respective implementations.

The signed mode is able to delegate its work to human experts and other qualified personnel. Hence, initial implementations can simply delegate, where subsequent

---

[4]   In holonic systems, this person will be considered to be part of the product holon, which is an aggregate/composite holon (or holarchy) with a possibly time-varying membership.

versions implement the lessons learned as the development team sees opportune or the users regard as necessary. Here, the ability to evolve the holonic execution systems becomes a major benefit.

The unsigned mode is allowed to "not always get it right" as it only serves to look ahead and arrange the activities more optimal and smoothly than current practice. When the unsigned mode gets it wrong, it creates a disturbance, where handling such kind of disturbances is a core competence of our holonic execution systems technology. Indeed, changes and disturbances are considered business as usual. Summarizing, the unsigned mode is allowed to achieve efficiency and low effort by tolerating a level of inaccuracy.

In addition, this unsigned mode need not account for its world-of-interest in more detail than required for its services. It must be able to estimate how (future) activities will be using resources while following a valid process plan (or therapy), including time estimates. For instance, a machine learning mechanism, trained by traces of past activities, may estimate what is needed without possessing a model that explains what would be happening in the corresponding reality. This is a possible manner to implement the unsigned mode (among many others).

4.3   Discussion

This section addressed the application of the NEU protocol and holonic execution systems to multiple application domains. Importantly, the enhancement needed to cover a new domain is compatible with the earlier-addressed application domains. Stronger, it typically will be useful for other domains (e.g. in our HMES proof of concept trials within an industrial setting). Consequently, a single holonic execution systems platform suffices; it is unnecessary to establish or maintain multiple versions.

Another example of such cross-fertilization, not affecting the NEU protocol, is privacy. The issue first appeared in networked production in which factories have different owners. Data and information disclosure needed addressing. Trust and reputation handling constitutes another aspect that is relevant in multiple application domains.

The design of our holonic execution systems, comprising communicating software processes mirroring the corresponding reality, proved to be highly suited to address this privacy aspect. Indeed, it is easy to have holons exchange data on a need-to-know basis and to divide responsibilities across holons, each belonging to a data protection area.

In healthcare, similar issues and requirements appear. The past development will be useful and new developments for e-health are likely to be useful in networked production, intelligent traffic, smart grids, etc. Thus, achieving critical user mass becomes easier.

5   Conclusion

This paper presents the NEU protocol that enables the holons in execution systems to evolve without affecting others. It shows how a product holon remains agnostic about instances and specializes in type-specific knowledge. Conversely, it reveals how order holons delegate all type-related information processing to their order holon.

As a result, product holons do not notice changes in order holons and order holons do not perceive changes inside their product holon. The overall effect is an evolvable execution system. This allows to develop, maintain and operate execution systems incrementally. Furthermore, with an Erlang/OTP implementation, such execution systems can be adapted, extended, upgraded while remaining on-line and operational.

In a next step, we applied the developed technology to a new application domain (e-health) and discussed its relevance/usefulness for this domain. The NEU protocol was enhanced without rendering it (too) complicated, and this enhancement answered a demand already encountered during an exercise in an industrial setting, demonstrating HMES short-term forecasting capabilities. Importantly, a single software basis will serve multiple domains; there is no need to support more than one implementation.

Finally, the NEU protocol and its fine-grained interaction suffices because of the delegate multi-agent systems in our holonic execution systems. Indeed, through virtual execution, the system allows to generate information requiring more complicated formats and larger chunks of information, where each holon collects whatever fits its internal representation/format. Each holon preserves its internal expressiveness without the need for system-wide standards or conventions.

References

1. Van Brussel, H., Valckenaers, P.: Design for the Unexpected: From Holonic Manufacturing Systems towards a Humane Mechatronic Society. Butterworth-Heinemann (2015)
2. Valckenaers, P., Van Brussel, H.: Holonic Manufacturing Execution Systems. CIRP Annals - Manufacturing Technology **54**(1), 427–432 (2005)
3. Verstraete, P.: Integrating Existing Scheduling Techniques into the Holonic Manufacturing Execution System. PhD thesis, KU Leuven, Leuven (2009)
4. Van Belle, J.: A Holonic Logistics Execution System for Cross-docking. PhD thesis, KU Leuven, Leuven (2013)
5. Leitão, P.: An Agile and Adaptive Holonic Architecture for Manufacturing Control. PhD Thesis, University of Porto, Porto (2004)
6. Pach, C.: ORCA: Architecture hybride pour le contrôle de la myopie dans le cadre du pilotage des Systèmes Flexibles de Production. PhD thesis, University of Valenciennes (2013)
7. Valckenaers, P., Van Brussel, H., Bongaerts, L., Bonneville, F.: Programming, Scheduling, and Control of Flexible Assembly Systems. Computers in Industry **26**, 209–218 (1995)
8. Jang, P., Son, Y., Cho, H.: Elaboration and Validation of AND/OR Graph-based Non-linear Process Plans for Shop Floor Control. Int. J. Prod. Research **41**(13), 3019–3043 (2003)
9. Kruth, J.-P., Detand, J., Van Zeir, G., Kempenaers, J., Pinte, J.: Methods to Improve the Response Time of a CAPP System that Generates Non-Linear Process Plans. Advances in Engineering Software **25**(1), 9–17 (1996)

ARUM: Adaptive Production Management

Adaptive Production Management
Using a Service-Based Platform

Usman Wajid[1($\boxtimes$)], Vadim Chepegin[2], Despina T. Meridou[3],
Maria-Eleftheria Ch. Papadopoulou[3], and José Barbosa[4]

[1] The University of Manchester, Oxford Road, Manchester M15 6PB, UK
usman.wajid@manchester.ac.uk
[2] TIE Kinetix, De Corridor 5d, 3621 ZA Breukelen, Netherlands
vadim.chepegin@tiekinetix.com
[3] School of Electrical and Computer Engineering, National Technical University of Athens,
Heroon Polytechniou 9, 15773 Athens, Greece
{dmeridou,marelpap}@icbnet.ece.ntua.gr
[4] Polytechnic Institute of Bragança, Apartado 1134, 5301-857 Bragança, Portugal
jbarbosa@ipb.pt

Abstract. This paper presents a platform for adaptive production management developed in the ARUM[1] (Adaptive pRodUct Management, http://arum-project.eu/) project. The design of ARUM platform started with applying a traditional enterprise Service-Oriented Architecture (SOA) paradigm to solving an integration problem for the production ramp-up of highly customized products such as aircrafts, ships, etc. The production of such articles is exceptionally challenging for planning and control, especially in small lot sizes. Often requests for changes at any stage of the production, immature products and processes bring serious additional risks for the producers and customers. To counter such issues requires new strategies, the core elements of most of them include early detection of unexpected situations followed by rapid mitigation actions. Furthermore, human beings cannot cope any longer with processing a massive volume of data that comes with a high velocity from various sources that is a requirement for any modern production shop floor. The traditional IT solutions also fall short when trying to satisfy all those requirements and this motivates the need for ARUM platform to help in effective decision making.

Keywords: System architecture · Adaptive manufacturing · Enterprise service bus

1   Introduction

Automation of conventional processes and wider adoption of service oriented system design approaches mean services are playing an increasingly important role in modern

---

[1] This project has received funding from the European Union's Seventh Framework Programme for research, technological development and demonstration under grant agreement no 314056.

V. Mařík et al. (Eds.): HoloMAS 2015, LNAI 9266, pp. 133–144, 2015.
DOI: 10.1007/978-3-319-22867-9_12

manufacturing domain. Currently there are two trends for designing service-based systems competing in the market that many researchers and practitioners consider mutually exclusive, namely service-oriented architecture (SOA) and REST style. To design a service-based system that brings together and integrates different entities SOA advocates the use of an Enterprise Service Bus (ESB) for integration pattern and functional decomposition of system level entitiesogies. However, at enterprise level the implementation of SOA is usually associated with large investments in IT infrastructures in terms of time and funds. On the contrary, REST integration style is capitalizing on the existing Web infrastructure. It supports P2P communications, lightweight protocols and message formats for interaction between different services, and does not require large upfront investments. The success and rapid growth of the Internet is often seen as a proof of success for the REST style. REST services are globally used for delivering new business functions via exploiting existing polyglot infrastructure (execution environments, persistency) and continuous delivery approach.

This paper describes a service-based platform that enables the manufacturing industry to benefit from using both of the paradigms together taking an example based on the experience and lessons learnt from the European funded ARUM (Adaptive pRodUct Management) project. ARUM aims at solving hard planning problems during a production ramp-up of complex and highly customised products such as new aircrafts with help of Multi-Agent Systems (MAS). The ARUM approach is based on the combination of innovative lines of commercial SOA-based products such as *TIE Smart Bridge* (TSB), a lightweight message and service bus that strongly supports SOA principles, along with *TIE Smart Integrator* (TSI) and a semantic mapping and transformation tool. TSB and TSI together provide facilities for data exchange and integration from a vast variety of services and legacy systems that cannot be reached using REST/HTTP on its own. Although, businesses in the manufacturing domain are typically dealing with common industrial formats and systems, within the ARUM context in order to satisfy the needs of knowledge-based MAS; TSI was enriched employing micro-services approach to take care of transforming data from legacy systems into the Web ontological models [2]. Both of the tools (TSI and TSB) can be exposed and be used via REST APIs, TSB has a support for workflows, and is designed to operate with SOAP and REST Web services, and altogether this solution paves the link between two integration paradigms, SOA and REST [4]. Moreover, TSB and TSI can be provided within the Cloud as Software-as-a-Service (SaaS) to help in integrating business services dispersed all over the Internet running on their own distributed Virtual Machines (VM) and Virtual Environments.

Thus, the proposed ARUM solution speeds up and facilitates delivery of the new value for the businesses by quickly setting up a foundation for communications in heterogeneous distributed environments that require intensive data exchange among context bubbles but run on various platforms and speak different vernaculars. Within the ARUM context, such an environment is realised by designing a SOA-inspired platform that is primarily designed to support ramp-up systems for manufacturing, where there are conflicts between the need for control and rigour and the reality of rapid changes. To address such challenges and industrial requirements the architecture of ARUM platform integrates the key features of service-oriented-architecture, holonic multi-agent systems and legacy systems and links them via an enterprise service bus (ESB) [1], providing communication, monitoring, interoperability and aggregation of information across existing legacy systems at all production levels to support real-time automatic negotiation, planning, scheduling and optimization within and across factories. The envisaged technologies of distributed multi agent system within a holonic architecture is expected to help in integrating legacy systems, information aggregation from high level systems (MES, ERP, etc.) to factory floor automation (e.g. metal cut and assembly systems). Based on such requirements reflected in the system architecture, the main functionalities of ARUM platform include scheduling, planning, production management and manufacturing process supported by information delivered from a variety of sources e.g. legacy systems, sensors, and users.

The use of multi-agent system and service-oriented architectures in manufacturing is not new, and other approaches have already been promoted, mainly focusing the lower-level control and interaction [10, 0]. Despite this, the ARUM project differentiates from those, by promoting the integration of different layers of the ISA-95, namely the planning and scheduling, aggregated by the use of a common communication infrastructure and a well-define data access process flow.

The rest of the paper is organized as follows: Section 2 presents the ARUM architecture, briefly describing its components and tools, while Section 3 describes the technical background that supports that architecture. Section 4 describes, by means of two practical examples, the usage of the ARUM architecture, particularly the data retrieval and the strategic planning actions. At last, Section 5 rounds up the paper with the conclusions.

2   ARUM Platform Architecture

Based on the user and domain specific requirements as well as the underlying SOA principles, the architecture of the ARUM platform is closely coupled with the goal of enabling prediction in the pre-planning phase and real-time control in the production phase in highly dynamic ramp-up production domains. Figure 1 depicts the system architecture and its key components and services that make up the ARUM platform, as well as the interrelations between them, making it easier to understand the functionality offered and realise the potential benefits of the ARUM platform.

As shown in Figure 1, the SOA inspired **Enterprise Service Bus** constitutes the core of ARUM intelligent ESB (i-ESB) platform and provides a common communication infrastructure for the interoperability of different tools and services, such as the Strategic Planner, Ontology Service, FND&SD service and others described below.

The Ontology Service and the MIDAS/Azimov tool are considered as the **knowledge base** of the system. The **Ontology Service** is the major data provider to the ARUM tools as it holds the schema of the ARUM Ontologies (Core, Scene, Events and Policy Model) and manages production-related data expressed based on the appropriate schema in a triple store, a special data structure for semantic data.

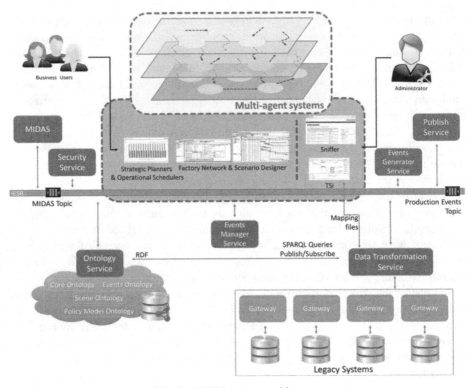

Fig. 1. ARUM system architecture

The Legacy Systems, the ARUM tools and services, as well as the Production Events Topic are the three data sources from which data are acquired by the Ontology Service. In the first case, data in various formats coming from the Legacy Systems on demand by the aforementioned tools are converted into RDF by the Data Transformation Service before sending them to the Ontology Service. In the second case, semantic data resulting from scheduling and planning processes operated by the related tools, such as the current state of the factory used by the Operational Scheduler for what-if games, are sent to the Ontology Service for the purpose of storage and/or reasoning. Finally, in the third case, each iESB service publishes any production-related event in the Production Events Topic by exploiting the schema of the ARUM Events Ontology. The **MIDAS/Azimov** [8] tool receives the production-related events via the **MIDAS Topic** supported by a publish/subscribe messaging model and analyses them by taking also into account their respective solutions. In this respect, all information is processed and in order to facilitate the troubleshooting procedure the estimated troubleshoot time is provided for given production events, typically non-conformities in the production/manufacturing processes.

Day-to-day data of current manufacturing practices contained in existing systems known as **Legacy Systems** are integrated in the platform via gateways of the **Data Transformation Service,** which transforms data from heterogeneous sources (e.g. legacy systems) into the RDF format according to the ARUM ontology. The mapping between the schema of legacy systems data and the ARUM ontology, based on which the Data Transformation Service performs the transformation of the data, is created by the **TIE Semantic Integrator** (TSI).

An innovative feature of the ARUM architecture is the support for multiple iESB services that serve generic purposes providing support for the whole infrastructure. To be more specific, the **Security Service** is mainly responsible for authenticating users as well as making access control decisions based on policies specified by the Policy Model Ontology when. This service plays a crucial role to the ARUM infrastructure by acting as a mediator in the communication for data exchange between the iESB services, thus ensures trust. The **Publish Service** used by other services to distribute messages in a publish-subscribe manner posts any received message to a corresponding topic to which other services are subscribed. The **Event Generator Service** used by the Scenario Designer tool for obtaining generated hypothetical production-related events on request is useful in what-if game simulations and in this way it supports planning in the manufacturing domain. The **Production Events Topic,** as mentioned above, receives production-related event messages by an ARUM console, legacy systems, or any other service such as FND&SD.

The main tasks of the ARUM platform regarding scheduling and planning are carried out by **Multi-Agent Systems** [6] **as a set of intelligent services (MAS realm)**. These services mainly carryout the scheduling and planning activities, which effectively are the main features of the ARUM platform. More specifically, the **Operational scheduler** as a tool computes one or more valid schedules as a set-up of start and end times of (manufacturing) jobs and allocation of resources based on input data about jobs to be done, their precedencies and required resources. The **Strategic Planner** [3] assists the professionals taking managerial decisions, particularly at the tactical level by enabling them to identify and analyse which and where resources must be allocated in order to cope with production demand as well as at the strategic level by helping them decide if, e.g., building an extra production line is required.

The presentation tier of the ARUM platform, based on open source technologies and products (such as Apache Rave and Wookie) that can support widget based environments or LifeRay for portlet-based dashboards, helps in creating an iterative user-centred experience. Moreover, the **Factory Network and Scenario Designer (FND&SD) Service** acts as the gateway between the ESB and the user interface. Its GUI provides users with functionalities such recording and processing production events. Finally, the **ESB Sniffer** GUI [7] provides a list of messages going through the ESB together with their details, showing a visualization of the message flow, being particularly useful for debugging problems in inter-service communications.

3   Architecture Support for Technical Solution

The support from the above described SOA-inspired architecture enables ARUM platform to bring together a new generation of innovative *Multi-Agent Systems (MAS) that can build plans and schedules in real time* based on the information collected from different resources including legacy systems (e.g., MES, ERP, etc.), data generated by workers, sensors, MAS themselves, etc. and *enterprise integration platforms that follow different paradigms* in order to guarantee fast delivery of business value, maximal coverage of systems accepted by the platform, and a security - the high-level overview of ARUM platform is shown in Figure 2.

An extra challenge of ARUM platform lay in the fact that MASs need a massive flow of information into them up-front and continuously during their execution to make their work effective. This is a well-known so-called "knowledge bottleneck" problem but in case of ARUM velocity and volume of data are also playing an important role since a schedule for workers that does not factor in the latest figures over the articles in the local warehouse or the outcomes of the recent quality checks would have no value. And to make it even more challenging providers of business tools in ARUM requested platform providers to support ontologies and triple stores for the convenience of their communications among each other and with other data sources. This solution also helps them to focus on their functionality and delegate all the heavy lifting work to the platform.

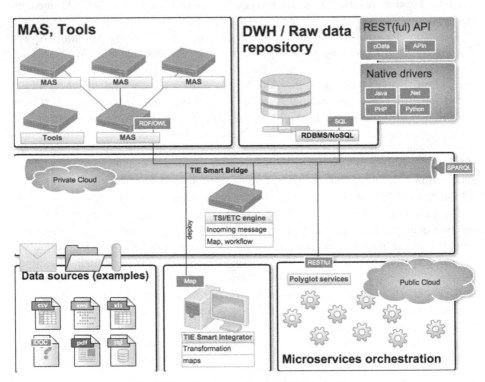

Fig. 2. High-level overview of ARUM platform

The architecture also support ARUM platform to take advantage of the realm of Internet of Things and Knowledge-based systems such as Multi-agent systems (MAS) and thus consists of many independent services and data sources that reside on various platforms spanning from legacy monoliths to notebooks, and tablet PCs. Cooperation via interaction of all those systems (hardware and software) is the intrinsic characteristic of the ARUM platform. Integration with legacy and off-the-shelf monolith systems is important because tones of valuable data are already there and those systems are tightly integrated into the enterprise business processes and they will not be replaced any soon. Legacy nature of those systems (such as CAD, CRM, HR, etc.) also means that those systems most of the time does not have common interaction mechanisms, Web Service interface and cannot communicate via HTTP protocol. As mentioned above, the the ARUM Intelligent ESB (iESB) platform employs a combination of two message-service busses, namely TIE Smart Bridge (TSB) and JBoss ESB. This combination was suits the requirements since it allows interoperability and interplay between different programming paradigms (e.g. .Net and Java) that cover most of the traditional enterprise integration spectrum.

This also allows integration of different proprietary and open source products. In addition to the combination of two service buses, any other ESB can be connected to the platform that follows ARUM approach of a shared stack of message queues and common service registry. Because queues are hosted in the cloud environment it is possible to dynamically manage them, for instance, in order to react to the spiky loads. A service registry supports a dynamic discovery, which adds agility to the whole infrastructure by allowing on-the-fly discovery and service binding. Of course, all other ARUM added-value services that constitute the complete iESB are also deployed in the cloud and can benefit from using the same dynamic discovery and elasticity along with a polyglot persistency and service execution environments. This become especially valuable when ARUM had faced a need of integrating new wave of service and data providers that reside on the hand-held devices of the shop floor personnel such as tablets or notebooks used by workers and managers next to the working stations.

An example scenario for such integration is the interplay of TIE Smart Bridge (TSB), a lightweight message and service bus that strongly supports SOA principles, with TIE Smart Integrator (TSI), a semantic mapping and transformation tool. TSB has a history of successful business brokerage for different sizes of commercial projects and a rich set of off-the-shelf functionality for integration with a wide spectrum of legacy systems as well as with services and data providers that are hosted in the cloud. TSB relies on TSI for doing explicit declarative maps that describe how elements of a source schema correspond to elements of a destination schema. Transformation engines use those maps in the data exchange and integration scenarios. Both of these tools can be exposed and used via REST APIs, and altogether this solution paves the road between two integration paradigms, SOA and REST.

A typical scenario starts when a factory-floor worker sends a message via a specialized mobile application to the platform about finishing his or her job. This message is accepted by the data warehouse using a REST API, and the appropriate data is added or updated. Other devices or software services that are connected through RESTful APIs or use native drivers, such as ODBC or JDBC (see Figure 1), can get access to this new state right away. But that is not all, since ontologies have to be supported to enable meaningful information exchange between different components and systems. Consequently, a service responsible for managing knowledge within the platform, namely the Ontology Service, is subscribed to a publish-subscribe endpoint in TSB that can manage different queries in SPARQL format – a W3C standard for querying Web ontologies. In this respect, the Ontology service can manage internal logic and requests from its main clients, namely planners, schedulers, and other knowledge-based tools.

Although in theory any service can subscribe to this pub/sub point, the only one practical subscriber at the moment is the Ontology Service. The Ontology Service focuses on providing a clean API and language understood by knowledge-based systems; it intensively manipulates knowledge in a triple store, searches for implicit relationships using different inference mechanisms, and it is ready to reply to complicated analytical queries.

Furthermore, in order to satisfy the needs of knowledge-based systems, TSI was enriched to deal with the transformation of data into the Web ontology format OWL. Thus when a SPARQL request arrives:

1. It is rewritten into one or more SQL queries.
2. Data is retrieved from the target systems.
3. It is transformed using existing maps into the destination format.

All three steps are implemented via micro-services, and they can be executed in parallel when possible. Implementation of a scale-out strategy here also helps in increasing the throughput of the system and decreases its latency. A similar situation exists between the platform's data warehouse and legacy systems. TSB is used to subscribe or to poll legacy resources through its gateways. When data is emitted by any of the data providers, TSB starts an appropriate workflow that contains necessary transformations, and data is finally pushed into the data warehouse.

The above scenario describes a normal operational routine of our solution, when data comes in small chunks from different directions. There is another mode used for the initial setup. In this mode, TSB collects data from the connected legacy systems, transforms it using TSI and stores it in the data warehouse, and then performs a massive batch transformation into ontological format followed by the upload of that data into the Ontology Service. This is necessary so that a new system does not suffer from a "cold start" — a term used in knowledge-based systems to describe a situation in which they cannot make any meaningful suggestions due to a lack of available information.

Together TSB and TSI can be provided within the cloud as software-as-a-service (SaaS), and they can help in integrating business services dispersed all over the Internet running on their own distributed virtual machines (VMs) and virtual environments (VEs; e.g., Docker) with a diversity of operating systems. Thus, the proposed solution speeds up and facilitates delivery of the new business value by quickly setting up a foundation for communications in heterogeneous distributed environments that require intensive data exchange among context bubbles but run on various platforms and speak different vernaculars

4   Usage Scenarios

We have carried out the validation of the proposed architecture and the resulting platform in the context of ensuring that architecture supports the perceived functionalities and the platform can handle the system level operations with the help of the following data retrieval scenarios.

Example of the interaction of the Factory Network & Scenario Designer with the Ontology ServiceIn this scenario (as shown in Figure 3), a user of the ARUM platform, such as a Station Manager, wants to design a new scene, i.e., a new snapshot of the current state of the station and associate it with a particular product, which is processed at the aforementioned station. This operation can be performed through the **User Interface (UI) of the Factory Network & Scenario Designer (FNDSD).**

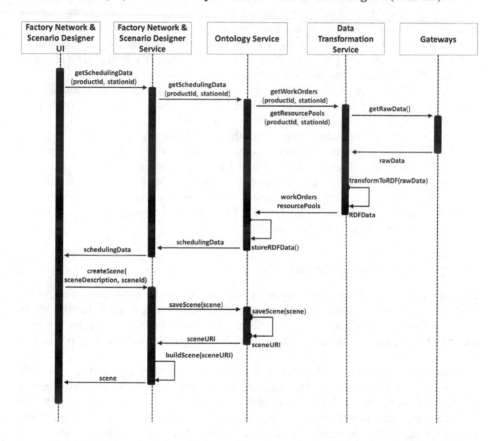

Fig. 3. Sequence diagram for the legacy systems data retrieval scenario

Before the creation of the scene is possible, certain pieces of data, which will be later used as part of the scene during the scheduling process, need to be acquired. Once such a request is sent by the FNDSD UI to the **FNDSD service**, the latter sends the appropriate request to the Ontology Service. Since, initially, the legacy data are kept in the legacy systems, the FNDSD service requests the Ontology Service to fetch all data that are needed for the scheduling of the operations concerning the processing of the aforementioned product to the station, where it is allocated.

In this respect, the **Ontology Service** decomposes the query into sub-queries that are then sent to the Data transformation service. The reason for decomposing the initial query is that various pieces of data are spread over different legacy systems. Basically, the requested data contains the set of operations to be performed, their precedencies, durations, required human resources with particular skills, required parts, availability of resources, etc. This communication does not go over the ESB, but rather via a Web service based API of the Data Transformation service. In particular, the requests are reflected by means of SPARQL queries.

Then, the **Data Transformation Service** issues several requests to appropriate Gateways, each of which is designed to retrieve data from particular legacy MES or ERP system. The retrieved data are returned back to the Data Transformation Service in its native format. The Data Transformation Service then converts the acquired data into the semantic format (RDF) using semantic mappings generated by TIE Semantic Integrator and the ARUM Core and Scene ontologies as target schemas. The resulting pieces of RDF data are returned back to the Ontology Service.

When the Ontology service receives the RDF data, it aggregates it in a dedicated triple store and then returns it to the FNDSD service. Local storage is intended for easy and faster data access in case such data is requested again.

Having received the scheduling data, the FND&SD service returns it to the FNDSD UI, which is now able to issue a request to create a new scene. This request is sent back to the FNDSD service, which in turn asks the Ontology Service to save it in the triple store. The result of the action performed by the Ontology Service is the generation of a new unique URI for the scene, which is sent to the FNDSD service. The latter builds a scene and sends it back to the FNDSD UI. The scene will be then used as a holder of input data for the Scheduler.

4.1   Strategic Planning Operation

The higher hierarchical levels of any manufacturing company must take strategic decisions that culminates, among others, in the construction of a new production site or in a shop-floor re-organization, e.g., by means of the use of additional degrees of freedom (DoF), such as the introduction of extra working hours or of a new production line.

In such way, the Strategic Planner (SP) in the ARUM platform combines the agility and flexibility provided by the software agent technology with the optimization levels provided by classical mathematical models [5] – as shown in Figure 4. The SP tool is a bundle composed of a User Interface (UI) and a Multi-Agent System (MAS) that encapsulates the mathematical solver, as depicted in Figure 4. Both components interact within the ARUM platform using a standardized message mechanism that combines the standard service communication process with the interaction protocols facilitates offered by the agent world, namely the FIPA (Foundation for Intelligent Physical Agents) interaction protocols.

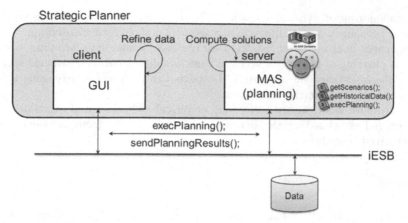

Fig. 4. User interface and multi-agent system planning interaction

The planning process, each time the user wants to use the tool, in reaction to an external event or to perform exploratory studies, starts by the request of the available data, i.e. the system current status. After this, the user designs the conditions to be tested, e.g., a product demand increase or costs variation, and requests the computation of a solution. At this stage, the agents within the MAS cooperate in order to provide the requested plan with the details of associated tasks, activities and resources - leading to the solution (or a set of best solutions) [9].

5   Concluding Remarks

ARUM is aimed at the development of a flexible and adaptive ICT solution for production management and control of highly complex, small lot productions such as in aircraft and shipbuilding industries. Small lot manufacturers have to deal with specific challenges such as the high investments in the product design and ramp-up due to the complexity of the final product and very small production batches.

This paper provides an overview of the ARUM platform that uses SOA-inspired design principles to narrow the gaps that current practices cannot do in small-lot production and ramp-up of highly customized and complex products. The key objectives of ARUM platform include ensuring purposeful and unobstructed flow of information between decision makers, intelligent planning, scheduling, optimization, control tools and legacy systems.

To support the stakeholders in small lot manufacturing and complexity of product design and ramp-up stages, the architecture of ARUM platform presented in this paper promotes the view of services as Intelligent Services that are defined as independent pieces of software and are expected to provide a particular result either produced by the intelligent services themselves or by requesting support from other intelligent services. Seamless communication between intelligent services is supported by adopting the SOA-inspired Enterprise Service Bus solution. The use of a combination of ESBs in ARUM platform also facilitates other operational features such of knowledge acquisition and sharing by exploiting different ontologies, integration of legacy systems, monitoring of dynamic interactions by reviewing the flow of high volume of message exchanges, service lifecycle management and platform distribution.

This paper does not cover the details or research behind the scheduling, optimisation and planning of production services. Functionality details and software specification of these services and other ARUM aspects can be found by exploring different pieces of work in the references section.

In our future work, we are performing empirical and user-based assessment of the platform and associated services in order to determine their effectiveness in delivering the perceived benefits.

References

1. Marín, C.A., Mönch, L., Liu, L., Mehandjiev, N., Lioudakis, G.V., Kazanskaia, D., Chepegin, V.: Application of intelligent service bus in a ramp-up production context. In: CAiSE 2013, Valencia, Spain, June 17-21, 2013
2. Inden, U., Mehandjiev, N., Mönch, L., Vrba, P.: Towards an ontology for small series production. In: Mařík, V., Lastra, J.L.M., Skobelev, P. (eds.) HoloMAS 2013. LNCS, vol. 8062, pp. 128–139. Springer, Heidelberg (2013)
3. Leitão, P., Barbosa, J., Vrba, P., Skobelev, P., Tsarev, A., Kazanskaia, D.: Multi-agent system approach for the strategic planning in ramp-up production of small lots. In: SMC 2013, Manchester, UK, October 13-16, 2013
4. Marin, C., Moench, L., Leitao, P., Vrba, P., Kazanskaia, D., Chepegin, V., Liu, L., Mehandjiev, N.: A conceptual architecture based on intelligent services for manufacturing support systems. In: SMC 2013, Manchester, UK, October 13-16, 2013
5. Biele, A., Mönch, L.: Using a math-heuristic to optimize mixed model assembly lines in low-volume manufacturing. Informs Annual Meeting, Minneapolis, Minnesota, USA, October 2013
6. Leitão, P., Barbosa, J.: Adaptive scheduling based on self-organized holonic swarm of schedulers In: ISIE 2014, Instanbul, Turkey, June 1-4, 2014
7. Vrba, P., Myslik, M., Klima, M.: JBoss ESB sniffer: message flow visualization for enterprise service bus. In: ISIE 2014, Instanbul, Turkey, June 1-4, 2014
8. Stellingwerff, L., Pazienza, G.E.: An agent-based architecture to model and manipulate context knowledge. In: Demazeau, Y., Zambonelli, F., Corchado, J.M., Bajo, J. (eds.) PAAMS 2014. LNCS, vol. 8473, pp. 256–267. Springer, Heidelberg (2014)
9. Ferreira, A., Pereira, A., Rodrigues, N., Barbosa J., Leitão, P.: Integration of an agent-based strategic planner in an enterprise service bus ecosystem. In: 13th IEEE International Conference on Industrial Informatics (INDIN 2015), Cambridge, UK, July 22-24, 2015
10. Rocha, A., di Orio, G., Barata, J., Antzoulatos, N., Castro, E., Scrimieri, D., Ratchev, S., Ribeiro, L.: An agent based framework to support plug and produce. In: 2014 12th IEEE International Conference on Industrial Informatics (INDIN), vol. 504, no. 510, pp. 27–30, July 2014
11. Karnouskos, S., Colombo, A.W., Bangemann, T., Manninen, K., Camp, R., Tilly, M., Sikora, M., Jammes, F., Delsing, J., Eliasson, J., Nappey, P., Hu, J., Graf, M.: The IMC-AESOP Architecture for Cloud-Based Industrial Cyber-Physical Systems. In: Colombo, A.W., Bangemann, T., Karnouskos, S., Delsing, J., Stluka, P., Harrison, R., Jammes, F., Lastra, J.L. (eds.) Industrial Cloud-Based Cyber-Physical Systems, pp. 49–88. Springer International Publishing, Cham (2014)

Agent-Based Production Scheduling for Aircraft Manufacturing Ramp-up

Pavel Vrba[1(✉)], Ondřej Harcuba[1], Martin Klíma[2], and Vladimír Mařík[2]

[1] Czech Technical University in Prague, Prague, Czech Republic
pavel.vrba@ciirc.cvut.cz, harcuond@fel.cvut.cz
[2] Certicon a.s, Prague, Czech Republic
{martin.klima,vladimir.marik}@certicon.cz

Abstract. The paper presents a solution for scheduling of the aircraft production during the ramp-up phase. The developed scheduler features a combination of multi-agent systems and classical constraint logic programming algorithms. The concept of multi-agent systems is used to break down the complexity of the scheduling problem into smaller, independent sub-problems that can be solved independently and in parallel by individual agents. The selected use case is the Airbus A350 assembly line organized as a sequence of several assembly stations. Each station's schedule is computed by a single agent, however the coordination among agents takes place to handle situations when particular jobs cannot be finished in the original station, for instance due to missing parts, and have to be passed in the next station. The presented solution was developed within the European FP7 project ARUM.

Keywords: Multi-agent systems · Ramp-up · Aircraft manufacturing · Assembly · Scheduling

1 Context and Motivation

This paper presents one of the main outputs of the European project ARUM – Adaptive Production Management, which is carried out within the EU's Seventh Framework Programme. The ARUM project is aimed at increasing the effectiveness of production of highly complex and individualized products, such as aircrafts. The most challenging is the ramp-up period, which starts when the design of a new product is finished and the production of first products is initiated, and ends when the full capacity of the production line is reached. In case of the aircraft assembly, which is in focus of ARUM, such a period usually lasts about two to three years, but in reality may take even several extra years. An example is the grounding of fifty operating Boeing 787 airplanes in January 2013 because of the fire hazards from a new type of Lithium-Ion batteries, which stalled the production for several months [1]. Airbus A380 was also delayed in 2009 because of the design failures identified at ramp-up [2].

The reasons for lengthening of the ramp-up period are frequent disturbances that halt the assembly operations. The typical examples are missing parts caused by the

© Springer International Publishing Switzerland 2015
V. Mařík et al. (Eds.): HoloMAS 2015, LNAI 9266, pp. 145–156, 2015.
DOI: 10.1007/978-3-319-22867-9_13

delayed deliveries from external suppliers, non-conformant parts that are either damaged or do not conform to drawings, or late change requests from customers.

This is the case of the currently ongoing ramp-up of a new long-range aircraft Airbus A350, which represents the main test case of the ARUM project. The main goal is to develop new software tools that provide enhanced decision-making support to production managers, team leaders, and assembly line workers. The existing ERP (Enterprise Resource Planning) systems used for production planning and scheduling do not sufficiently cope with disturbances in form of provisioning the real-time updates to planned activities in order to mitigate the impacts of such disruptions. The reallocation of workers and assembly operations across the production line is done by station managers, relying mainly on their knowledge and experiences. The problem of finding the suitable work allocation is however too complex to be mastered in an optimal way, considering hundreds of depending operations in different state of completion, the varying availability of workers and materials, the currently existing disruptions like non-conformities, etc. The goal of ARUM project was thus to develop the real-time scheduling software (Scheduler in short) that supports the station managers to make relevant decisions regarding the failures mitigation. Additionally, there was a requirement to design the mobile application for workers, which keeps them updated on the assigned jobs and enables them to electronically report about the work progress as well as about any disturbances. Such detailed reporting provides a real-time feedback to the station managers as it enables them to see the actual overall status of production and helps them to decide, having the Scheduler running behind the scenes, to reorganize the work.

The job scheduling problem itself can be addressed by various means. There are mathematical optimization methods, AI-based methods, simulation-based methods, multi-agent based approaches, and others, as reviewed in Sect. 2. The approach taken in ARUM, discussed in Sect. 3, is a combination of multi-agent systems and mathematical optimization. The overall ARUM solution, described in Sect. 4, is designed according to the enterprise service bus (ESB) software architecture model, in which the loosely coupled software components – services – communicate via message exchange. One of the services is the presented Scheduler; other services are for instance the User interface service mediating the interaction with users, or the Ontology service responsible for gathering data from the legacy software systems [4]. The conclusions and prospects for future work are given is Sect. 5.

2   Related Work

In the job shop scheduling there is a set of *jobs* that must be executed in given chronological order. Each job has a given the execution time and requires particular resources such as a machine, a tool, a material, or a worker with specific skills. For given set of jobs and available resources the scheduling problem is to calculate a time table of all jobs, called *schedule*, which defines exact times at which the jobs are intended to take place and specifies which resources will be allocated to the jobs. There are multiple constraints to be satisfied such as the capacity constraints (one machine can execute only one job at the same time) or precedence constraints (jobs must be executed in given order). A solution to the scheduling problem is a schedule that satisfies all the constraints. There exist multiple solutions to the same scheduling problem, thus the goal is to find "good" solutions with respect to minimizing or maximizing given performance indicators, called *objectives*. The most common objective function is the *makespan*, which means that all the operations should be finished as soon as possible.

Production scheduling is a complex NP-hard problem, where the number of solutions grows exponentially with the problem size. There are no computationally efficient methods that find optimal solution, however the importance for manufacturing domain is indisputable. The job shop scheduling has been thus attracting researchers from different domains over the decades. As a result multitude of methods and algorithms has been designed.

A substantial part of research was devoted to *mathematical optimization algorithms*, which model the scheduling problem as mixed integer programming, solved often by the branch and bound (BB) method. BB method explores all feasible schedules by constructing a tree representation of the solution space, from which large branches of unpromising solution candidates are cut off on the basis of estimated lower and upper bounds. BB methods guarantee finding the optimal solution but due to the NP-hard nature of the scheduling problem it is applicable only on small-scale problems [3]. Instead of finding optimal solutions many approximation methods to find good near-optimal solutions were developed. It is for instance shift bottleneck procedure [4], tabu search [5], simulated annealing [6], beam search [7], genetic algorithms [8] or machine order space search [9].

In industrial practice there are more simplistic methods, such as *dispatching rules*, often used instead of elaborate mathematical algorithms. A dispatching rule tries to determine the sequence of jobs execution on a basis of some simple criteria. This can be for instance earliest due date rule that prioritizes jobs based on their due dates, or shortest process time rule that sets higher priorities for operations with shorter process times [10].

Various *artificial intelligence techniques* to scheduling problems have been developed. Examples include rule-based scheduling [11], constraint-directed search [12] and case-based reasoning [13]. A lot of attention was paid to applying expert systems technology by emulating the decision-making process of human schedulers [14]. A substantial contribution is the constraint-directed search method that uses the beam search powered reasoning engine guided by the constraints represented with schema representation language [15].

The *multi-agent system* (MAS) has been recognized as a promising conceptual framework for developing production planning and scheduling systems. Using MAS the complex system is modeled as a community of autonomous and intelligent agents that cooperate on common goals via the message-based communication. Several MAS-based methods and software prototypes for planning and scheduling have been developed, such as the methodology for real-time job-shop scheduling problems [16], the FABMAS multi-agent-system for production control of semiconductor manufacturing [17], the Production 2000+ system for scheduling and control of engine cylinder heads production [18], the ExPlanTech multi-agent planning and scheduling system deployed in Skoda Auto engine assembling workshop [19], a multi-agent system for real-time scheduling and optimization of workshop resources deployed at Axion-Holding Izhevsk factory [20], or the agent-based discrete production scheduling and control system deployed at packing line [21]. There are also several works that combine multi-agent approaches with the classical methods, such as with the dispatching rules [22], with the beam search method [23], or with the genetic algorithms [24]. A detailed review of agent-based systems for planning and scheduling can be found in [23] and [25].

3   Agent-Based Scheduler for Aircraft Manufacturing

3.1   Use-Case Description

The use-case of the ARUM project is the Airbus A350 XWB assembly line (Fig. 1). As it is usual in similar small lot productions, the line is organized as a sequence of several stations, in which the semi-finished products (in this case A350 XWB fuselages) are equipped with various components. When the assembly in a given station is completed, the product moves to the next station. This process must be synchronized across all the stations as there can be only a single product in a station at a time.

Fig. 1. Airbus A350 XWB first front fuselage in final assembly line in Toulouse, France (source: http://www.airbus.com/galleries/photo-gallery/)

The production time in the station is called a *cycle time*. At the beginning of ramp-up the actual cycle time is usually much longer than planned because of the frequent disruptions caused by late deliveries and non-conformities. As the ramp-up progresses the volatility of assembly processes settles down and consequently the cycle time shortens. The cycle time represents in fact one of the key KPIs (Key Performance Indicators) to be optimized as it has a direct correlation with the assembly line throughput.

The key challenge for the station managers is to make right decisions regarding the strategy for allocating jobs and resources to achieve a balanced production across the line with minimized impact of the actual disruptions. Because of the dependencies of jobs even a single non-conformity that caused halting a given job causes halting other dependent jobs and as a result lengthens the station's cycle time. It effects also subsequent stations in the line since they have to wait until the problem is fixed in the preceding station. It is obvious that the workers originally assigned to the impacted job have to be released and assigned to another jobs. This applies also to workers allocated to all dependent jobs, not only in the original station but also in all other stations down the line. Achieving the work balance across the whole production line therefore requires coordination of multiple station managers and thus exceeds the area of responsibility of each single one.

Besides a strategy for halting a production in a station until the problem is fixed there is another possible strategy of leaving the impacted jobs unfinished and moving them together with the product to subsequent station(s). It is for instance known that a missing part will be delivered within few days so the completion of affected jobs can be postponed to the next stations when the part arrives. This implies another challenge for station managers to coordinate their activities as the extra work caused by moving jobs can be covered either by next station's "own" workers or by borrowing the workers from the original station. In both cases a rescheduling of work across the stations has to be done again to achieve the optimal state.

3.2   Proposed Agent-Based Scheduler

The proposed scheduler features a combination of mathematical optimization methods and multi-agent systems. As seen in Fig. 2 the scheduling problem for a production line composed of N stations is represented as $N \times N$ matrix, where lines represent the stations $S = \{S_1, S_2, ..., S_N\}$ and columns represent the cycle times $C = \{C_1, C_2, ..., C_N\}$.

In each cell of the matrix the scheduling task is defined as n-tuple:

$$T^{i,j} = \{J^{i,j}, D^{i,j}, SK^{i,j}, R^{i,j}, O^{i,j}\}, i = 1, ..., N; j = 1, ..., N$$

where:

- $J^{i,j} = \left\{J_1^{i,j}, ..., J_{M^{i,j}}^{i,j}\right\}$ is a set of $M^{i,j}$ jobs to be performed on a product; each job has a given duration $dur\left(J_x^{i,j}\right)$;
- $D^{i,j}$ is a set of job dependencies represented as doubles $\{J_a, J_b\}, J_a, J_b \in J^{i,j}; a \neq b$ for which holds $endtime(J_a) \leq starttime(J_b)$;

- $SK^{i,j}$ is a set of skills required to perform particular jobs; $SK^{i,j} = \left\{SK_1^{i,j}, ..., SK_{M^{i,j}}^{i,j}\right\}$, where $SK_x^{i,j}$ is a set of skills required by job $J_x^{i,j} \in J^{i,j}$
- $R^{i,j} = \left\{R_1^{i,j}, ..., R_{M^{i,j}}^{i,j}\right\}$ is a set of available resources, where $R_x^{i,j}$ is a set of the skills provided by the x-th resource;
- $O^{i,j}$ is the objective function to assess the quality of solutions.

The goal of scheduling is for each job $J_x^{i,j} \in J^{i,j}$ to compute its start time $starttime\left(J_x^{i,j}\right)$ and end time $endtime\left(J_x^{i,j}\right)$, such as the constraints on durations of the jobs expressed as $starttime\left(J_x^{i,j}\right) + dur\left(J_x^{i,j}\right) = endtime\left(J_x^{i,j}\right)$ are met and there are resources with required skills available during the job's execution times. Some of the resources might be modeled as *cumulative constraints*, meaning that there is k units of the resource available at the same time, while the given job consumes $l, l \leq k$ units of the resource.

In detail, Fig. 2 depicts a case of a beginning of the current cycle C_1, with the product P_N that has just entered the first station of the line, while other products $P_{N-1}, ..., P_1$ were moved one station ahead. At the same time the product P_0 (not shown in Fig. 2) left the last station S_N. In the next cycle C_2 the same scenario repeats – P_{N+1} enters the line, P_1 leaves it and all other products move ahead (shown as diagonal movement in the matrix).

If only the mathematical optimization algorithms would be used to solve the scheduling problem then the model would have to be built from the complete matrix $T = \{T^{i,j}\}, i = 1, ..., N; j = 1, ..., N$ because of the interrelations between particular matrix cells, especially due to unfinished jobs allowed to move across stations. Considering the NP-hard character of the problem this might imply serious issues regarding the unrealistic computation times.

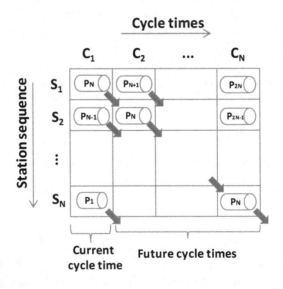

Fig. 2. The graphical representation of the scheduling problem, considering N stations and a scheduling horizon given by N cycle times

To reduce the complexity the mathematical optimization methods were combined with the multi-agent systems concept. In this approach each scheduling task $T^{i,j}$ is solved independently by an agent and, if needed, the coordination between the agents takes place to deal with the traveling jobs. The *Station agent* responsible for computation of task $T^{i,j}$ uses the constraint logic programming engine – the open-source Choco solver (http://choco-solver.org/). The model for the solver includes variables, representing the start times and end times of jobs and their durations. The constraints are expressed as mathematical functions of the variables, such as `job_starttime + job_duration = job_endtime` or `job1_endtime ≤ job2_starttime`. The solver explores the state space and searches for such values of variables so that all the constraints are met. Different heuristics are applied to limit the searched state space, such as placing the jobs with higher amount of dependencies first, etc. (detailed discussion is out of scope of this paper).

The solver generates multiple valid solutions, which are evaluated using the objective function $O^{i,j}$ to find the "good" ones. Two different objective functions are considered:

1) $O^{i,j} = min\left\{max\{endtime(J_x^{i,j})\}\right\}$, $\forall J_x^{i,j} \in J^{i,j}$, which is translated to finding such a configuration in which the last job is finished as early as possible. It is in fact equal to minimizing the *make span*. The main motivation is to create an "empty space" at the end of the cycle time, as shown in Fig. 3. There are two reasons for this: (i) to have a reserve for possibly delayed jobs in the same station, and (ii) to be able to accommodate traveling jobs from previous station.

2) $O^{i,j} = min\left\{\sum_{J_x^{i,j}} f\left(starttime(J_x^{i,j}), dur(J_x^{i,j})\right)\right\}$, which purpose is to find such a configuration in which all the jobs are finished as early as possible. The idea is to divide the time interval $\langle starttime(J_x^{i,j}), endtime(J_x^{i,j})\rangle$ to pieces of the length 1 and give the penalty to each of that piece equal to the absolute position of the piece in time from the beginning of the cycle time. If, for example, $starttime(J_x^{i,j}) = 10$ and the job has duration equal to 3 time units, there are three pieces of length 1 placed at positions 10, 11, and 12, penalized by same values 10, 11, and 12, respectively. It gives the total penalty equal to 33. It is in fact a sum of integer numbers in a given interval, the function $f(\cdot)$ from the formulae above is thus:

$$f(\cdot) = \frac{\left(starttime(J_x^{i,j}) + \left(starttime(J_x^{i,j}) + dur(J_x^{i,j}) - 1\right)\right) \cdot dur(J_x^{i,j})}{2}$$

The decomposition of work among the Station agents is done by the *Scheduler agent*. Its task is to obtain the complete data set for the scheduling matrix, decompose it into sub-problems $T^{i,j}$ and orchestrate the computation done by Station agents. First, the Station agents in the first column of the matrix compute their results and return them back to the Scheduler agent, marking the jobs that cannot be suitably placed, for instance due to the missing resource needed for the execution. The Scheduler agent analyzes the results and makes a decision about the failed jobs. If the strategy is to halt the production until the problem is fixed then the cycle time is extended according to the expected date and time of the fix ($[S_i, C_{j+1}]$ in Fig. 3). In case of traveling work, the affected jobs are left marked and are then handled in the next step.

In this step the Station agents for the next column in the matrix are requested to compute their schedules, giving them their "own" jobs plus the additional traveling jobs from the previous station (see the highlighted job moving from $[S_i, C_j]$ to $[S_{i+1}, C_{j+1}]$ in Fig. 3). Handling the extra jobs follows another two strategies: (i) using the target station's own resources ($[S_{i+1}, C_{j+1}]$), or (ii) borrowing the resources from the original station. In the latter case however, it does not mean to borrow from $[S_i, C_j]$, but in fact from $[S_i, C_{j+1}]$ to be in the right cycle time. This situations is handled in such a way that the two involved agents agree on choosing one of them as a master, which then combines data, including the jobs and resources, from both $T^{i,j+1}$ and $T^{i+1,j+1}$ cells and lets its solver to compute the result. The result is then split by the master agent back to two groups according to the original belonging of the jobs to stations. However, the result contains the information about some resources (mainly the humans) that will be requested to move from one station to the other one to work on the traveling jobs.

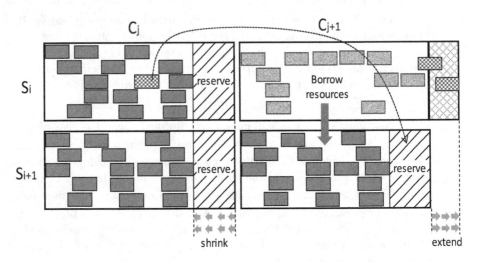

Fig. 3. Possible scheduling results – shrinking or extending the cycle time; moving jobs between stations with borrowing resources

This procedure is repeated until the computation for the last cycle time is finished. Finally, the overall solution for the whole matrix is assembled by the Scheduler agent, which then computes the global KPIs (key performance indicators). The KPIs are presented to the station manager as a quality of found solution. It is the number of traveling jobs, the human utilization and the station flexibility representing the ratio of the reserve at the end of cycle time to the cycle time length (see Fig. 3).

As the production progresses and the disruptive events are occurring the station manager can decide to run the re-scheduling process. The goal is to find a solution that is as close to the previous one as possible. It is mainly because the just-in-time delivery of parts that would be harmed if the jobs would be shifted in time too much. For this reason the Station agents use the last found solution as a starting point for the solver to begin searching the state space.

It is shown in Fig. 3 that besides extending the cycle time it is also possible to decide shrinking it, if the time reserve is achieved in all the stations in the same cycle time. This is one of the main contributions of the presented soultion as it results in speeding up the production and achieve higher throughput of the line.

4   Integration of the Scheduler into the Overall ARUM Solution

The ARUM system is designed according to the Enterprise Service Bus (ESB) software architecture model, which is one of the implementations of the Service Oriented Architecture (SOA) paradigm. The software modules are designed as self-contained loosely-coupled services that communicate via messages over the messaging bus.

Fig. 4 shows services that are involved in the scheduling task. It is naturally the *Scheduler Service* implemented as a multi-agent system. It includes a MAS-ESB gateway, which was designed to enable the agents, implemented in JADE agent platform (http://jade.tilab.com/) to interact with the JBoss ESB (http://jbossesb.jboss.org) services [26].

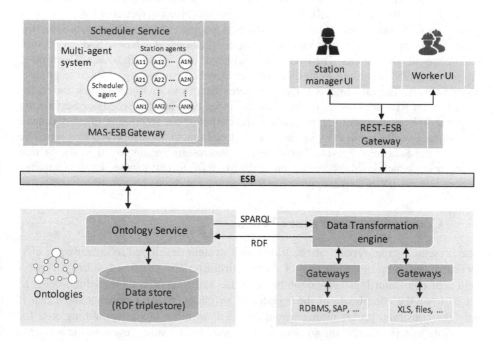

Fig. 4. Integration of the Scheduler (Scheduler Service) with the Ontology Service providing it with data and the user interfaces from which the scheduler is controlled

The *REST API Service* provides means for integration of lightweight clients with the heavyweight Enterprise Service Bus (ESB) messaging system via the HTTP-based RESTful API [27]. These clients are primarily the user interfaces for both the station managers and workers. The *Station manager UI* provides the station manager with the real-time process monitoring and control. It gives a detailed overview of the progress of work in the stations, such as a number of finished/unfinished jobs, estimated lead time, current throughput, utilization of resources, occurred events, etc. Through this user interface the station manager creates a new schedule at the beginning of the cycle time as well as at the beginning of each work shift. He/she can also decide to update the schedule any time when coming to a conclusion that the events such as missing parts and non-conformities disrupt the currently running production to such extent it is necessary to re-organize the production and re-allocate the workers. The Station manager UI interacts over the REST-API Service with the Scheduler Service requesting it to compute a new or update an existing schedule. When finished, the results are displayed to the station manager, who decides to apply them to a running production.

The new allocation of work is propagated down to workers that are equipped with a smart phone/tablet running the *Worker UI*. Through this mobile application the worker checks the list of jobs he is supposed to execute during the work shift, reports on the progress of work (starting and completing the job) and also report on any disturbances such as missing/broken parts or other non-conformities.

The *Ontology Service* is responsible for gathering data from the legacy software systems and converting them into a common data format. It was decided to use ontologies to model the data structures in ARUM in a semantic, machine interpretable form. The Ontology Service queries the Data Transformation engine, which gathers data over the Gateways from various legacy systems, such as relational databases, SAP, Microsoft Excell spread sheets, etc. Then data is converted into RDF (Resource Description Framework) [28] according to an ontology developed for modeling of discrete production processes. The Ontology Service aggregates data from multiple sources and stores them into an RDF triplestore. In this way the input data for the Scheduler Service are prepared. When the scheduling is finished, the output of the scheduling (the assignment of resources to jobs, and job's planned start and end times) are also stored in a semantic form by the Scheduler Service. Subsequently, the results are displayed in the Station manager UI, which involves conversion of data in RDF format handled by the Ontology Service into the JSON format appropriate for lightweight clients.

5   Conclusions and Future Work

The presented paper reports on the scheduling system developed to increase the efficiency of the ramp-up production of Airbus aircrafts. The solution features a combination of constraint logic programming and the multi-agent systems, which helps to break down the complexity of the scheduling problem. The experiments show that if only the constraint programming would be used, with the model containing data for the whole matrix (Fig. 2), the solution is not found by the solver even within a couple of hours. Using the agents finding a good enough solution takes couple of minutes; of course due to the NP-hard character of the problem, it is not the globally optimal one.

We are currently preparing experiments that should give the estimates of improvement of the production performance when the presented solution is deployed in the real factory. The experiments will employ an emulator of the disruptive events that uses a statistical data of the real occurrence of failures gathered during the ongoing A350 ramp-up. The goal is to compare the real performance with a state when the continuous rescheduling would be applied. The expectations are quite high, going up to 30%.

The presented solution obviously gives better results than the manual ad-hoc rescheduling done by the station managers, for it considers the interrelations between the particular stations instead of relying on the local view of individual station managers only. In addition to the presented use case, the Scheduler is supposed to be used also in a combination with the strategic planner to validate different possible configurations of the production line. The attention is paid to so-called "parking station", where the product, which production is halted due to a disruptive event, can be put aside and wait until the problem is fixed. In this way the flow in the main line would be not affected. The challenge here is to determine a proper moment when to put the product from the parking station back to the line, in which all the stations are occupied by other products. It requires to speed up the production in part of the line and simultaneously slow down the progress in the preceding part of line to vacate a given station in between, to which the product from the parking place will be returned. This again requires a coordination among the Station agents in terms of negotiating about reallocating people from the between the parts of the line to achieve a requested misbalance.

Acknowledgements. This research was supported by the European Union FP7 Programme under the ARUM project No. 314056, and also by the Ministry of Education, Youth and Sports of the Czech Republic under the grant No. 7E13001.

References

1. Dreamliner Grounded Until At Least End Of May. In: Sky News, February 25, 2013 (accessed June 12th 2015). http://news.sky.com/story/1056514/dreamliner-grounded-until-at-least-end-of-may
2. Kingsley, J.M.: Airbus slows A380 final assembly ramp-up. In: Flightglobal, May 14, 2009 (access February 25th 2013). www.flightglobal.com/news/articles/airbus-slows-a380-final-assembly-ramp-up-326416/
3. Jain, A.S., Meeran, S.: Deterministic job-shop scheduling: Past, present and future. European Journal of Operational Research **113**(2), 390–434 (1999)
4. Adams, J., Balas, E., Zawack, D.: The shifting bottleneck procedure for job shop scheduling. Management Science **34**(3), 391–401 (1988)
5. Amico, M.D., Trubian, M.: Applying tabu search to the job-shop scheduling problem. Annals of Operations Research **41**(3), 231–252 (1993)
6. Van Laarhoven, P.J.M., Aarts, E.H.L., Lenstra, J.K.: Job shop scheduling by simulated annealing. Operations Research **40**(1), 113–125 (1992)
7. Ow, P.S., Morton, T.E.: Filtered beam search in scheduling. International Journal of Production Research **26**(1), 35–62 (1988)
8. Jensen, M.T.: Generating robust and flexible job shop schedules using genetic algorithms. IEEE Transactions on Evolutionary Computation **7**(3), 275–288 (2003)
9. Choi, S.H., Yang, F.Y.: A machine-order search space for job-shop scheduling problems. International Transactions in Operational Research **10**(6), 597–610 (2003)
10. Pinedo, M.: Scheduling: Theory, algorithms, and systems. 4th edn. Springer Verlag (2012)

11. Bruno, G., Elia, A., Laface, P.: A rule-based system to schedule production. IEEE Computer **19**(7), 32–40 (1986)
12. Fox, M.S., Smith, S.F.: ISIS-a knowledge-based system for factory scheduling. Expert systems **1**(1), 25–49 (1984)
13. Miyashita, K., Sycara, K.: CABINS: a frarnework of knowledge acquisition and iterative revision for schedule improvement and reactive repair. Artificial Intelligence **76**(1–2), 377–426 (1995)
14. Metaxiotis, K.S., Askounis, D., Psarras, J.: Expert systems in production planning and scheduling: a state-of-the-art survey. Journal of Intelligent Manufacturing **13**, 53–260 (2002)
15. Fox, M.S.: Constraint-directed search: A case study of job-shop scheduling, Ph.D. Thesis, Carnegie Mellon University, Intelligent Systems Laboratory, The Robotics Institute, Pittsburgh, PA, CMU-RI-TR-85-7 (1983)
16. Choi, S.H., Yang, F.Y.: A machine-order search space for job-shop scheduling problems. International Transactions in Operational **10**(6), 597–610 (2003)
17. Mönch, L., Stehli, M., Zimmermann, J., Habenicht, I.: The FABMAS multi-agent system prototype for production control of water fabs: design, implementation and performance assessment. Production Planning & Control **17**(7), 701–716 (2006)
18. Bussmann, S., Schild, K.: An agent-based approach to the control of flexible production systems. In: 8th IEEE International Conference on Emerging Technologies and Factory Automation, vol. 2, pp. 481–488 (2001)
19. Pěchouček, M., Říha, A., Vokřínek, J., Mařík, V., Pražma, V.: ExPlanTech: Applying Multi-agent Systems in Production Planning. International Journal of Production Research **40**(15), 3681–3692 (2002)
20. Andreev, M., Ivaschenko. A., Skobelev, P., Tsarev, A.: Multi-agent platform design for adaptive networks of intelligent production schedulers. In: 10th International IFAC Workshop on Intelligent Manufacturing Systems, pp. 78–83 (2010)
21. Vrba, P., Radakovič, M., Obitko, M., Mařík, V.: Semantic extension of agent-based control: the packing cell case study. In: Mařík, V., Strasser, T., Zoitl, A. (eds.) HoloMAS 2009. LNCS, vol. 5696, pp. 47–60. Springer, Heidelberg (2009)
22. Merdan, M., Moser, T., Sunindyo, W., Biffl, S., Vrba, P.: Workflow scheduling using multi-agent systems in a dynamically changing environment. Journal of Simulation **7**(3), 144–158 (2012)
23. Gang, K.S., Hong, C.: Multi-Agent Based Beam Search for Real-Time Production Scheduling and Control: Method, Software and Industrial Application. Springer, London Heidelberg New York Dordrecht (2013)
24. Shen, W.: Implementation of genetic algorithms in agent-based manufacturing scheduling systems. Integrated Computer-Aided Engineering **9**(3), 207–218 (2002)
25. Shen, W., Hao, Q., Yoon, H.J., Norrie, D.H.: Applications of agent-based systems in intelligent manufacturing: an updated review. Advanced Engineering Informatics **20**(4), 415–431 (2006)
26. Vrba, P., Fuksa, M. Klíma, M.: JADE-JBossESB gateway: integration of multi-agent system with enterprise service bus. In: IEEE International conference on System, Man, and Cybernetics, pp. 3663–3668 (2014)
27. Harcuba, O., Vrba, P.: Unified REST API for supporting the semantic integration in the ESB-based architecture. In Proceedings of IEEE International Conference on Industrial Technology (2015)
28. Manola, F., Miller, E., McBridge, M.: RDF 1.1 primer (2014) (accessed June 12, 2015). http://www.w3.org/TR/2004/REC-rdf-primer/20040210

Adaptive Production Management for Small-Lot Enterprise

Daria Kazanskaia[1(✉)], Yaroslav Shepilov[1], and Bjorn Madsen[2]

[1] SEC "Smart Solutions", 1201-17 Moskovskoye Shosse, Samara, Russia
{kazanskaya,shepilov}@smartsolutions-123.ru
[2] Multi-Agent Technology Ltd., 3 Ashbourne Close, London, UK
bm@multiagenttechnology.com

Abstract. Currently the methodology of eliminating the negative effects of the issues in ramp-up stage mostly involves the increase in investment and updating the design data. In the paper the authors consider an approach that can be applied on every level of ramp-up production: from suppliers to shopfloor operators. The architecture of the system is described and the first implementation results are given.

Keywords: Adaptive planning · Small-lot production · Ramp-up production · Multi-agent technologies · Production management

1 Introduction

The ramp-up stage is typical for the modern enterprise since new products are developed and introduced frequently to keep up with the market needs. The key challenge for management at this stage is to cope with disruptive events, whilst having to increase production volume at short notice. To put this into the context, production usually operates with period-based plans (usually, monthly or, in the best case, daily).

However, this perfect plan rarely fits the reality. In fact, the range of unexpected factors can influence its execution:

1. Suppliers failures (including non-conformities, not delivered parts and delayed deliveries);
2. Overestimated production rate;
3. Unpredictable time in decision-making;
4. Urgent additional orders.

Since the plan is not revised after it is issued to the production the lack of adjustments result in a growing backlog for products. For consecutive periods (week, month, year) the effect is accumulative. The main task for management is therefore to increase the productivity to eliminate the backlog systematically.

Despite understanding this, contemporary systems for production planning still tend to use traditional methods [1] that cannot reflect the environment that is changed almost every moment.

© Springer International Publishing Switzerland 2015
V. Mařík et al. (Eds.): HoloMAS 2015, LNAI 9266, pp. 157–168, 2015.
DOI: 10.1007/978-3-319-22867-9_14

The attempt to cover the typical issues of ramp-up production together with supply chain was taken in Adaptive Ramp-Up Management (ARUM) project by the FP7 of the European Commission. The approach considered in this project was described in the several papers [2,3] and is based on the combination of using the multi-agent planning to deal with the unexpected changes in the scheduler, ontology to gather and store information about the domain, intelligent service-bus to provide the interaction between the different modules.

In the first section of the paper we will describe the current production process of one of the industrial partners of the project (Iacobucci Holding Ferentino, IHF). In the second section the main production issues are highlighted. The third section describes the architecture of the ARUM system. In the fourth section we describe how the system addresses the main challenges, while chapter five provide the results of the experiments.

2   Production Process

The case study considered in the ARUM project covers production (including testing, warehouse and management), interfaces to development, finance, procurement and logistic of IHF. At the center of this study is the production area that is divided into a number of production lines for specific product types:

1. Coffee machines (CM) and espresso machines (EM), which are the most popular products. The assembly lines for these two products are interchangeable including the operators, who can apply the same skillset.
2. Trash compactors (TC), which is an expensive long-term durable product. The current demand for TC is on less than coffee machines, but the ordering profile is more volatile.
3. Induction heating units (IHU) – commonly known as ovens – represent a recently introduced product, which currently is experiencing growth in demand (ramp-up). Ovens are produced at a relatively slow rate with potential for increase in throughput through the ARUM system.

There are eight functions involved in IHF's production:
1. **Production engineering,** which provides the specifications for production and suppliers, such as assembly instructions, technical drawings of parts etc.
2. **Procurement**, which is responsible for supplier contracts and ordering of the parts, required for production the production line.
3. **Customer Service**, which manages the customer contact and maintains the overview of planned and forecasted orders.
4. **Production planning**, which constructs the production schedule to which everyone else is working (from procurement to dispatch of quality certified products). Production planning interfaces with customer service to assure that customers are kept informed about progress.

5. **Warehouse incoming inspection**, which is responsible for receiving and inspecting supplies and to indicating if any parts are delivered short, missing, broken or otherwise non-conform.
6. **Warehouse pick & packing**, which picks the assembly-kits that are consumed by the production line.
7. **Production**, which assures the assembly according to certified processes.
8. **Quality Assurances** (QA), which test all products before dispatching to the customers. This final QA interacts with the product developments quality management department, which is involved in the investigation of any non-conformity from the certified process, and feeds back into product development.

Information about orders, bill-of-materials and inventory is stored and processed in an AS400-database, which was developed in-house. All other information is managed in office documents (PDF, Excel).

The ARUM system influences the order-to-delivery process, whereby it is essential for the reader to understand the sequence of activities where the ARUM system can contribute to improvement of productivity during ramp-up. The process is illustrated below (Fig. 1):

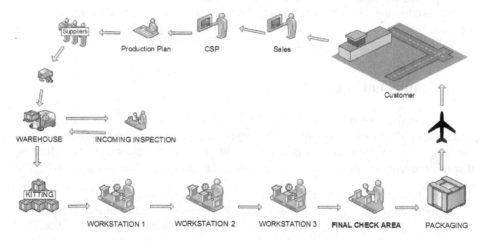

Fig. 1. Order-to-delivery process in IHF

The processing of a new order starts when customer service receives a customer order with a requested date of delivery. Orders vary in quantity, frequency and content/choice of products. As a guideline, orders are given 90 days in advance to ensure receipt of parts from suppliers and shipping to the customer. Some customers provide long-term orders to establish a periodic (re-)delivery of the products during the year, whilst others come with notices as short as 45 days. A key in prioritization criteria is whether the order is for a brand-new aircraft or as replacement for older ones, as delay of delivery to brand-new aircrafts delays the delivery of the aircraft as a whole, and therefore is unacceptable. In either case customer service is the key contact point for interpretation of the commercial priorities and evaluation of the consequence of any changes given by account managers at short notice.

The ability to fulfill the order on time is verified with other departments (checking capacity, production capability, required supplies etc.) which finally is approved by CEO and released into AS400 database as confirmed demand which need to be incorporated into the production plans. The production is coordinated at the highest level with reference to a master plan, which uses the data from the AS400. Based on the master plan, the production planning department provides the detailed production plan which clarify which products are to be produced by the end of the month at the level of serial numbers including any units made to stock. The detailed plan is then aggregated into work orders, which reflect the number of products that a single assembly line can produce per week. Each work order is then assigned to the assembly lines according to the types of product types, which the line is certified for. The release of the work order to all departments is a used as a trigger for authorization of staffing, purchase of parts by procurement, kitting for the production line by the warehouse, etc.

The material flow is logical: Procured materials are received, inspected, stored, picked to kits, consumed sequentially on the assembly line, tested, labeled for traceability, packed on pallets and shipped to the customer.

The production planning department provides a weekly report on the progress, which is tied into the regular management meetings, though daily trouble-shooting is done directly between the departments

3   Main Challenges

From the analysis of IHF processes and interviews with employees, a wide range of issues were identified which inhibit the ramp-up process from being efficient. From planning through production to delivery of the goods to the customer, the following disruptive events are of key importance (following the order-to-deliver process):

1. Sales and customer service:
   (a) Extra demand: An example is a sudden request of a major airline for the delivery of about 100 TC within four months (at a planned capacity of about 140 units per year). When the a large amount of products is to be produced in short time, two issues have to be solved:
      (i) Resource reallocation. The demand for one type of products may require moving the operators from the lines that assemble other products. If the resources are still not enough, additional capacity can be gained by involving office personnel that has the required certification or staff from EASA 45 line that mostly operates the maintenance of the units supervised by EASA authorities.
      (ii) Keeping the delivery dates. It is obvious that the delivery dates for the other orders must be kept as much as possible. However, if there is no chance to prevent the violation of the due date, the orders should be planned to reduce the penalty. New delivery times should be communicated and negotiated with the customers.

(b) Contract problems (supplier & customers): Prices are based on annual quantities which allow the supplier to operate effectively, but volumes ordered by procurement are not divisible in batch-sizes that are viable for the supplier to deliver. This causes shortage or over delivery.

(c) Updates to orders: Change in delivery dates or required amounts, cancellation of orders trigger the changes that will result in completely new delivery schedule for the current period. That results in the problems with the supplies and affects the delivery dates of other products.

(d) Updates to forecast: When forecast is wrong, there is request from customer to provide additional number of products. Usually the company can handle small amounts (2-3 products); however, these additional orders should be approved by warehouse, procurement and production.

2. Production planning: Production planning has to deal with the daily updates from production and sales. All the data is collected manually, usually in talks and phone calls. Then the plan has to be manually updated in Excel sheets.

3. Procurement:

(a) Delivery delays. Though the orders to the suppliers are communicated year in advance, the suppliers have issues on their side that result in violation of agreed supply dates.

(b) Quality flaws. The parts received from the supplier may be different from the required design because of production flows or inconsistent design data given to the supplier. This results in insufficient stock.

4. Incoming inspection: Materials do not reflect drawings and instructions provided by design engineering. Incoming inspection is a potential bottleneck, since there is no way to learn that the material is delivered/not delivered or if it is conform until if passes the incoming inspection. Therefore, any major issues that require involving the incoming inspection personnel may result in delay in delivery the materials to the production.

5. Warehouse: The warehouse employees discover that there is a lack of certain part only when they start preparing the assembly kits.

6. Production line:

(a) Production capability: in the case of the IHF primarily supply problems are to be expected. Nevertheless, the very cost- as well as quality-effective technology may kindle the demand faster than currently planned. Typical ramp-up problem: incoming inspection has checked the part against the drawing (usually used in hardcopy on-site, available in electronic form in the shared folder) while they were changed or updated (electronic form), so they and the part are not correct anymore. This must create the task that the stock that was inspected under the old inspection instructions are re-inspected under the new instructions.

(b) Defects: Instruction on assembly line is different from physical materials. The defect may result in that a certain part of stock becomes unavailable. Moreover, sometimes the decision regarding the defect resolution requires the coordination of several departments.

(c) Incomplete assembly kits. Sometimes the assembly kits arrive in the production lacking several parts that means that certain subassemblies cannot be completed. If the required supplies will not arrive before the subassembly starts, the management will need to solve this problem.

4   ARUM System

4.1   System Architecture

The architecture of the ARUM system is designed within the context of ramp-up systems for manufacturing, where there are conflicts between the need for control and rigor and the reality of rapid changes. Ramp-up systems often require end-to-end integration from strategies, systems to tools (i.e. at all control and optimization levels). Further, vertical integration is required from MES down to shop floor and horizontal integration from engineering to production system planning to steady state production processes.

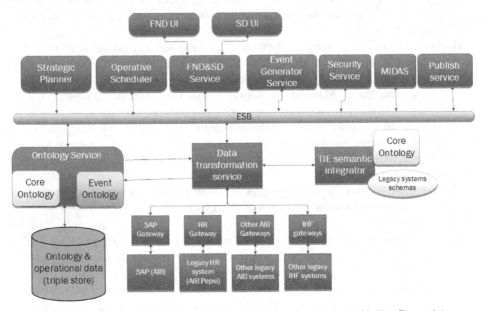

Fig. 2. ARUM system architecture (image courtesy: Cesar Marin, Vadim Chepegin)

The address the above challenges and industrial requirements the ARUM architecture integrates the key features of service-oriented-architecture, holonic multi-agent systems and legacy systems and links them via an enterprise service bus (ESB), providing communication, monitoring, interoperability and aggregation of information across existing legacy systems at all production levels to support real-time automatic negotiation, planning, planning and optimization within and across factories. The envisaged technologies of distributed multi agent system within a holonic architecture is expected to help in integrating legacy systems, information aggregation from high level systems (MES, ERP, etc.) to factory floor automation (e.g. metal cut and assembly systems). Based on such requirements reflected in the system architecture, the main functionalities of ARUM system include planning, planning, production management and manufacturing process supported by actual information delivered from a variety of sources such as legacy systems, sensors, and user inputs.

Based on the user and domain specific requirements as well as on the results of previous research and implementation [4,5] the logical view of ARUM system not only identifies the key components and services that make up the ARUM system but also demonstrates the interrelations between them, as depicted in Figure 2.

This architecture was considered in more details in [6]. In the paper we will highlight only the key elements of the architecture to support the case of IHF that include:

- Gateways to extract data from the legacy systems.
- Ontology to describe the domain to the system.
- Multi-agent adaptive scheduler to create the plans for the production.
- User interface for production and planning managers to create schedule and ensure its execution.
- User interface for the shopfloor operators to receive the tasks according to the schedule, report their completion and discovered problems.

4.2   Method of Planning

The core of the system is the world of agents consisting of multiple agents that interact with each other by exchanging messages notifying on the certain events the agent is subscribed to.

The message exchange is implemented with the special mechanism called message whiteboard. The whiteboard itself is a high-level agent that coordinates the tasks between the agent that requires the resources (i.e. demand agents) and the agents that can provide the resources (i.e. resource agents). The agents can indicate their demands and resources by making the matching rules. Each agent sends its rule with the demands and resources to the whiteboard. According to these rules, the whiteboard selects the most optimal matches.

With this mechanism, the schedule is not created from the scratch every time, but adjusted according to the events in real time. There adjustments are the result of conflicts, negotiations and compromises between the agents.

The current version of the system implements multi-threading planning mechanism with the ability of the agents to process their messages in parallel in different CPU threads. After an agent processes its message, the thread becomes free and it is ready to receive another agent for operation (or the same agent with a new message). Processing of different messages can take different time, however, it is does not result in additional delay since the agents work asynchronously and occupy different processor threads.

There are four types of agents in the implemented multithread planning system that comply with the demand-resource classification described in [1]:

The *employee agent* (resource) represents an employee that can perform a certain type (or types) of jobs, has specific skills, can use the equipment and is ready to perform any relevant job.

The *equipment agent* (resource) represents a unit of equipment that has the specific model that can be used by the employee to perform specific type of jobs.

The *workshop agent* (resource) is looking for jobs and services from other workshop agents to perform them in their facilities.

The *job agent* (demand) is representing a technological operation that is looking for its allocation in the schedule according to the given criteria (employee, equipment). To satisfy the requirements of the job agent, the employee agent must be able to perform the job of this type, have required skills and be able to work on the specific equipment model required for the job.

The system calculates the schedule in the real-time mode, when the agents go through the cycle of initialization, interaction and achieving the results:

1. *Start.* At this stage the world of agents is created. In the world there exist and interact the instances of applications implementing the required agents functions including the basic agent interaction mechanisms.
2. *Data load.* The loading of the initial and updated data for the system operation;
3. *Creation of agents.* At the first stage the world of agents sends the creation and activation messages to all agents that were created ("wake-up" message);
4. *Agents initialization.* The agents define their goals, priorities, criteria according to the data they received from the agents world. Each agent decides to which updates from the specific agents it will be subscribed. At this stage the threads are started and the parallel operation of the agents can be started;
5. *Agents validation.* Agents specify how accurate their goals, priorities and criteria are defined;
6. *Agents operation.* The agents start operating according to their instructions to achieve their goal in parallel asynchronous mode;
7. *Achieving the compromise.* The agent finds the best solution by negotiating with other agents or on its own, after that the agent operation is stopped;
8. *Saving the results.* Solution achieved by the agents is saved;
9. *Receiving the events.* Notification on the events from the real world is received by the world of agents;
10. *Cycle repeated.* The data is uploaded or updated according to the received event (stage 2) and the cycle is repeated.

After the completion of the cycle, the agents transmit to the pending state when they do not perform any actions until they receive a specific message from other agents.

In this process, the job agent is the most active one: it reacts to the allocation request from the employee, can be initiated by the agent of the related job or just take part in the conflicts resolution. In order to be allocated to the specific slot in the schedule, the agent must satisfy all criteria. An employee agent must be relevant to the given parameters to satisfy the demands of the job agent. This can result in long interactions between the agents, that are avoided by using the message whiteboard described above. A job agent leaves the required demands in the rules while the employee agent leaves the resources that it can provide in the rules. Then the whiteboard agent analyses the rules and informs the agent on the matches found.

Negotiations take considerably long time since there is a huge number of job agents that want to be allocated to the best slot in the schedule, while at the same time many employee agents of and equipment can match many jobs. The number of agents considered during the allocation can be decreased by several criteria, e.g., priority, availability and response time.

The main planning process is done during the stage of achieving the compromise. The agent finds the best allocation option by the negotiations with other agents or by its own means. Then the agent activity is stopped and checked of the event planning accuracy starts. This check consists of correct event processing and the schedule consistency checks. The event processing check is required to ensure that all changes triggered by the planning were effected (for example, the fired employee has no operations in his schedule or a new order is completely scheduled). Only after the check for plan accuracy, the schedule is stored and available to the user.

The mandatory condition of agents operation is the existence of the world of agents. The world is considered as active if at least one agent is active. During its operation, the world runs the parallel operation of the agents by running the CPU threads. All CPU threads can be run simultaneously and work in parallel. For example, if the CPU has eight cores, a maximum of eight agents can process their messages at the same time. After the message processing is completed, the thread is disengaged and will be occupied by the agent that the scheduler chooses to activate. The threads can be free during a certain time, but a thread can be occupied only by one agent at a time.

5   Application of ARUM System

As it was shown in the above chapters, ARUM system covers most of the aspects of factory operation due to its structure and architecture. To provide the reader a clear picture, let us go through the problems that were highlighted above and describe how the system addresses them.

In the case of extra demand received by the customer service the solution is provided by the coordinated operation of strategic planner and operational scheduler. The strategic planner allows the managers to investigate different possible solutions (extra lines, change in workshop layout, etc.) and select the best one in terms of profit. Operational scheduler ensures that the resources will be allocated in the most efficient way (to cut the costs and keep the deadlines) within the set-up provided by the managers.

Contract problems with supplier and customers are solved by the operational scheduler considers not only the production process, but also the inventory profile of the required stock. Therefore, the management can put the orders for supplies according to the needs of production, which helps to eliminate shortage and over-stocking.

Any change in the orders or forecast reflected in one of the legacy systems (either Excel or AS400) is immediately processed by the operational scheduler that updates the current plan for production.

The issues of the production planning are resolved by the automatic updates to the plan done by the operational scheduler will cut the time for communication between the production planning and other departments. Instead of updating the numerous tables, the planning manager can focus on providing the required KPIs values by adjusting the planning properties.

If the required stock was not provided by the supplier in time or in insufficient quantity, the operational scheduler will indicate the problem and will reallocate the resources correspondingly.

The operational scheduler can provide the actual order priorities to the incoming inspection, therefore, the staff will know what parts should be processed first. The incoming inspection operators can be scheduled as production ones, while the two departments and their schedulers can communicate via p2p network. Moreover, when the problem is discovered in the warehouse, the operational scheduler can reallocate the resources.

For the production line, the operator tablets with the installed operator UI ensure that all staff members have up-to-date engineering data that is updated automatically when the new product is assigned to the line. The time for line refurbishment is cut making production more flexible. The operator UI also helps to report the problem without any paperwork. The report can be later received by the managers and be an input in the process of problem resolution while the scheduler reallocates the resources to prevent idle time. In case of incomplete assembly kits the operational scheduler can allocate the operations of the current batch until the materials in the kit allow it. Then the operations from the next batch will be allocated to prevent idle time.

Furthermore, the ARUM system can provide the support in applying the lean principles by highlighting the bottlenecks and reacting to the events and the information received. The system also reduces the time required for communication between the departments and amount of the corresponding paperwork by providing the user interfaces by all roles relevant for the process.

6   Results

In the paper we will investigate the influence of the ARUM system on the production process of IHF in the following set of experiments:

1. The basic case. Describes IHF performance based on the data provided for year 2013.
2. The perfect case. We assume that all orders are known in advance and plan them in the most efficient manner.
3. The realistic case. The orders are received according to the 2013 data. They are planned in the efficient manner.

Considering the perfect case as an ultimate example, we will use its KPIs values to measure the other two cases.

Let us consider in more details the measures presented in the table. The productivity is calculated as following:

$$N = \frac{Q_{out}}{Q_{in}} = \frac{Q_{output}}{Q_{pt} + Q_{empl}},$$

where Q_{output} is the units output in euro, Q_{pt} is the input for part in euro, Q_{empl} is the input for employees in euro.

The delays are calculated as following:

$$D = T_{actual} - T_{contract},$$

where T_{actual} is the actual date of delivery, $T_{contract}$ is contract delivery date.
The utilization is calculated as following:

$$U = \frac{\sum_{i,k} j_{i,k}}{N_r \cdot (t_2 - t_1)},$$

where $j_{i,k}$ is a duration of the specific job, N_r is the number of the resources, t_1, t_2 are the start and the end of the considered time interval.

The assumptions on the resources based on the skill matrices and data provided by IHF representatives were considered in the evaluation presented in Table 1.

Table 1. Data *used in the tests*

Product	Number of lines	Operators per line	Total items per 2013	Order production, man-hours	Operator cost per hour, €	Unit parts cost, €
CM	4	2	768	20	6	679,5
TC	1	4	200	35,68	6	4737,8
IHU	1	2	12	61,07	6	5615

During the experiments, for each of three cases described above, the schedule for the period of one year was calculated. The results are given in Table 2.

Table 2. The *results of the experiments*

Scenario	Productivity	Delays, day			Utilization, %
		Min	Max	Average	
The basic case	1,45	0	434	32,5	99
The perfect case	1,47	0	287	0	70
The realistic case	1,47	0	363	0	67

The slight increase in productivity in the perfect and realistic case is achieved by reducing the penalties to be paid for the delayed orders. This indicator can be increased by taking the extra orders (in comparison with 2013 data).

Resource utilization is reduced in perfect and realistic cases by more efficient planning. That means that new orders can be taken to achieve the full workload. However, the company may would like to maintain the same customers demand, but reduce or reallocate the resources instead. Another possibility for the efficient use of capacity is taking the outsource orders.

Again, the efficient planning resulted in reducing the delays in order delivery thus reducing the penalties to be paid to the customers.

7   Conclusion

The results of the experiment shows that the improved coordination in planning can lead to reducing the delays in order delivery and free capacity. That means that despite the potential impact of the disruptive events, the company can take extra orders or eliminate the backlogs from the previous years. Therefore, the application of the ARUM system provides the possibility to increase the company profit with the same number of resources

Moreover, the experiments have proved that coordination with customers plays significant role, since the performance of the company depends not only on production, but also on the dates when the orders for supplies were placed. This opens the wide field for the further experiments and investigation.

Acknowledgment. The research leading to these results has received funding from the European Union Seventh Framework Programme FP7/2007- 2013 under grant agreement n° 314056.

References

1. Skobelev, P.: Multi-agent systems for real time adaptive resource management. In: Industrial Agents: Emerging Applications of Software Agents in Industry (Invited Chapter). Elsevier (2014) (in publishing)
2. Leitão, P., Barbosa, J., Vrba, P., Skobelev, P., Tsarev, A., Kazanskaia, D.: Multi-agent system approach for the strategic planning in ramp-up production of small lots. In: Proceedings of the IEEE International Conference on Systems, Man, and Cybernetics (IEEE SMC 2013), October 13-16, 2013, Manchester, UK, pp. 4743–4748 (2013)
3. Tsarev, A., Kazanskaia, D., Skobelev, P., Kozhevnikov, S., Larukhin, V., Shepilov, Y.: Knowledge-driven adaptive production management based on real-time user feedback and ontology updates. In: Proceedings of the EEE International Conference on Systems, Man, and Cybernetics (IEEE SMC 2013), October 13-16, 2013, Manchester, UK, pp. 4755–4759 (2013)
4. De Bra, P., Aroyo, L., Chepegin, V.: The next big thing: Adaptive web-based systems. Journal of Digital Information 5(1) (2006)
5. Chepegin, V., Perales, F., de la Maza, S.: CREATE Software architecture (2012). https://itea3.org/project/workpackage/document/download/862/10020-CREATE-WP-2-D21Architecture.pdf
6. Marin, C., Moench, L., Leitao, P., Vrba, P., Kazanskaia, D., Chepegin, V., Liu, L., Mehandjiev, N.: A conceptual architecture based on intelligent services for manufacturing support systems. In: Proceedings of the IEEE International Conference on Systems, Man, and Cybernetics (IEEE SMC 2013), October 13-16, 2013, Manchester, UK, pp. 4749–4754 (2013)

Approach to the Solution of Aerospace Product Lifecycle Management Problem Based on Network-Centric Principles

P.O. Skobelev[1(✉)], O.I. Lakhin[2], A.S. Polnikov[2], and E.V. Simonova[1,2]

[1] Samara State Aerospace University, 34 Moskovskoe Shosse,
Samara 443086, Russian Federation
petr.skobelev@gmail.com
[2] Smart Solutions Ltd., 17 Moskovskoye Shosse,
Business Center "Vertical", Office 1201, Samara 443013, Russian Federation
lakhin@smartsolutions-123.ru

Abstract. The paper proposes a new concept for product lifecycle management based on network-centric and multi-agent technology principles. Network-centric system Smart PLM is a superstructure over traditional PLM-systems, and is designed to increase efficiency of every stage of complex product lifecycle management. Key Smart PLM systems are also represented.

Keywords: Product lifecycle · Product lifecycle management · PLM-system · Decision support · Adaptive management · Network-centric architecture · Multi-agent technology · Strategic scheduling · Domain ontology

1 Introduction

Product lifecycle management (PLM) is a strategic business approach that consistently manages all life-cycle stages of a product, commencing with market requirements through manufacturing and maintenance to disposal and recycling [1]. For the aerospace industry, this includes such complex engineering objects as spacecraft and satellites, aircraft and rocket engines, their subsystems, separate instruments and components, etc. Due to ever-increasing complexity of lifecycle knowledge, intensifying market competition and high-level dynamics of changes from individual requirements to the finished product, it becomes critical to implement continuous and connected adaptive closed-loop PLM. Closed-loop PLM systems allow for information from middle lifecycle stages to support decision making in later lifecycle stages (recycling and re-purposing) and together for them to send feedback to the early lifecycle stages, improving the new generations of the product [2].

The paper suggests a new approach to aircraft and spacecraft lifecycle management based on implementation of network-centric organization. It will enable to create smart "system of systems" for increasing efficiency of every stage of PLM, from design and production to maintenance and recycling.

V. Mařík et al. (Eds.): HoloMAS 2015, LNAI 9266, pp. 169–178, 2015.
DOI: 10.1007/978-3-319-22867-9_15

2   Aircraft as a Complex System

Maintenance and technical support of aerospace PLM software is a complex task due to the high level of uncertainty, which is an inherent part of the product. The practice of operating an aircraft or spacecraft requires timely repairs of units from various systems that suffer malfunctions at unpredictable intervals. One can distinguish seven criteria of complexity that qualify establish product lifecycle as a complex system and postulate the major objectives for closed-loop PLM-systems [3]:

1) *Connectivity*. Aircraft consists of a very large number of components that can fail interdependently from one another due to their functional or proximity relations. The objective is to establish all possible malfunctions and their interdependencies, as well as conditions under which they are likely to occur. Additionally, a large number of personnel who operate and service the aircraft regularly cooperate and occasionally even compete with each other. The objective is to establish human factor effects on malfunctions, their dependencies and on repairs.

2) *Autonomy*. Complex systems possess the capability to make decisions without direct instructions, under given constraints, or within given rules. Physical components of aircraft have no functional autonomy but they appear to have autonomy of malfunction dynamics; intelligent components (e.g., software) may have a limited autonomy while personnel operating and servicing aircraft may have a considerable autonomy. The objective is to establish autonomy of every functional component and effects of this autonomy on malfunctions and repairs.

3) *Emergence*. The aircraft malfunction pattern emerges from the separate occurrences of individual malfunctions and is obviously unpredictable. The objective of is to establish *probable* patterns of malfunctions and repairs for each individual aircraft. If the possibility of malfunction for a particular component continuously increases and at some point exceeds a certain value, it might be prudent to replace the unit before its inevitable breakdown.

4) *Nonequilibrium*. A comparison can be made between a dynamic system, which may have no time to return to equilibrium between two disruptive events, and aircraft functionability, which may not return to the original state after a malfunctioning unit has been repaired or replaced. The objective is to establish effects of this on the future pattern of malfunctions and repairs.

5) *Nonlinearity*. A relatively insignificant malfunction may cause a catastrophic event when involving an aircraft. The objective is to identify possible catastrophic consequences of malfunctions and to influence reliability of an aircraft as a whole.

6) *Self-organization*. In response to a malfunction, some aircraft subsystems are capable of autonomously reconfiguring themselves with a goal to reducing or eliminating potential consequences. The objective is to identify self-organizing activities and their effects on malfunctions and repairs.

7) *Conjugacy*. Since the occurrence of aircraft malfunctions depends of working and servicing conditions, the malfunction and repair patterns will differ as these conditions change. In other words, malfunction and repair patterns of an individual aircraft and its functionability co-evolve with its working and servicing environment.

Despite significant progress in the past two decades, there are still considerable difficulties concerning the implementation of existing automated PLM-systems. The main problem is that while the declared goal is establishing closed-loop PLM, the implementation is frequently restricted to conceptual development and design lifecycle stages. In particular, implementation rates in the production, transportation and maintenance stages is quite low [4]. Another reason for reduced usability of implemented PLM-systems is due to lack of uniform modelling rules and related programming methods. Because most of knowledge in traditional PLM-systems is nonstructured, it becomes difficult to track information at various lifecycle stages. This leads to lack of feedback to design and production stages from the middle and the end of each particular item's lifecycle, restricting access to knowledge [5].

In time knowledge inevitably changes, which is why software dependent on it can swiftly become outdated. Both existing systems and those under development should react promptly to changes in knowledge about product during its lifecycle. The current solutions to the problem are complete or partial re-design of the system, investment in prolonged and expensive maintenance or complete termination of system's technical support, which inevitably leaves it outdated. Some estimates show that each year continuous maintenance and improvements of PLM software takes up to 25% of initial development cost [6]. The proposed alternative is to account for possibility of knowledge changes early in the development of PLM-system and implement solutions that support knowledge changes in the implemented software.

3   New Principles of Creating Intelligent PLM-Systems

To solve the presented challenge, a new approach for developing intelligent system for lifecycle management «Smart PLM» is suggested, based on principles of network-centric management, multi-agent technology and domain ontology (Fig. 1).

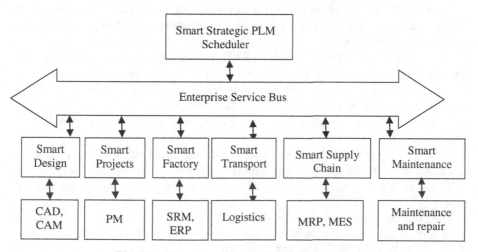

Fig. 1. Architecture of the distributed PLM-system

Smart PLM functions as a superstructure built on top of the traditional PLM-systems. The main level of the system is formed by autonomous intelligent systems using service-oriented architecture and Intelligent Enterprise Service-based Bus (iESB), which manages integration of data from all subsystems in a unified information space for achieving the current management goals [7,8]. In place of one unified PLM-system, there will exist an adaptive p2p network of multi-agent schedulers for separate lifecycle stages, enterprise departments and even employees, all interacting through iESB. The goal is to enable full coordination between every lifecycle stage due to dynamic interaction of all participants in real time.

The proposed network-centric intelligent system Smart PLM is based on using ontologies and multi-agent technologies. An ontology is a conceptual model of some aspect of the world that contains vocabulary describing various aspects of the modelled domain and provides an explicit specification of the intended meaning of the vocabulary by describing the relationships between different vocabulary terms [9]. An Agent is a software object capable of consulting knowledge base to ascertain what is necessary to achieve and how, composing and sending messages to other agents or humans, interpreting information found in knowledge base or received from other agents and electing from a set of options the action. A system of one or more swarms of agents competing or co-operating with each other with the aim of accomplishing a common task is a Multi-Agent System [10]. There have been previous successful cases of implementing Multi-Agent Systems during aircraft manufacturing lifecycle stage, characterized by high degree of customization between individual units, as part of the project ARUM (Adaptive Production Management) [11]. We propose to extend the same approach to all stages of PLM, allowing agents on various stages to exchange messages between each other, effectively creating a closed-loop PLM system.

Major component systems of Smart PLM are (Fig. 1):

1) *Smart Strategic PLM Scheduler* - provides product lifecycle planning for a prolonged time period as well as ensures cooperation between separate systems.

2) *Smart Design* – enables support of decision-making process during the design stage of the R&D Projects, helping individual components to self-organize according to proposed requirements.

3) *Smart Project* – management of R&D Projects in complex interdisciplinary teams with additional options for ongoing development oversight.

4) *Smart Factory* – scheduling and optimization of workshop resources such as workers, equipment, materials and others in real time.

5) *Smart Transport* – management of transportation (trucks, railway transport, sea transport, etc.).

6) *Smart Supply Chain* – procurement of external components during production, repair and maintenance lifecycle stages and updating of existing supply chains.

7) *Smart Maintenance* – support of service, maintenance and repair lifecycle stages.

The described systems will be integrated with existing traditional systems through iESB and will be used for decision-making and coordination efforts by the method of a virtual "round table". This approach allows developing reconfigurable systems by considering such biological inspired techniques as swarm intelligence and self-organization. In addition to an ability to react to sudden and unpredictable changes, modern reconfigurable systems should be easy in maintenance and use [12].

The proposed architecture is aimed at modular composition of models of multiple agents behavior, capability and self-reflection and enhancing the agent's performance by usage of semantics and knowledge ontology. Each of the systems will enable working with the domain knowledge models represented as ontologies based on se-mantic networks of concepts and relations between classes. This is necessary for the formation of the knowledge base as well as for search and comparison between possi-ble management solutions [13].

4   Network-Centric Approach to PLM-Systems Development

Due to high complexity of aerospace PLM, we suggest to divide the original goal into a sequence of local optimization tasks, which can be resolved as the disruptive events occur. This means using a network-centric method, in which plans are not formed hierarchically, but instead are generated though interaction of agents in different areas of ontology, which are connected to one another. This differs from direct optimization methods or common heuristics based on priority rules with centralized planning algorithms.

Network-centric approach to PLM will provide enough flexibility to accommodate needs from different industry sectors, which poses a challenge to the software compo-nent design of PLM systems [14]. A modular approach will be advantageous in long run, allowing the systems to work concurrently and asynchronically, while messaging each other in case of a disruptive event.

The suggested intelligent PLM system consists of individual subsystems for man-agement of separate stages with primary focus on the possibility of adaptive planning and coordinated adjustment of plans based on real-time events. In this scenario, coor-dination of decision-making between systems is provided through the multi-level adaptive p2p network between systems, unlike the traditional relations "master-slave" in a cascade model of enterprise business management (Fig. 2).

This architecture corresponds to one of the distinctive characteristics of network-centric software systems, because the communicating elements are essentially loosely-coupled sub-systems that work together only to solve a large and complex problem that cannot be solved by any individual element [15]. According to the net-work-centric approach, multi-level adaptive p2p network of intelligent PLM-systems contains system of long-term strategic schedulers and short-term tactical schedulers that can react to occurrence of disruptive events in real time. This is a major defining characteristic, considering that design, assembly and maintenance centers will be located far apart from each other.

Bottom level systems support product design (Smart Design), manufacturing (Smart Factory) and service (Smart Maintenance). Different maintenance centers of specific components will collect and process information about malfunction statistics, dynamics of performance indicators, etc. If one or several indicators go beyond the established limits, the scheduler sends inquiries for possibility of product re-design, changing product requirements and its construction or production characteristics.

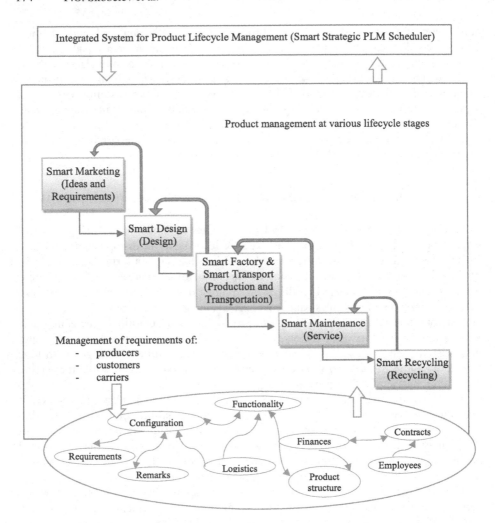

Fig. 2. Network-centric approach to distributed intelligent PLM-system

In such system, when the strategic scheduler makes an initial rough version of the plan, it sends it to the bottom-level adaptive schedulers for coordination. They will work autonomously and start negotiations horizontally for updating their existing plans. Non-contradictory plans will be send for approval and implementation, while emerging conflicts, on which individual systems cannot agree, will be sent to the top-level strategic scheduler for assistance in resolution of the conflicts and allocation of additional resources. After the solution has been approved, individual systems will be able to re-schedule their plans and come to a mutual agreement.

4.1   Models and Methods for Implementing the Network-Centric Approach

The proposed system is based on the multi-agent approach. Each element of the superstructure and every piece equipment has a correspondent program agent acting on behalf of its element. Tasks that emerge at various stages of product lifecycle and should be scheduled and then implemented in real time also have the correspondent agents. Behavior of multi-agent systems is not determined by a specific algorithm, but instead is formed organically as a result of interaction between its components. [7].

The basis of multi-agent PLM-system is a conceptual ontology-based product model. The model consists of elements organized in systems, where output of one element of the system serves as an input for another, establishing functional connections between elements. All elements and systems are also connected by spatial relations, which allows to detect development of deterioration, malfunction and emergency situations. For instance, if an element starts overheating and the temperature spike is detected, through the spatial relations it is possible to determine which neighboring elements be can influenced in their performance.

The conceptual model presupposes that every item has distinct features due to its unique lifecycle. These features enable to describe the item's state at each moment and to keep track of occurring changes by processing information from other systems. In addition, the features enable to support decision making about necessity of maintenance to increase component's safety.

5   An Example of Possible Implementation and Cooperation of PLM Systems

Suppose there is a conceptual model of an aircraft and its working conditions on which we can track various situations. Initially, two aircrafts from the same production line will be almost identical at the start of their lives. However, due to their different working conditions, different malfunction dynamics and periodic replacement of components, characteristics of these two aircrafts will start to differ significantly over time, requiring individual approach to their maintenance. For example, one aircraft may be operated in the northern latitudes with low temperatures while the other one is used in the tropics with high temperatures and humidity. Agents of all components will be constantly checking conditions under which the aircrafts are operated, calculating risks of malfunction and proposing either maintenance or replacement of components, which leads to rescheduling within the system. If the same component constantly malfunctions under certain working conditions, this information is send to Smart Design system in order to change the requirements to components and to their working conditions and to initiate redesign processes.

When the disruptive events occur, component agents are activated and begin to calculate their risks and probability of malfunction, then pass this information to agents of neighboring components, which in response either mitigate the risks by adjusting their plans of action, or increase them and in turn pass the message to their neighbors. For example, if the aircraft operating at low temperatures suffers from accelerated oil degradation, the oil agent takes into account the environment temperature and duration of service, proposing oil replacement more frequently than during under regular temperatures.

In this case, discovery of one problem launches a wave of malfunctions probability calculations for neighboring components in the ontology's semantic web, which identifies actions necessary to correct the situation. The system then displays the statistics of possible risks with the most critical ones having priority during scheduling, while the less critical ones have lower priority during scheduling and are taken into account by the system later, allowing scheduling to return the situation to an equilibrium on all levels.

Based on this data, the system can predict future malfunctions and make plans for maintenance and prevention of future emergencies in advance. By analyzing the probability of a certain problem and its effect on other systems using ontological relations, it becomes possible to trace the influence of emerging events on the overall characteristics of the aircraft and develop a plan for timely prevention of potentially dangerous situations.

In terms of user interface, the proposed solution contains virtual models undergoing changes concurrently with each individual aircraft and indicating which actions must be performed to ensure the required level of reliability. The visual interface based on a three-dimensional model of the aircraft will enable users to see highlight potentially unstable component or system and to track critical functional, spatial and other types of connections while calculating probability on whether the current problem will spread.

If the same unit continually breaks down under the same operating conditions, it could indicate a flaw in its design and once such conclusion is made in the Smart Maintenance system, all data about the product, its working conditions and malfunctions is send into the Smart Design system. Using this data, it may be suitable to perform a partial redesign of the product resulting in a new modification that will not be susceptible to such frequent malfunctions in the predetermined working conditions. Implementing prognosis of conditions for future aircraft maintenance early in design stages will result in major benefits in reduction of wasted spare component lifetime and overall improvement of maintenance efforts. A change from preventive maintenance towards a predictive, condition-based maintenance strategy can also significantly reduce cost and duration of maintenance downtime [16].

If reaching consensus within the system is impossible because the newly generated plans interfere with already implemented plans and functionability of other systems, the strategic scheduler becomes involved to resolve the contradictions. It corresponding requests to individual scheduling systems (Smart Design, Smart Maintenance, etc.) which interact with each other through iESB. At the same time, all plans on various levels are adjusted in order to return the situation to normal. For example, it might become necessary to replace a broken component during the next maintenance session, and if not in stock, an urgent delivery of a new unit to the maintenance station is required. This in turn will change the work schedule of ground delivery services, which means strategic plans will also have to be re-scheduled.

6   Conclusion

The proposed system can be used in stand-alone mode or be integrated with existing lifecycle management systems, which significantly expands the market for the finished product. Several individual components of the intelligent PLM system have already being realized using proposed models and methods. For example, «Smart Factory» was designed as a multi-agent system for machine-production factories characterized by complexity and dynamics of hand-made operations, as well as high uncertainty in supply and demand that require adaptability in reaction on unpredictable events, such as aircraft jet production [17].

Additionally, iESB is been developed and tested as part of ARUM, a collaborative project within the EC "Factory of the Future" initiative, which also utilizes knowledge-based multi-agent system for decision support in planning and operation to great success [18-20].

The multi-level distributed network of interacting intelligent PLM-systems will enable implementation of the holonic approach to aerospace industry management by creating an architecture that fully corresponds to the structure of the enterprise itself. Such approach will feature interaction of multi-agent systems and illustrate co-evolution of self-organizing systems. This provides such important advantages of the proposed system as the improvement of quality and efficiency of PLM solutions, operational efficiency, flexibility and productiveness, reliability and survivability, scalability and high level of integration of the whole PLM system. Moreover, this approach reduces the cost of PLM-system and their maintenance and mitigates risks during its implementation.

References

1. Thimm, G., Lee, S.G., Ma, Y.-S.: Towards unified modelling of product life-cycles. Computers in Industry **57**, 331–341 (2006)
2. Matsokis, A., Kiritsis, D.: An Ontology-based Approach for Product Lifecycle Management. Computers in Industry **8**, 787–797 (2010)
3. Rzevski, G.: Using complexity science framework and multi-agent technology in design. In: Alexiou, K., Johnson, J., Zamenopoulos, T. (eds.) Embracing Complexity in Design, pp. 61–72. Routledge (2010)
4. Verhagen, W.J.C.: An Ontology-Based Approach for Knowledge Lifecycle Management within Aircraft Lifecycle Phases. Thesis. Uitgeverij BOXPress (2013)
5. Ferrer, G., Apte, A.: Managing Life-Cycle Information of Aircraft Components. Defense ARJ **1**, 161–182 (2012)
6. Van Dijk, R., Zhao, X., Wang, H., Van Dalen, F.: Multidisciplinary design and optimization framework for aircraft box structures. In: 3rd Aircraft Structural Design Conference, At Delft, The Netherlands (2012). ISBN: 9781629931159
7. Skobelev, P.: Multi-agent systems for real time resource allocation, scheduling, optimization and controlling: industrial applications. In: Mařík, V., Vrba, P., Leitão, P. (eds.) HoloMAS 2011. LNCS, vol. 6867, pp. 1–14. Springer, Heidelberg (2011)
8. Marín, C., Mönch, L., Liu, L., Mehandjiev, N., Lioudakis, G.V., Kazanskaia, D., Chepegin, V.: Application of intelligent service bus in a ramp-up production context. In: Proc. CAiSE 2013, pp. 33–40 (2013)
9. Horrocks, I.: What are ontologies good for? Evolution of Semantic Systems, 175–188 (2013)

10. Rzevski, G.: Multi-agent technology for designing adaptive business processes. In: Proc. ICIS 2013, pp. 83–89 (2013)
11. Marin, C., Mönch, L., Leitao, P., Vrba, P., Kazanskaia, D., Chepegin, V., Liu, L., Mehandjiev, N.: A conceptual architecture based on intelligent services for manufacturing support systems. In: Proc. IEEE SMC 2013, pp. 4749–4754 (2013)
12. Terzic, I., Zoitl, A., Rooker, M., Strasser, T., Vrba, P., Mařík, V.: Usability of multi-agent based control systems in industrial automation. In: Mařík, V., Strasser, T., Zoitl, A. (eds.) HoloMAS 2009. LNCS, vol. 5696, pp. 25–36. Springer, Heidelberg (2009)
13. Ivaschenko, A., Khamits, I., Skobelev, P., Sychova, M.: Multi-agent system for scheduling of flight program, cargo flow and resources of international space station. In: Mařík, V., Vrba, P., Leitão, P. (eds.) HoloMAS 2011. LNCS, vol. 6867, pp. 165–174. Springer, Heidelberg (2011)
14. Hu, G., Wang, Y., Bidanda, B.: PLM systems for network-centric manufacturing. In: Proc. IERC 2006, p. 1227 (2006)
15. Chigani, A., Arthur, J.: The implications of network-centric software systems on software architecture: a critical evaluation. In: Proc. of the 45th Annual Southeast Regional Conference, NY, USA, pp. 70–75 (2007)
16. Hölzel, N., Schilling, Th.: An aircraft lifecycle approach for the cost-benefit analysis of prognostics and condition-based maintenance based on discrete event simulation. In: Proc. of the Annual Conference of the Prognostics and Health Management Society, Fort Worth, USA, pp. 442–457 (2014)
17. Goryachev, A., Kozhevnikov, S., Kolbova, E., Kuznetsov, O., Simonova, E., Skobelev, P., Tsarev, A., Shepilov, Ya.: "Smart factory": intelligent system for workshop resource allocation, scheduling, optimization and controlling in real time. In: Proc. Manufacturing 2012, Advanced Materials Research, vol. 630, pp. 508–513 (2013)
18. Leitão, P., Barbosa, J., Vrba, P., Skobelev, P., Tsarev, A., Kazanskaia, D.: Multi-agent system approach for the strategic planning in ramp-up production of small lots. In: Proc. IEEE SMC 2013, pp. 4743–4748 (2013)
19. Leitao, P., Barbosa, J.: Adaptive scheduling based on self-organized holonic swarm of schedulers. In: Proc. ISIE 2014, pp. 1706–1711 (2014)
20. Vrba, P., Kadera, P., Myslik, M., Klima, M.: JBoss ESB Sniffer. In: Proc. ISIE 2014, pp. 1724–1729 (2014)

Smart Grids, Complex Networks and Big Data

Towards a Design Methodology for Agent-Based Automation of Smart Grid

Gulnara Zhabelova[1(✉)] and Valeriy Vyatkin[1,2]

[1] Lulea University of Technology, Lulea, Sweden
gulnara.zhabelova@ltu.se, vyatkin@ieee.org
[2] Aalto University, Helsinki, Finland
vyatkin@ieee.org

Abstract. This paper proposes an agent-oriented design methodology specific to power system automation domain. The existing agent-oriented methodologies have some deficiencies when applied in industrial automation. Besides, there is lack of models, methods and guidelines for their systematic application. The proposed methodology combines familiar to domain engineer design process of the IEC 61850 standard and design flow of agent-oriented methodologies. The resultant agent-based system is modelled and implemented with IEC 61499. The transformation of IEC 61850 models into the IEC 61499 solution models is guided by the set of rules and supported by automated transformation tool. The methodology has a set of models, their transformation methods and well defined steps that enable systematic design of the agent-based solutions for power system. The methodology is exemplified here on a Smart Grid protection application.

Keywords: Design methodology · Agent-oriented methodology · IEC 61499 · IEC 61850 · Power system automation · Distributed grid intelligence · Smart grid · Agent

1 Introduction

Issues with energy generation, transmission, distribution and consumption, are driving the research and development of the Smart(er) Grid. To control complex and highly distributed infrastructure, the Smart Grid has to employ distributed automation and control systems, i.e. Distributed Grid Intelligence (DGI) [1], that is a network of distributed nodes performing intelligent control to achieve local goals and participating in overall Smart Grid operation and control to achieve system objectives. These nodes can be seen as autonomously operating agents, reacting on the environment and proactively negotiating among themselves to achieve the system objectives, exhibiting a kind of social behaviour. Thus, DGI of Smart Grid is best realized as a distributed multi-agent system (MAS).

There is a large body of work investigating application of agent technology to solve power system problems [2].

© Springer International Publishing Switzerland 2015
V. Mařík et al. (Eds.): HoloMAS 2015, LNAI 9266, pp. 181–194, 2015.
DOI: 10.1007/978-3-319-22867-9_16

With the growth of the agent technology and its application, researchers realized the importance of the methodology to capture agent specific concepts such as roles, tasks, responsibilities, capabilities, goals, beliefs, agent organizational model and interactions. As a result, many agent-oriented methodologies were developed: Gaia [3], Tropos [4], CoMoMas [5], Burmeister [6], Promethus [7], AgentUML [8] and many other. These agent-oriented methodologies require prior experience with agent technologies in order to design agent-based solutions.

In power system automation domain, researchers tend to follow custom, often ad-hoc design methodology when developing agent-based solutions. Many of them do not focus on the methodology while designing the developed agent-based systems. While concentrating on developing specific control algorithms, often design methodology is left as an afterthought.

There is a need to develop a power system domain specific agent-oriented design methodology, where design process is driven by system requirements and specification.

This work is aimed at developing a methodology which is based on current design practice in power system automation domain, and yet, allows to capture agent-specific concepts. The proposed agent-oriented methodology utilizes the IEC 61850 power system automation design process.

IEC 61850 is a standard for communication networks in power utility automation [10]. The standard does not specify the design process itself, but provides a necessary set of concepts and models for accurate design of automation systems according to the customer requirements. The standard provides comprehensive models of the system at different design stages with different abstraction levels and details [10, 11]. These models are captured with specifically developed substation configuration language (SCL) [11]. It is based on XML allowing for semi-formal description of the system, its functionalities, configuration and communication. SCL enables computer-aided design of single line diagrams (SLD), so that resulted XML file facilitates the further design process by enabling automated processing. SCL based device models provide easy configuration of IEC 61850 compliant intelligent electronics devices (IED). Abstraction levels of the IEC 61850 models allow for both top-down and bottom-up system design. Thanks to the SCL and supporting tools, design can be exchanged between projects and can be reused as a base for new projects. As shown in [12], the design flow of IEC 61850 can be used as a backbone for a comprehensive automation system engineering tool chain for power systems.

The paper is structured as follows. Next chapter presents definition of the design methodology and describes the proposed agent-oriented methodology. The proposed methodology is supported by the automated transformation method and tool described in Chapter III. The methodology is exemplified on Smart Grid protection application and described in chapter IV. The paper concludes with short evaluation of the proposed methodology.

2   Design Methodology for Agent-Based Smart Grid Automation

2.1   Definition of a Design Methodology

A methodology is a logical set of steps to guide a designer through the development process. It is especially important for large complex projects, where a methodology reduces ambiguity around design process. Methodology provides known plan of a design process, as opposed to the "ad-hoc". In this manner steps taken to develop a solution are well-known and design is traceable. This definition of a methodology is derived by Bussmann [9] building on works of Hubmann [13] and Budgen [14]. A methodology is composed of following components:

- a *problem space*, where the methodology is applied;
- a set of *models* capturing aspects of the problem domain and different stages of the solution;
- a set of *transformation methods* converting one model into another;
- a set of *procedural guidelines* which describe rules for the systematic application of sequence of steps.

There are two requirements to a design methodology [9]: *model appropriateness* and *method prescriptiveness*.

Model appropriateness. Design process involves transformation of models, eventually leading to the model of the solution. Initial model should be based only on problem domain concepts familiar to the domain engineer and then every successive model should relate to previous to bridge the gap between problem and solution concepts. This is aimed at helping a designer to understand relations between problem and the design models. An important stage is an introduction of the solution models with agent-oriented concepts.

Method prescriptiveness. The transformation methods should prescribe details or rules of how to derive the next model. An important transformation is deriving an agent-based solution model and it is important to provide unambiguous transformation rules. Here the process can benefit from an automated model transformation tool.

2.2   Proposed Design Methodology

The methodology relies on two enabling technologies: IEC 61850 and IEC 61499, while combining the above-mentioned design processes.

In this methodology agents are modelled and implemented with IEC 61499 following the architecture based on logical node concept (LN) of IEC 61850 proposed in [15, 16]. This architecture models LN as an agent, and each agent is implemented as IEC 61499 composite function block (FB).

The use of IEC 61499 to implement agents is motivated by lack of practically usable agent architectures [16]. Agent technology in the power system domain is the realm of theory and laboratory simulation [17]. The challenge is to enable an agent to be executable on field devices and operate within industrial environment such as power system. Being an industrial standard for developing distributed systems in the domain of industrial automation, IEC 61499 provide native support for distributed multi-agent systems (MAS) and ensures their execution on the field devices such as programmable logic controllers (PLC). Moreover, IEC 61499 is an open standard, enabling interoperability, re-configurability and portability of the system; these capabilities are the must for large scale MAS. Furthermore, changing requirements of power system automation drive the need for open standard-based development environment and standard-based engineering, which promise to enable system flexibility, multi-vendor systems and cost efficiency. It is also step forward towards enabling smart substation. The potential benefits of IEC 61499 are in both design efficiency and system performance areas.

The idea to use IEC 61499 for developing and implementing agents have been proposed and investigated in [9, 18, 19, 20, 21].

Combination of both industrial standards IEC 61850 and IEC 61499 facilitates migration of the designed agent-based system into industrial practice. IEC 61499 based agents can be directly executed on field devices.

Applying agent-oriented design principles of proposed methodology will help to capture agent-specific concepts. Employing the IEC 61850 design process will help to capture power system requirements and specification unambiguously and accurately. Therefore, the methodology will help to develop appropriate set of agents.

The proposed methodology defines two stages of the design process: design within the problem and solution domains. Design within the problem domain is based on elaborating IEC 61850 models of the automation system. Within solution domain an engineer defines internals of an agent: concrete architecture (structure), internal states and behaviour. Solution domain implements the agent-based system. Transformation process from problem domain to solution domain is supported by automated transformation method with clearly defined rules.

After the solution has been modelled and implemented within the IEC 61499 framework, it can be simulated and tested. Thanks to the capabilities of IEC 61499, the developed solution is directly executable, so deployment of the control code is straightforward. Due to re-configurability provided by IEC61499, the system can be tested with various system topologies.

Proposed design process is shown in Fig. 1. The design methodology is built around the concept of LN as an agent.

Input into the design process is a SLD and desired system functionality. Refining these requirements into system specification and designing system configuration is the first half of the process, i.e. problem domain (steps 1-4). It follows the design process with IEC 61850 described earlier.

Designing system specification description (SSD) corresponds to the *Requirements analysis* and *Task/role decomposition* steps of the agent-oriented methodology. By designing the SSD model, the system is decomposed into LNs, i.e. functions. Designer specifies all possible functions or tasks within the automation system and their relation to the physical components (equipment, bays and voltage levels).

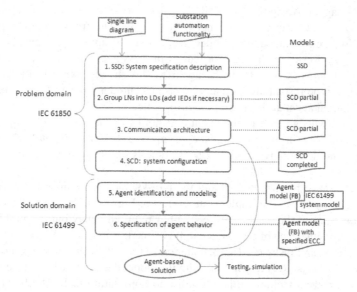

Fig. 1. Proposed agent-oriented methodology specific for power system domain.

Step 2 grouping LNs into LD (Fig. 1), covers for three corresponding steps in the IEC 61850 design process: identify LNs grouping, select devices and allocate LNs to the devices. By performing LN grouping according to their functionality, location, relations and interactions, an engineer has performed *specification of an agent organizational model* step in agent-oriented methodology.

Step 2 captures necessary information into a partial SCD model, which is used for designing communication topology (step 3). This step defines physical network topology, configuration of the sub-networks, horizontal and vertical data exchange (GOOSE, Reporting, Logging and etc.) and communication addresses of the IEDs. Detailed design (step 4) specifies data flow between devices and LNs. In this step following two activities are completed: *Specification of agent organizational model* and *Agent interactions modelling*. By defining details of communication topology, organizational model is completed. The agent interactions are specified by defining data flow between LNs and devices, as well as by necessary communication services. This involves specifying communication control blocks such as GOOSE, sampled values, reporting and etc.

So far, the process follows the design flow familiar to the domain engineer. The second half of the methodology is in the solution domain of agent-based systems. The transition method should be prescriptive for the domain engineer to accurately transfer the designed system configuration model into the solution domain model. This process is guided with transformation rules and supported by automated transformation tools. This activity contributes to the next design step 5 *Agent identification and modelling* (Fig. 1).

The LN class is the foundation of the agent architecture, enabling straightforward identification of the agents. Each LN specified in SSD or SCD models defines the corresponding agent. An agent is modelled by a IEC 61499 composite FB [16]. Then, SSD or SCD models transform into network of FBs. The transformation preserves system topology, communication architecture, agents grouping and their allocation to physical devices. Result of the transformation process is the agent-based system, implemented as a network of FBs. If the agent model already exists in the LN FB library, then it can be instantiated. Otherwise, a placeholder FB will be created, which will evolve into an agent at the agent modelling stage.

LN forms knowledge base of the agent and define agent's top level goal. Decision making is modelled in the *Intelligence* composite FB. *Intelligence* FB contains both reactive and deliberative modules. More details on the architecture can be found in [16].

Once agents have been modelled and their tasks and interactions are defined, behaviour of each agent can be implemented (step 6, Fig. 1). Behaviour of the agent is driven by functions of the respective LNs. Other required behaviours should be added and, if necessary, interface of the agent can be refined.

LNs, functions and tasks need to be categorized into two groups: time critical and non-time critical tasks. Reactive module should model decisions which have to satisfy timing constraints: protection, some control and automation tasks Deliberative layer models more complex, long term tasks, which are not time sensitive. More details on the architecture are provided in [16].

Derived individual agent specification is complete and modular, which allows implementing them individually. IEC 61499 models are directly executable. Consequently, designed agent-based solution can be deployed to hardware and be tested in the co-simulation framework (Fig. 1). The issues uncovered during testing can be traced and addressed.

The methodology is supported by models and prescriptive methods. An important step within the design is the transformation method from the problem domain model to the solution domain.

3   Rule Based Transformation Method from IEC 61850 to IEC 61499 Models

Industrial standards IEC 61499 and IEC 61850 address comparable design issues and promote design which abstract from implementation [10, 22]. As a result the standards have similar high-level concepts. As shown in the Fig. 2, both standards introduce system level specification - desired system functionality. System configuration includes defined communication and devices.

The difference is that IEC 61850 to some extent standardizes representation (modelling) of the system to be developed. Since IEC 61850 developed for power system automation, the provided model of the domain is detailed and standardized [11]. In the other hand, IEC 61499 does not define standard model of the system to be developed. It is a tool specifically designed to develop distributed systems.

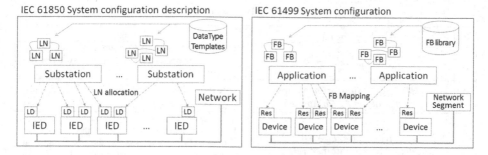

Fig. 2. System configurations in IEC 61850 and IEC 61499.

Power system and more so future smart grid, are highly distributed systems with complex automation schemes employed. IEC 61499 is a natural fit for designing and implementing distributed automation solutions, while IEC 61850 provides standardized domain model across various applications of smart grid automation. IEC 61850 artefacts can be appropriately mapped to the IEC 61499 concepts and refined into executable specification. This mapping was formalized as a set of rules and described in [16] and presented in Table 1.

These rules are illustrated in Fig. 2, and Table 1represent their formal description. The rules are straightforward. However, in case of mapping rule 4, an additional explanation is necessary.

Mapping rule 4 defines allocation of the LNs to the IEDs. IEC 61850 automation functions in the form of LNs are grouped into Logical devices (LDs) and allocated to IEDs (Fig. 2).

In IEC 61499 architecture, such allocation of function is defined by a mapping element Map_i, describing allocation of FB instances at the application level to the devices. *Mapping* is defined as a tuple:

$$Map_i = (From, To),$$

where *From* is reference to the FB at the application level in the format $From = "App_i.FBI"$; and *To* is reference to the corresponding resource of the destination device in the format $To = "Dev_i.Res_i"$.

The proposed transformation method is supported by the developed automated tool. Mapping rules defined in previous sections are implemented using Computer Aided Engineering Exchange (CAEX) universal data format [23]. It is based on XML and has defined a XML schema.

Power system automation solution in the form of IEC 61850 SSD or SCD is modelled as CAEX *InstaceHierarchy*. IEC 61499 system configuration and all its artifacts are modelled by *SystemUnitClassLib*. *InstanceHierarchy* is a set of instances of the *SystemUnitClassLib*. That is, IEC 61850 SSD or SCD elements are instances (i.e. objects) of the IEC 61499 classes, instantiated according to the mapping rules. Mapping is specified by defining corresponding system unit class (SUC, that is representing IEC 61499) for each instance in IEC 61850 hierarchy.

Table 1. Mapping rules.

	Mapping rule	Comments
1	$M_{system}: SCL \rightarrow S$	IEC 61850 System Configuration Description SCL is mapped to the IEC 61499 System Configuration S.
2	$M_{substation}: Substation \rightarrow App$ $Substation \in SCL, App \in S$	A $substation$ section of the SCD file is mapped to IEC 61499 $application$.
3	$M_{LNode}: LNode_i \rightarrow FBI$, $LNode_i \in LNodeContainer, FBI \in App$ $FBITeype_{LNode}: LNode_i \times FBI \rightarrow FBType$	$LNode$ references at the $Substation$, $VoltageLevel$, Bay and any subclass of the $LNodeContainer$ class are mapped to the FB instance at the application level. $FBITeype_{LNode}$ function assigns matching $FBType$ to the FBI based on information in $LNode_i$ and FBI.
4	$M_{map1}: LNodeContainer_i \times LNode_j \rightarrow Map_i$, $Map_i \in S, LNodeContainer_i \in SCL$, $M_{map2}: Substation_i \times LNode_j \rightarrow From$, $From \in Map_i$ $M_{map3}: iedName \times ldInst \rightarrow To$, $To \in Map_i; ldInst \in LNode_j$, $iedName \in LNode_j$, $LNode_j \in LNodeContainer_i$	IEC 61850 $LNode_j$ and the $Substation$, $Voltage$ $level$, $bays$ and all subclasses of $LNNodeContainer$ class, to which the $LNode_j$ belongs, determines IEC 61499 mapping Map_i of a FB instance at the application level App to the device Dev.
5	$M_{IED}: IED \rightarrow Dev$, $IED \in SCL, Dev \in S$	An IED physical device of IEC 61850 is mapped to device Dev (i.e. physical controller) of IEC 61499.
6	$M_{LDevice}: LDevice \rightarrow Res$, $LDevice \in IED_i, Res \in Dev_i$	IEC 61850 logical grouping of automation functions in the form of logical device is mapped to IEC 61499 resource.
7	$M_{LN}: ln \rightarrow FBI$ $ln \in IED_i, ln \in LDevice_j, FBI \in FBN$, $FBN \in Res_j$	IEC 61850 LN at the IED and logical device level is mapped to an instance of a FB at the resource levels.
8	$M_{DataTypeTemplates}: DataTypeTemplates \rightarrow$ $FBLib$, $DataTypeTemplates \in SCL$; $M_{LNodeType}: LNodeType \rightarrow cFB$, $LNodeType \in DataTypeTeamplates$, $cFB \in FBLib$	IEC 61850 data type template can be mapped to the IEC 61499 system configuration FB library $FBLib$, where all necessary FB types are defined. A LN type in $DataTypeTemplates$ of IEC 61850 is mapped to composite FBType of IEC 61499 FB library
9	$M_{com1}: SubNetwork_i \rightarrow Seg_i$ $SubNetwork_i \in Communicaiton, Seg_i \in S$; $M_{com2}: ConnectedAP_j \rightarrow Link_j$ $ConnectedAP_j \in SubNetwork_i, Link_j \in Seg_i$; $M_{com3}: BitRateMbPerSec \rightarrow Parameter_j$, $BitRateMbPerSec \in SubNetwork_i$ $Parameter_j \in Seg_i, Seg_i \in S$	Each subnetwork in communication section of IEC 615850 SCD file is mapped to IEC 61499 communication segment; and access point of IEC 61850 is mapped to the link connecting corresponding device of IEC 61499 to the segment. Speed of each IEC 61850 subnetwork and addresses of IEC 61850 services of the access points are mapped to parameters of mapped communication segment.

SCD or SSD model with the CAEX rule file are the inputs into the transformation tool. Fig. 3 shows the diagram of the transformation tool. The software tool was implemented using *.Net* framework. There are two major modules: *Parser* and *Transformation engine*. *Parser* generates corresponding SCL object hierarchy using IEC 61850 class library. *Transformation engine* loads the given set of mapping rules and IEC 61499 and IEC 61850 class libraries. The output of the transformation tool is the solution domain model - IEC 61499 system configuration. The tool generates an agent for each LN with the architecture as mentioned earlier. Resultant agents must then be further designed, completing steps 5 and 6 of the methodology: agent modelling and behaviour specification (Fig. 1).

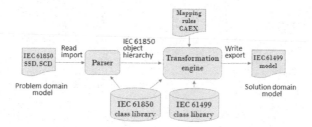

Fig. 3. Diagram illustrating concept of developed automated transformation tool.

4   Use Case: Developing Smart Grid Protection Using Proposed Methodology

This chapter presents the application of the proposed methodology. The chapter described how to use this methodology on the example of the design process of the Intelligent Fault Management (IFM) system for FREEDM distribution network model called Green Hub [24].

Green Hub is a Matlab model of the distribution network shown in Fig. 4. The system consists three 200kVA 7.2kV - 0.12kV solid-state transformers, which controls energy flow between connected solar generation, battery and load.

The main concept is to divide the system into zones with circuit breakers (CBs 1-4 on Fig. 4). The protection scheme is divided into three zones and an overall zone 0, not shown on the figure. Within a zone, the primary protection is the numerical differential scheme and the secondary protection is overcurrent scheme.

Due to space constraints the design process will be explained in short.

First steps are to develop problem domain models: SSD and SCD. System functionalities are modelled with the corresponding LNs: PIOC for overcurrent and PDIF for differential; TCTR LN for a current transformer and XCBR for a circuit breaker. Fig. 4 shows required functionality. SCD model captures the LN interactions required for the protection scheme, LN grouping, physical topology of the system (number of IEDs) and communication topology. An excerpt from resultant SCD model of the Green Hub system is shown in Fig. 5. Step four will detail additional information.

The next step is to transform the SCD model into a solution domain model (step five). Using the developed transformation tool, IEC 61499 system configuration "*GreenHub*" was generated. The resultant system has an FB application "*substation1*" with the list of FBs. FBs are instantiated from the library, which was created during transformation. Fig. 6 shows IEC 61499 "*GreenHub*" system configuration.

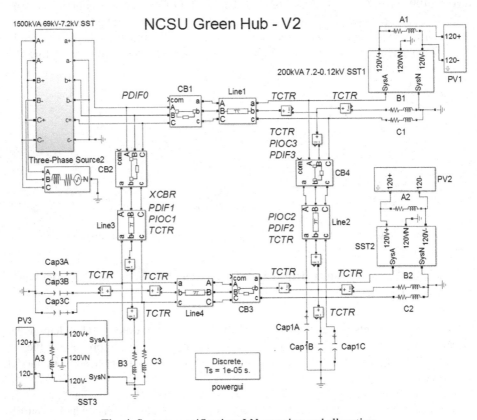

Fig. 4. System specification: LN mapping and allocation.

Now that the model is in the solution domain, the agent identification and modelling step can begin. The identification of the agents is straightforward. An agent corresponds to LNs. Hence there are PIOC, PDIF and XCBR types of agents in the system (denoted as iPIOC, iPDIF, iXCBR). Each instance of the LN is an instance of the respective agent. Next step is to model behaviour of each agent. Protection related functions have to meet the specified time constraints and therefore these agents have only reactive layer. Implementation of behaviour of each agent is explained in [24].

The methodology concludes with the IFM agent-based system for the Green Hub distribution network. Fig. 7 shows the developed IFM solution. Developed automation system is executed on IEC 61499 compliant Beckhoff PLCs.

The proposed methodology has resulted in a set of agents, specific to power system domain. The agent architecture allows accurate modelling of system requirements and decision making, while decomposing and structuring it in a problem specific way.

```
⊟ SCL version="2007"; revision="A"; xmlns="http://www
  ⊞ Header id="GreenHubIFM"; version="4.2.0"; revisi
  ⊟ Substation name="substation1"; desc="GreenHub IF
    ⊞ VoltageLevel name="voltageLevel1";
  ⊟ Communication
    ⊞ SubNetwork name="ProcessBus"; type="8-MMS";
  ⊟ IED name="ied2_Zone3";
    ⊞ Services
    ⊟ AccessPoint name="APied2";
      ⊟ Server
        ├ Authentication
        ⊟ LDevice inst="1Device1";
          ⊞ LN0 lnClass="LLN0"; lnType="LLN01"; inst
          ⊞ LN lnClass="LPHD"; lnType="LPHD1"; inst=
          ⊞ LN lnClass="XCBR"; lnType="iXCBR"; inst=
          ⊞ LN lnClass="PDIF"; lnType="iPDIF3"; inst
          ⊞ LN lnClass="PIOC"; lnType="iPIOC"; inst=
  ⊞ IED name="ied1_Zone1_2";
  ⊞ DataTypeTemplates
```

Fig. 5. Excerpt from SCD model of Green Hub system.

By applying familiar design steps of IEC 61850 an engineer is enabled to design agent-based systems. The methodology does not require experience in agent technology and yet enables an engineer to appropriately capture agent-specific concepts in the final design. An important step within the design is the transformation method from the problem domain model to the solution domain. The method is supported by the automated tool allowing a designer to accurately convert an SCD (or SSD) model into the agent-based solution model.

```
⊟ System Name="GreenHub";
  ┈ Identification Standard="61499-1";
  ┈ VersionInfo Organization=""; Version=""; Author="Gulnara Zhabelova"; Dat
  ⊞ Application Name="substation1"; Comment="DESC: GreenHub IFM system'
  ⊟ Device Name="ied2_Zone3"; Type="NXT_RMTDEV"; Namespace="nxtC
    ┈ Parameter Name="MGR_ID"; Value="localhost:61499";
    ┈ Parameter Name="HMI_ID"; Value="localhost:61498";
    ┈ Parameter Name="WATCH_ID"; Value="localhost:61497";
    ⊟ Resource Name="1Device1"; Type="EMB_RES"; Namespace="IEC61·
      ⊟ FBNetwork
        ┈ FB Loaded="true"; x="740"; y="180"; Namespace="UoA.Gree
        ┈ FB Loaded="true"; x="1640"; y="180"; Namespace="UoA.Gre
        ┈ FB Loaded="true"; x="180"; y="880"; Namespace="UoA.Gree
        ┈ FB Loaded="true"; x="180"; y="1580"; Namespace="UoA.Gre
        ┈ FB Loaded="true"; x="180"; y="2280"; Namespace="UoA.Gre
      ⊞ FBNetwork
  ⊞ Device Name="ied1_Zone1_2"; Type="NXT_RMTDEV"; Namespace="nx
  ┈ Segment Name="ProcessBus"; Type="localhost"; Comment="TYPE: 8-MM
  ┈ Link SegmentName="ProcessBus"; CommResource="ied2_Zone3";
  ┈ Link SegmentName="ProcessBus"; CommResource="ied1_Zone1_2";
```

Fig. 6. Generated IEC 61499 solution domain model of IFM system.

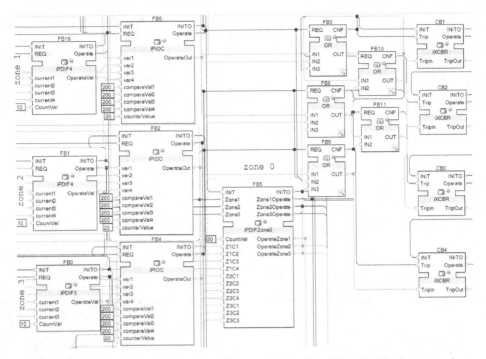

Fig. 7. Resultant agent-based IFM solution designed for Green Hub distribution network.

5   Conclusion

This work is aimed at facilitating design process of the agent-based systems and thus the application of agent technology in power system. The proposed methodology allows development of agent-based solutions for power system automation, while capturing specifics of the domain.

The methodology has defined a *problem space*, which is power system automation. A set of IEC 61850 *models* are utilized to capture concepts of the problem domain. Provided set of *transformation methods* converts one model into another.

The methodology allows modelling of agent-oriented aspects of a power system automation and control. Underlined agent architecture is based on IEC 61850, using a logical node a foundation of an agent. A domain engineer, when operating with IEC 61850 models, would identify agents, their organizational model and interactions in the system with this concept in mind. The resultant set of agents is specific to the power system automation domain, reflecting given functional and non-functional requirements. In the solution domain, model of an agent captures reactive and deliberative characteristics of the agent.

Provided models satisfy the *appropriateness* requirement. Each consecutive model relates to the previous. The solution is designed incrementally, building up on each model and avoiding sudden and abrupt transition between design models. The methodology provides *prescriptive* methods. Transition from problem domain to solution domain is guided by the clearly defined method. Mapping rules from IEC 61850 models to IEC 61499 agent-based system are formally defined. The transformation is supported by automated tool. Appropriate models, prescriptive methods and formalized agent architecture guide a domain engineer through the design process and help to capture agent-oriented concepts for the solution specific to power system automation domain.

References

1. Huang, A.Q., Crow, M.L., Heydt, G.T., Zheng, J.P., Dale, S.J.: The Future Renewable Electric Energy Delivery and Management (FREEDM) System: The Energy Internet. Proceedings of the IEEE **99**(1), 133–148 (2011)
2. Vrba, P., Mařík, V., Leitão, P., Zhabelova, G., Vyatkin, V., Siano, P., Cecati, C., Strasser, T.: A Review of Agent and Service-oriented Concepts applied to Intelligent Energy Systems. IEEE Transactions on Industrial Informatics **10**(3) (2014)
3. Wooldridge, M., Jennings, N.R., Kinny, D.: The gaia methodology for agent-oriented analysis and design. In: Autonomous Agents and Multi-Agent Systems. Kluwer Academic Publishers, The Netherlands, pp. 285–312 (2000)
4. Bresciani, P., Perini, A., Giorgini, P., Giunchiglia, F., Mylopoulos, J.: Tropos: an agent-oriented software developemnt methodology. In: Autonomous Agents and Multi-Agent Systems. Kluwer Academic Publisher, The Netherlands, pp. 203–236 (2004)
5. Glaser, N.: Conceptual Modelling of Multi-Agnet Systems: the Comomas Engineering Environment. Kluwer Academic Publisher, Dordrecht (2002)
6. Burmeister, B.: Models and methodology for agent-oriented analysis and design. Daimler-Benz, Ressearch Systems Technology, Berlin (1996)
7. Padgham, L., Winikoff, M.: Prometheus: a practical agent-oriented methodology. In: Henderson-Sellers, B., Giorgini, P. (eds.) Agent-Oriented Methodologies. Idea Group (2005)
8. Wooldridge, M.: An introduction to Multiagent Systems. John Wiley & Sons Ltd., UK (2009)
9. Bussmann, S., Jennings, N.R., Wooldridge, M.: Multiagent systems for manufacturing control: A design methodology. Springer, Germany (2004)
10. International Electrotechnical Comission, IEC 61850 Communication networks and systems for power utility automation, ed. 2, Switzerland (2009)
11. International Electrotechnical Commission, Part 6. Configuration description language for communication in electrical substatioins related to IEDs, In: Communication Networks and Systems for Power Utility Automation, 2.0 ed. International Electrotechnical Commission, Switzerland (2009)
12. Yang, C.-W., Zhabelova, G., Vyatkin, V.: SysGRID: IEC 61850 and IEC 61499 Standard Based Engineering Tool for Smart Grid Automation Design. EAI Endorsed Trans. on Energy Web **3** (2015)
13. Hubmann, H.: Formal Foundations For Software Engineering Methods. LNCS, vol. 1322. Springer, Heidelberg (1997)
14. Budgen, D.: Software Design. Addison-Wesley (2003)
15. Zhabelova, G., Vyatkin, V.: Multiagent Smart Grid Automation Architecture Based on IEC 61850/61499 Intelligent Logical Nodes. IEEE Transactions on Industrial Electronics **59**(5), 2351–2362 (2012)

16. Zhabelova, G., Vyatkin, V., Dubinin, V.: Towards industrially usable agent technology for Smart Grid automation. IEEE Transactions on Industrial Electronics **PP**(99), 1 doi:10.1109/TIE.2014.2371777
17. Leitao, P., Marik, V., Vrba, P.: Past, Present, and Future of Industrial Agent Applications. IEEE Trans. Ind. Inf. **9**(4), 2360–2372 (2013)
18. Paolucci, M., Sacile, R.: Agent-based manfacturing and control systems: New Agile Manufacturing Solutions for Achieving Peak Performance. CRC Press, USA (2005)
19. Vyatkin, V.: IEC 61499 as Enabler of Distributed and Intelligent Automation: State-of-the-Art Review. IEEE Transactions on Industrial Informatics **7**, 768–781 (2011)
20. International Electrotechnical Commission, Part 7-2. Basic information and communication structure - Abstract Communication service interface (ACSI). In: Communication Networks and Systems for Power Utility Automation. International Electrotechnical Commission, Switzerland (2010)
21. Pala, D., Tornelli, C., Proserpio, G.: An adaptive, agent-based protection scheme for radial distribution networks based on IEC 61850 and IEC 61499. presented at the Integration of Renewables into the Distribution Grid, CIRED 2012 Workshop, Lisbon (2012)
22. International Electrotechnical Commission, IEC 61499-1 Fulnction blocks - Architecture, ed. 1, Switzerland (2005)
23. International Electrotechnical Comission, IEC 62424 Representation of process control engineering - Requests in P&I diagrams and data exchange between P&ID tools and PCE-CAE tools, ed. 1.0, Switzerland (2008)
24. Zhabelova, G., Vyatkin, V., Nair, N.: Standard-based Engineering and Distributed Execution Framework for Intelligent Fault Management for FREEDM System. In: 37th Annual Conference of the IEEE Industrial Electronics Society (IECON 2011), Melbourne, Australia (2011)

An Open Source-Based and Standard-Compliant Smart Grid Laboratory Automation System: The AIT SmartEST Approach

Filip Andrén, Georg Lauss, Roland Bründlinger, Philipp Svec,
and Thomas Strasser[(✉)]

Electric Energy Systems – Energy Department, AIT Austrian Institute
of Technology, Giefinggasse 2, 1210 Vienna, Austria
thomas.strasser@ait.ac.at

Abstract. The large-scale roll out of distributed renewable energy resources has led to a change in the planning and operation of the electric power grids. Proper approaches and concepts are necessary in order to cope with the higher complexity in such systems. The Smart Grid vision has the potential to significantly contribute to a more stable and secure electricity supply but technologies, methods as well as corresponding validation approaches need to be further developed. This includes also the necessary laboratory equipment.

The SmartEST laboratory established by AIT provides such a necessary research infrastructure and corresponding testing methods. Its automation and control system is based on open source tools as well as on international Smart Grid standards which is discussed in this paper. Therefore, this environment provides the necessary basis for the realization of a flexible and highly configurable laboratory automation supporting the design and validation of new methods and concepts in the domain of Smart Grid systems.

Keywords: Automation · Communication and control systems · Open source tools · Power utility automation · Renewable energy sources · Smart grids · Standards · Supervisory control and data acquisition

1 Introduction

The large-scale roll out of Distributed Energy Resources (DER) from renewable sources (solar, wind, biomass, hydro, etc.) in several regions in the world during the last decade has led to a change in the planning and operation of the electric power systems [1]. Renewables are becoming nowadays visible on all voltage levels in distribution and partly also in transmission systems. This creates additional challenges for power system and utility operators due to their stochastic generation behavior [2–4].

Proper approaches and concepts are necessary in order to cope with the higher complexity in such systems. The Smart Grid vision integrating power

© Springer International Publishing Switzerland 2015
V. Mařík et al. (Eds.): HoloMAS 2015, LNAI 9266, pp. 195–205, 2015.
DOI: 10.1007/978-3-319-22867-9_17

system, automation and Information and Communication Technology (ICT) has the potential to significantly contribute to a more stable and secure electricity supply [3,5–7]. However, the necessary technologies but also corresponding validation as well as testing concepts for Smart Grid systems and components need to be further developed. Besides technical issues also training and education is a very important point which has to be covered, too [8]. This includes also the necessary laboratory equipment and corresponding training courses.

The "Smart Electricity Systems and Technologies Laboratory" (SmartEST) established by the Austrian Institute of Technology (AIT) provides such a research infrastructure and corresponding testing methods to analyze the interactions between components and the power grid under realistic conditions in a cyber-physical manner. Potential candidates for validation and testing range from inverter-based DER, energy storage systems, grid controllers, communication infrastructure through to charging stations for electric vehicles [9]. This facility is also being used for educational and training purposes.

In order to operate such a multi-functional validation and testing infrastructure for Smart Grid systems a flexible automation environment is necessary. The main aim of this paper therefore is to introduce and discuss the main elements of an automation system for the SmartEST laboratory which is based on open source tools, technologies realizing holonic principles [6,7] and international Smart Grid standards [10,11]. It provides the necessary basis for the realization of a flexible and configurable laboratory automation supporting the design and validation of new methods and concepts in the domain of Smart Grids.

The remaining part of the paper is organized as follows: Section 2 provides a brief overview of the laboratory environment, the validations scenarios for its usage and the main requirements for an open, extensible automation system. The main contribution of this paper, the proposed open source-based automation and control environment is presented in Section 3. Finally, the paper is concluded in Section 4 with the main findings and the planned future work.

2   AIT SmartEST Laboratory

2.1   Overview

The SmartEST laboratory provides a flexible and multi-functional environment for validating and testing Smart Grid research and development results. It is featuring highly flexible possibilities of different low-voltage network configurations, which gives a huge impact on the research of complex power grid problems. The main laboratory components and electrical sources implemented are the following one's:

- 3 independent low-voltage laboratory grids for testing power equipment up to 1000 kVA, configurable star point settings and grounding systems,
- 2 independent high bandwidth grid simulators (i.e., 0 to 480 V, rated 800 kVA, 3-phase balanced or unbalanced operation),
- 3-phase balanced or unbalanced operation,

– Facilities for Low-Voltage Ride-Through (LVRT) and Fault Ride-Through (FRT) tests, and
– 5 independent dynamic PV array simulators (i.e., 1500 V, 1500 A, 960 kVA).

A brief overview of the key elements of the laboratory environment available in SmartEST are given in Figure 1.

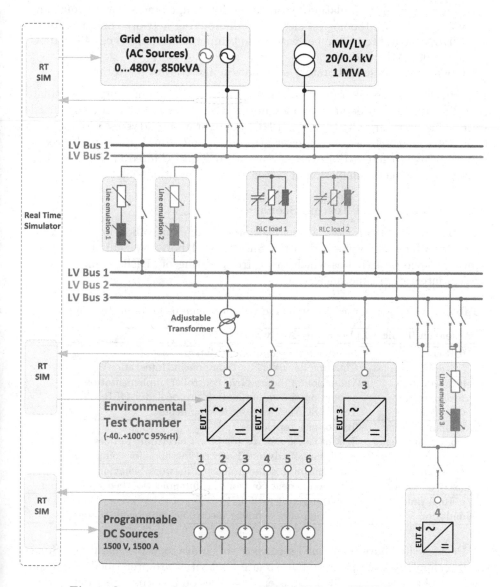

Fig. 1. Overview of the structure of the AIT SmartEST laboratory

In addition, dedicated devices and machinery for state-of-the-art research and education related ot Smart Grids is listed up in the following:

- Multicore Opal-RT real-time simulator for Hardware-in-the-Loop (HIL) experiments and real-time simulations,
- Power-HIL (PHIL) and Controller-HIL (CHIL) experiments at full power in a closed control loop [12],
- Line impedance emulation (adjustable line impedances for various low-voltage network topologies: meshed, radial or ring network configuration),
- Environmental test chamber with wide temperature range (i.e., -40C; 100C, up to 98% rH), and
- Open source-based laboratory automation and control platform.

The concept of the laboratory additionally offers the opportunity to simulate complex electrical grids in real-time and connect them to the laboratory hardware. This necessary CHIL and/or PHIL configuration allows real components to be integrated into a virtual power grid environment and tested under realistic conditions in interaction with the laboratory grid. Moreover, it also allows connecting offline co-simulation of power and ICT solutions [5].

2.2   Validation and Testing Scenarios

The following table provides a brief overview of different validation and testing scenarios which are performed in the SmartEST laboratory. This list includes a broad range of activities which range from testing of (DER) components to system integration experiments.

Table 1. Overview of the validation and testing scenarios performed in SmartEST

Research Topic	Laboratory Activities
DER component validation	– Inverter tests (component, integration) – Charging devices tests (component, integration)
ICT/controller development & validation	– Validation of Smart Grid controller implementation – Validation of communication protocols for DER – Test of SCADA system developments
Development of new network components (power electronics)	– Test of new topologies – Test of new materials for power electronic devices – Validation of advanced control methods for components
Co-simulation based validation	– Grid control & communication network behavior testing – Grid/component control & communication behavior testing
Real-time simulation & HIL	– Integration test for DER – Validation of new power electronic component topologies

Besides the above mentioned scenarios which are focusing mainly on Smart Grid technology issues, also training related activities are preformed. For example, the laboratory is used to train energy utilities on new (remote-)control functions provided by inverter-based DER components (e.g., voltage and frequency control). Furthermore, it is also used in university courses presenting Smart Grid systems and automation topics to students.

2.3   Requirements for Laboratory Automation

As introduced above, the SmartEST laboratory provides a flexible and configurable multi-functional design, validation and testing environment for Smart Grids. Therefore, also the corresponding automation system has to be flexible as possible. Table 2 provides an overview of the main requirements for the realization of the proposed laboratory automation concept.

Table 2. Main requirements for realizing the SmartEST automation system

Category	Major Requirements
Hardware environment	– *Flexibility:* Possibility of different power grid configurations in the laboratory environment – *Scalability:* Possibility to integrate new grid components in the laboratory automation system
Software application environment &	– *Configurability:* Easy and fast change of laboratory automation software configuration – *Portability and control application distribution:* Fast and easy deployment of control solutions to different controller platforms – *Hardware independence:* Automation solution has to be provided in an execution independent format
Simulation environment	– *Offline simulation:* Possibility to include power system and ICT offline simulation in the laboratory automation – *Real-time simulation:* Possibility to include real-time simulation and HIL experiments in the laboratory automation
Open & standard compliance	– *Interoperability:* Compliance to major IEC Smart Grid standards [10,13] – *Open communication interfaces:* Support of major IEC Smart Grid communication approaches [10,13] – *Free & open source approaches:* Usage of free and open source software and tools

3   Open Source-Based Automation System

Based on the above listed major requirements an open source and standard compliant automation environment has been developed for the SmartEST laboratory. In order to fulfill these requirements and future needs the realized concept is based on principles from the holonic systems domain using the IEC 61499 reference model as control environment [6,7]. In the following, more details about this development are provided.

3.1   General Concept

One of the main goals of the hard- and software architecture of the SmartEST automation environment is to have a flexible and rapidly adaptable system architecture. It allows a fast adaptation to new laboratory hardware without changing the core control/automation software. Figure 2 provides such an approach using the IEC 61499 reference model for distributed control as basis [10,11,14] achieving the aforementioned main design goal and requirements. IEC 61499 is a possible way to implement control logic in Smart Grid systems as suggested by DKE and IEC [10,11] and it has therefore been used in the SmartEST approach.

It consists of embedded control devices executing different control and monitoring functions as well as corresponding applications, either local on the device or distributed. These devices are connected through a communication network to a Supervisory Control and Data Acquisition (SCADA) systems or a Distribution Management System (DMS). For the interacting with the controlled process the process interface is used. It connects these devices with offline and/or real time simulation environments but also with the real laboratory environment (i.e., laboratory hardware). With the decoupling of control applications for different purposes (i.e., SCADA_APP, CONTROL_APP, IO_APP, and SIM_APP; for details see Figure 2) a hardware independent realization is possible. With this concept in hand the above mentioned requirements can be fulfilled.

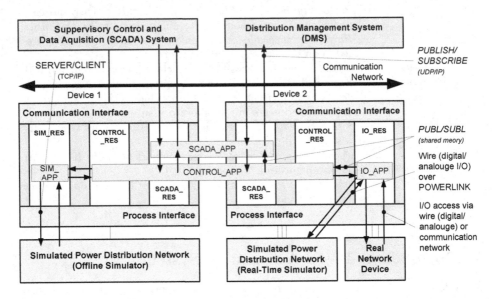

Fig. 2. Hard- and software architecture supporting a flexible setup of Smart Grid laboratory projects; based on the IEC 61499 reference model for distributed automation

3.2   Realized Hardware and Software Environment

The automation and control environment of the SmartEST laboratory is mainly based on open source software. Figure 3 provides a brief overview of the main components of the implemented open source approach. It contains mainly a SCADA layer and a control layer to configure, monitor and operate this Smart Grid laboratory. The flexible and adaptable system architecture is also used in

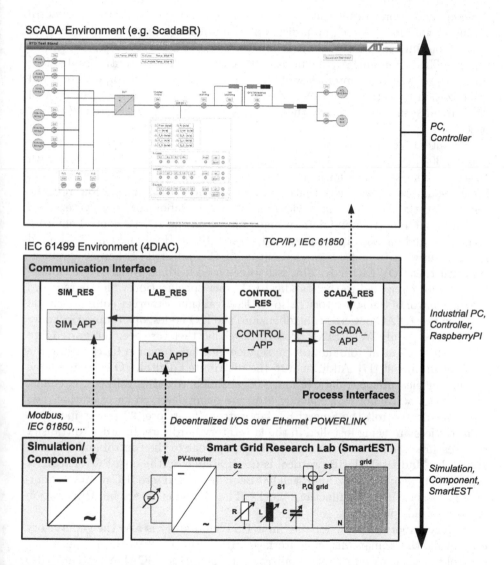

Fig. 3. Architecture of the open source-based automation and control environment for the SmartEST laboratory

a simulated environment in related curricula to educate master students – as discussed in [8].

The open source-based and IEC 61499 compliant distributed control environment 4DIAC is used for the implementation of the control functions [15,16]. It provides a function block-oriented programming model together with a hardware configuration model setting up a distributed automation platform which can be execute on different execution environments (e.g., Windows, Linux, Embedded Linux). This environment is being used to execute different control and safety functions as well as to interact with the superior monitoring, supervisory and visualization layer (i.e., SCADA). It has to be mentioned here that the control layer architecture also supports the connection to Multi-Agent Systems (MAS)-based tools.

For interacting with the physical hardware (i.e., the laboratory environment) about 1.300 digital I/O's are being installed using a distributed I/O system with 16 nodes. They are used for controlling the actuators (i.e., the power switches, breakers, and relays) as well as getting feedback and status information from the sensors and the measurement devices located in the laboratory hardware.

The communication and data exchange between the 4DIAC control environment executed on two Linux-operated Industry PC's (IPC) and the distributed I/O system with 16 nodes is carried out using the industrial Ethernet specification Ethernet POWERLINK. This Ethernet-based fieldbus provides deterministic behavior compared to the standard Ethernet specification which is required for the control of the laboratory. Also for the real-time Ethernet communication between the 4DIAC powered controllers and the I/O nodes, open source software is used. The openPOWERLINK protocol stack has therefore been integrated into IEC 61499 compliant communication service interface function blocks using the 4IAC environment [17]. Additional to the distributed digital I/O system a large amount of measurement data (about 700 channels covering voltages, currents, active and reactive power, frequency, etc.) are being observed for operating (i.e., monitor and control) the SmartEST laboratory. Therefore, 22 power measurement devices are being installed in the laboratory hardware. In order to transfer the measured values from the laboratory equipment to the control and SCADA layers the Modbus TCP/IP protocol is used. Similar to the openPOWERLINK integration, an open source approach has been integrated into IEC 61499 communication service interface functions blocks. The libmodus library implementation is used for this purpose.

A very important topic for the SmartEST laboratory is also the supervisory control and the Human-Machine Interface (HMI). Since 4DIAC covers mainly the control functions without any visualization possibilities a SCADA system is also used. In this system the HMI and visualization of the laboratory environment is implemented. Moreover, high-level supervisory, monitoring and control functions are mainly executed in the SCADA layer. For this purpose the open source implementation ScadaBR is being used. Figure 4 provides an overview over the implemented HMI. It provides an overview of the chosen configuration of the

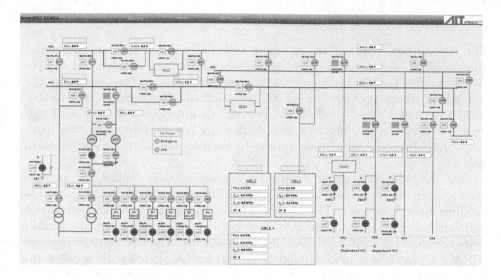

Fig. 4. Implemented SCADA HMI

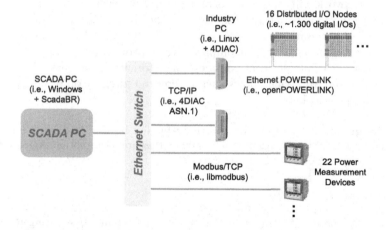

Fig. 5. Resulting open source-based automation environment.eps

low-voltage test grids as well as the status of the laboratory and its connected components to the operator.

The communication and data exchange with the control layer (i.e., 4DIAC environment) is carried out using a TCP-based protocol suggested by IEC 61499 which is implemented in the ScadaBR and 4DIAC. An overview of the resulting automation hard- and software as well as the communication infrastructure used for operating the SmartEST laboratory is provided in Figure 5.

4   Summary and Conclusions

For the further development of Smart Grid solutions a flexible and multi-functional laboratory environment is necessary. It should allow to test components but also their integration into the power systems. In this paper the AIT SmartEST laboratory environment has been introduced allowing such enhanced validation and testing possibilities. For the automation and control of this research infrastructure different and challenging requirements from the hardware and software point of view have to be fulfilled which have been discussed, too.

For the realization of the SmartEST automation and control environment mainly open source tools like 4DIAC, ScadaBR, openPOWERLINK, and libmodbus have been used. This time consuming integration of freely available software was necessary to realize a very flexible and highly configurable software environment fulfilling challenging requirements. The IEC 61499 compliant 4DIAC approach was used as kind of an integrating middleware between the hardware components and the supervisory control. It provides the core of the proposed automation system.

The future work will mainly focus on the further development of automation and control functions which are required by specific testing methods. Furthermore, additional communication approaches like OPC UA or smart metering need to be integrated as well. Compared to a proprietary and closed source approach mainly available from commercial automation vendors, the provided open source-based approach allows such a required integration of new concepts, methods and protocols.

Acknowledgments. This work was partially funded by the Austrian Climate and Energy Fund with the support of the Austrian Research Promotion Agency (FFG) under the project *"DG-EV-HIL"* (No. 827987).

References

1. Liserre, M., Sauter, T., Hung, J.: Future Energy Systems: Integrating Renewable Energy Sources into the Smart Power Grid Through Industrial Electronics. IEEE Industrial Electronics Magazine **4**(1), 18–37 (2010)
2. European Commission: European SmartGrids technology platform: vision and strategy for Europe's electricity networks of the future. Directorate-General for Research-Sustainable Energy Systems (2006)
3. Farhangi, H.: The path of the smart grid. IEEE Power and Energy Magazine **8**(1), 18–28 (2010)
4. IEA: Smart grid insights. Technical report, Int. Energy Agency (IEA) (2011)
5. Gungor, V., Sahin, D., Kocak, T., Ergut, S., Buccella, C., Cecati, C., Hancke, G.: Smart Grid Technologies: Communication Technologies and Standards. IEEE Transactions on Industrial Informatics **7**(4), 529–539 (2011)
6. Strasser, T., Andren, F., Kathan, J., Cecati, C., Buccella, C., Siano, P., Leitao, P., Zhabelova, G., Vyatkin, V., Vrba, P., Marik, V.: A Review of Architectures and Concepts for Intelligence in Future Electric Energy Systems. IEEE Transactions on Industrial Electronics **62**(4), 2424–2438 (2015)

7. Vrba, P., Marik, V., Siano, P., Leitao, P., Zhabelova, G., Vyatkin, V., Strasser, T.: A review of agent and service-oriented concepts applied to intelligent energy systems. IEEE Transactions on Industrial Informatics **10**(3), 1890–1903 (2014)
8. Strasser, T., Stifter, M., Andrén, F., Palensky, P.: Co-Simulation Training Platform for Smart Grids. IEEE Transactions on Power Systems **29**(4), 1989–1997 (2014)
9. Bründlinger, R., Strasser, T., Lauss, G., Hoke, A., Chakraborty, S., Martin, G., Kroposki, B., Johnson, J., de Jong, E.: Lab Tests: Verifying That Smart Grid Power Converters Are Truly Smart. IEEE Power and Energy Magazine **13**(2), 30–42 (2015)
10. SMB Smart Grid Strategic Group (SG3): IEC Smart Grid Standardization Roadmap. Technical Report Ed. 1.0, International Electrotechnical Commission (IEC), Geneva, Switzerland, June 2010
11. DKE: The German Standardisation Roadmap E-Energy/Smart Grid. Technical report, German Commission for Electrical, Electronic & Information Technologies of DIN and VDE, Frankfurt, Germany (2010)
12. Steurer, M., Edrington, C., Sloderbeck, M., Ren, W., Langston, J.: A megawatt-scale power hardware-in-the-loop simulation setup for motor drives. IEEE Transactions on Industrial Electronics **57**(4), 1254–1260 (2010)
13. Strasser, T., Andrén, F., Merdan, M., Prostejovsky, A.: Review of trends and challenges in smart grids: an automation point of view. In: Mařík, V., Lastra, J.L.M., Skobelev, P. (eds.) HoloMAS 2013. LNCS, vol. 8062, pp. 1–12. Springer, Heidelberg (2013)
14. SC 65B: IEC 61499: Function blocks. Technical report, International Electrotechnical Commission (IEC), Geneva, Switzerland (2012)
15. Zoitl, A., Strasser, T., Valentini, A.: Open source initiatives as basis for the establishment of new technologies in industrial automation: 4DIAC a case study. In: 2010 IEEE International Symposium on Industrial Electronics (ISIE), pp. 3817–3819, July 2010
16. Vyatkin, V.: IEC 61499 as Enabler of Distributed and Intelligent Automation: State-of-the-Art Review. IEEE Transactions on Industrial Informatics **7**(4), 768–781 (2011)
17. Andrén, F., Strasser, T.: Distributed open source control with industrial ethernet I/O devices. In: 2011 IEEE 16th Conference on Emerging Technologies Factory Automation (ETFA), pp. 1–4 (2011)

Applying Agents and Genetic Algorithms for Reducing Peak Consumption in District Heating

Petr Kadera[✉] and Martin Macaš

Czech Institute of Robotics, Informatics, and Cybernetics, Czech Technical
University in Prague, Zikova 4, 166 36 Prague, Czech Republic
{petr.kadera,martin.macas}@ciirc.cvut.cz
http://www.ciirc.cvut.cz

Abstract. Energy efficiency and occupant's comfort are two primary
concerns for evaluating the performance of a building control system.
This paper introduces an optimization method based on integration of
genetic algorithms for local optimization and agent-based approach for
integration of the locally optimal solution into a global solution that is
close to the global optimum. The approach is validated on a case study
that models a cluster of eight buildings sharing resources of a district
heating system.

Keywords: Building energy and comfort management · Intelligent
buildings · Multi-agent systems · Genetic algorithms · Optimization

1 Introduction

Energy efficiency and occupants comfort are two primary concerns for evaluating the performance of a building control system. The effort to improve energy efficiency of buildings while preserving the user comfort is a long lasting process with roots in the early 1970s during the world's first big energy crisis. This crises was the first warning that the natural energy resources are limited and deserve an economical exploitation. The second driving factor for advent of intelligent buildings was the increasing awareness of the ecological impact caused by building energy consumption.

For decades, space heating and cooling (space conditioning) accounted for more than half of all residential energy consumption. Estimates from the most recent Residential Energy Consumption Survey (RECS), collected in 2010 and 2011 and released in 2011 and 2012, show that 48% of energy consumption in U.S. homes in 2009 was for heating and cooling, down from 58% in 1993. Factors underpinning this trend are increased adoption of more efficient equipment, better insulation, more efficient windows, and population shifts to warmer climates. The shift in how energy is consumed in homes has occurred even as per-household energy consumption has steadily declined [1].

© Springer International Publishing Switzerland 2015
V. Mařík et al. (Eds.): HoloMAS 2015, LNAI 9266, pp. 206–216, 2015.
DOI: 10.1007/978-3-319-22867-9_18

This paper is focused on reducing peak demands for heat in district heating systems. A district heating system consists of heat producers, a distribution network and a set of consumers. The producers heat up water which is then circulated through the distribution network (sometimes in the form of steam). The consumers use this medium to heat buildings and/or tap water. Usually the heating systems in the buildings are separated from the distribution network, and make use of heat exchangers in order to transfer heating energy from the primary distribution network to the secondary system within the buildings.

The gap between supply and demand can also be reduced by incorporating Demand Side Management (DSM) techniques at the distribution end of the heating system. One of the goals of DSM is to encourage customer participation in reducing the peak demand and shifting of the peak according to the heat production. One such mechanism is Demand Response (DR), in which the system allows end users to change their heating profile to decrease the global peak of the system.

This research is motivated by a task of heating control of a cluster of eight buildings that is located within the Italian National Agency for New technologies, Energy and Sustainable Economic Development (ENEA) Casaccia research center and includes buildings F66, F67, F68, F69, F70, F71, F72, and F73 positioned in two different blocks. The first block, consisting of three contiguous buildings is oriented along the axis NWSE, while the second block consists of five buildings and its main orientation is NESW as shown in Fig. 1. The buildings have similar characteristics both from a structural and HVAC (Heating, Ventilation, and Air Conditioning) point of view. Moreover, all the buildings are offices and hence serve the same purpose. All buildings consist of a single floor except building F67, which also includes a basement. Buildings are composed of a concrete external wall with a thickness of 30 cm, and an internal paneling of insulating material of about 5 cm. The windows are sliding with an aluminum frame. The control of solar radiation in the offices is obtained through external venetian blinds.

The proposed solution is based on agent-based integration of locally optimized (using genetic algorithm) heating profiles of individual buildings into an aggregated system heating profile. This global heating profile has to meet the requirements on the physical constraints (e.g. maximal available heat-flow at particular time window). The agents are implemented in Jade [3] and they use price alteration in order to find balance between demand and supply.

2   Related Work

Smart buildings are becoming a trend of next-generations commercial buildings, which facilitate intelligent control of the building to fulfill occupants needs. The primary challenge in building control is that the energy consumption and the comfort level in a building environment often conflict with each other.

In building control, many different objectives can be defined – e.g. small energy consumption, costs, or environmental impact, high thermal comfort and air quality. Such multiple objectives must be followed in the underlying control task.

Fig. 1. Cluster.

One approach is to reformulate the optimization problem. For example, instead using the thermal comfort as an objective, it can be used as a constraint. The two-objective problem is thus replaced by uni-objective constrained optimization - minimization of energy consumption subject to keeping a discomfort measure below a predefined threshold. For Predicted Mean Vote (PMV) value, the value of the threshold can be adopted from international standards or recommendations (i.e. ISO EN 7730, CR 1752 or ASHRAE 55). This approach is used in [5], where the control is defined as a discrete optimization problem by enabling only integer set points and solved branch and bound method.

More popular approach to is the aggregation of the objectives into one scalar value. Most often, a weighted sum is used. In [2], thermal comfort, air quality and energy consumption are controlled simultaneously by maximizing an aggregation of objectives by gradient-based optimization. The three objectives are squared errors of the values of controlled variables from their desired value and are aggregated by weighted sum. Another approach of optimization with multiple objectives is represented by multi-objective particle swarm optimization [7], and [4].

Deployment of agents for building automation has been summarized in [6]. This work shows the potential of agents from multiple perspectives including personalized space, policy management, building performance quotient, wireless sensor network, and building automation/management system to provide an intelligent environment. Yang and Wang [8] developed a multi-agent system that is capable of facilitating the building to interact with its occupants for realizing user-centered control of buildings.

3   Solution

3.1   Problem Definition

Let $\mathbf{x}_i = [x_{i1}, x_{i2}, \ldots, x_{iD}]^\top$ be the input heat flow profile for building i, where D is the number of time slots inside the optimized horizon. Let $\mathbf{p}$ be the vector of D price values for each time slot of the horizon. Let f_D is the thermal discomfort expressed as the maximum difference of the temperature caused by heat flow $\mathbf{x}_i$ from a target (comfort) temperature (here the target temperature is 21.5°C). Thus, on the local level, the optimizer inside each ith of N agents solves the following

$$\mathbf{x}_i^* = \arg\min(\mathbf{p}^\top \mathbf{x}_i + f_D(\mathbf{x}_i)). \tag{1}$$

The global constraint is simple. For all time slots, the total heat consumption (sum of marginal heat flows of all N buildings) does not exceed the maximum capacity x_{MAX} of the thermal plant, i.e.: for all time slots j,

$$\sum_{i=1}^{N} x_{ij}^* <= x_{MAX}. \tag{2}$$

3.2   Simple Genetic Algorithm

Genetic algorithms are population based optimization techniques inspired by biological evolution. They use a set $\mathcal{Q}$ of L candidate solutions and at each iteration, this set is modified using operators analogical to evolutionary mechanisms in nature. Namely, the operators are selection, crossover, mutation and replacement. The *selection* selects a subset $\mathcal{Q}' \subset \mathcal{Q}$ according to a predefined strategy based on the cost values. The selected candidate solutions are used for creating new candidate solutions by *crossover*. Then, a random change called *mutation* is applied on the new candidate solutions. Finally, the old set of candidate solutions is replaced by a *replacement* strategy. Table 1 describes general pseudocode of a simple genetic algorithm (SGA) that was used to optimize local load profiles.

Particularly, we used tournament selection (tournament size=50), 2-point crossover and mutation with rate decreasing linearly from $2/D$ to $1/D$. These settings were used after some preliminary experimental tuning.

3.3   Agent-Based System

The multi-agent part of the solution is based on JADE platform. The system consists of four types of agents - Building, Aggregator, Occupancy Forecast Service, and Weather Forecast Service (see Fig. 2). Building agents represent individual buildings and communicate with the aggregator agent (in this case, only one aggregator agent is considered), who controls that the global demand does not exceeds the available resources and also triggers the negotiation. Occupancy Forecast Service and Weather Forecast Service agents are only agent-like wrappers that provides required information to the building agents.

Table 1. Simple Genetic Algorithm (SGA)

1: initialize randomly $\mathcal{Q}(0) = \{\mathbf{x}_i(0)\}_{i=1...L}$
2: **repeat**
3:    compute cost values $f(\mathbf{x}_i(t))$
4:    $\mathcal{Q}' =$selection$(\mathcal{Q})$
5:    $\mathcal{Q}'' =$crossover$(\mathcal{Q}')$
6:    $\mathcal{Q}''' =$mutation$(\mathcal{Q}'')$
7:    $\mathcal{Q}(t+1) =$replacement$(\mathcal{Q}''', \mathcal{Q}(t))$
8: **until** stopping condition is true

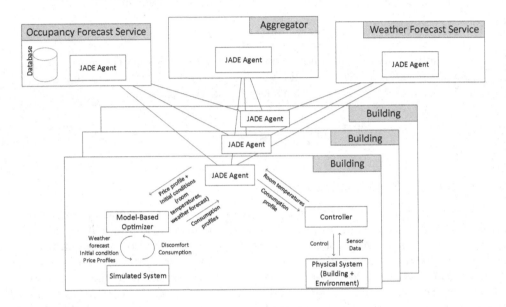

Fig. 2. System Architecture.

The negotiation schema is described in pseudo-code in Table 2. The algorithm starts with search of individual buildings for local pareto-optimal heating profiles that are send to the aggregator. Then, the aggregator performs a complete search over all combinations of the received profiles and tests if there is such a combination that does not exceed the estimated future heating performance of the resources.

Main requirements on the system cooperation are as follows:

– Assurance of convergence
– Utilization of available heating resources

A crucial property of any algorithm for distributed heating is its ability to converge to a solution. In general, the system can be operated in two basic regimes and the convergence has to be guaranteed in both:

Table 2. Multi-Agent negotiation

1: $U_{max} = 0$
2: $heatingProfiles = null$
3: **repeat**
4:    $localoptimization$
5:    aggregation of local results by the aggregator
6:    **if** $U > 100\%$ **then**
7:       Increase price
8:       break;
9:    **else if** $U > U_{max}$ **then**
10:      $U_{max} = U$
11:      $heatingProfiles = tmpHeatingProfiles$
12:      Decrease price
13:   **end if**
14: **until** stopping condition is true

1. The available resources fully **DO** satisfy the heating demand.
2. The available resources fully **DO NOT** satisfy the heating demand.

In the first case, the system does not require any coordination performed by the aggregator. Each building utilizes only its local optimization in order to achieve the optimal heating profile that balances the user comfort and heat consumption. On the other hand, if the resources cannot cover the global demand, the aggregator applies a price-based mechanism that increases the price for the heating in the time slots where the demand exceeds the available amount of heat. The updated price profile is then distributed to the building agents that repeats their local optimization respecting the new prices. The convergence of the algorithm is guaranteed by the fact that the prices can only grow. Based on this, the buildings are motivated to reduce their overall consumption at the expense of comfort at step by step iterate to a solution that is feasible.

However, this approach cannot guarantee that the final solution will soundly utilize the available resources. It depends on the price-update strategy how quickly the system converges to a feasible solution and what is the utilization of the resources. Simply saying, the negotiation is a trade off between speed and preciseness. If the aggregator increases the price steeply the system converge to a solution quickly, but it can significantly overshoot the optimal price and consequently the buildings do not exploit the available resources. In order to face this issue, the proposed method observes the utilization percentage of the available resources and if the proposed solution does not meet a predefined utilization threshold, the prices are decreased. Anyway, the feasible solution is remembered and serves as an back up solution in case there is no better solution before the negotiation deadline.An important benefit of the proposed method is the fact that it can fully utilize the available computational resources. The more powerful the computational resources are the more iterations can be performed and the better solution found.

4   Validation Study

As it has been already stated in the introduction, the research was motivated by the challenge of controlling a cluster of buildings. However, the validation study is not based directly on the real system, but on its simplified Simulink model. A model of one building is depicted in fig. 3. In the underlying experiments, the optimization is performed every hour. Horizon consisted of $D = 6$ hours and population size $L = 20$ was used.

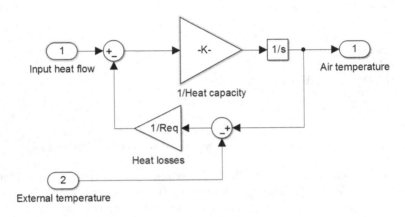

Fig. 3. Simple model of a hypothetical benchmark house.

The following plots captures the achieved results of simulation runs during which the system was trying to achieve indoor temperature of 21.5°C between 7:00 and 19:00. The first couple of figures illustrates the behavior of the system without implementation of the peak-shaving mechanism (i.e. with no constraint on the global heat consumption). It shows that the comfort is guaranteed (see fig 4), but the overall heat consumption of the cluster has a significant peak around 7:00 am (see fig 5), when a workday starts.

The second pair of plots shows behavior of the system controlled by the proposed algorithm and with a constraint on the overall consumption (6.8×10^8 W). In this case the system spreads the load in a wider time window in order to preheat the buildings in advance. Although the comfort is decreased, it is close to the theoretical maximum under this conditions (performance of the heating resource) and remains on an acceptable level (see fig 6). The peak-shaved heatflow profile is depicted in fig. 7.

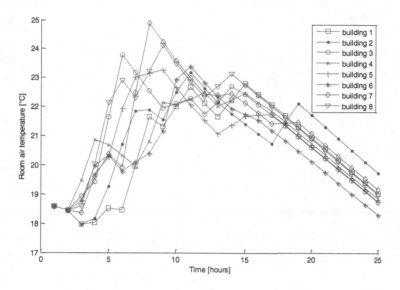

Fig. 4. Temperatures with a peak.

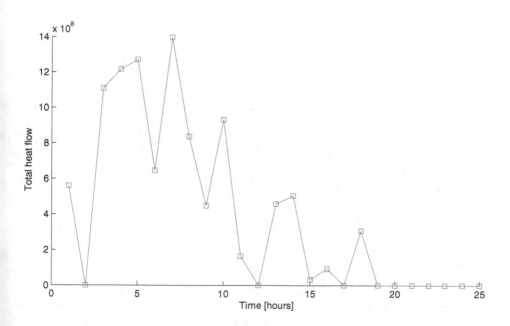

Fig. 5. Heatflow with a peak.

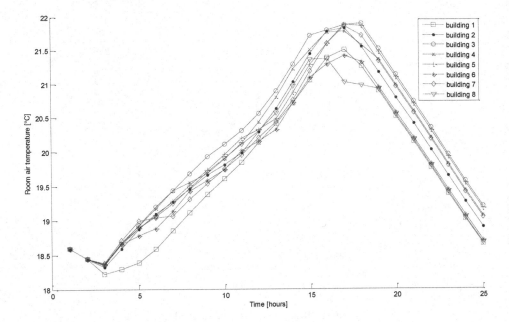

Fig. 6. Temperatures without a peak.

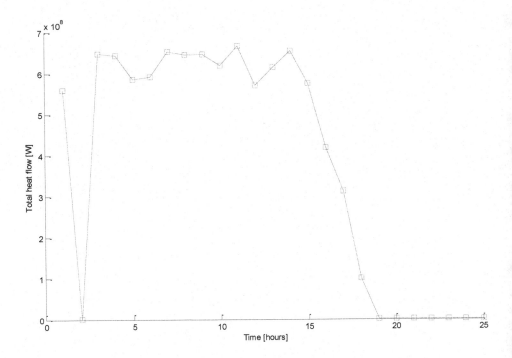

Fig. 7. Heatflow without a peak.

5   Conclusion

The proposed solution enables to combine local optimization utilizing genetic algorithms with price-based coordination of consumers represented as a multi-agent system. The advantage of this approach is its scalability, because the local optimization runs in parallel. The agent-based part of the solution combines the locally optimal sub-solution into a global solution. A central entity guarantees that the global solution does not violate any constraint (e.g. maximal available heating resources). This is achieved by adoption of an iterative pricing mechanism. Simply, if demand is above supply the prices are increased. This is done for the every time slot within the considered horizon separately. This approach motivates the involved building to shift their consumption into hours with low consumption (e.g. accumulate the cheaper energy from off-peak hours in form of the heat) and, in fact, it is a peak-shaving mechanism that balances the consumption between peak and off-peak hours. Moreover, this is done with respect to the specifics of the involved building, i.e., a well insulated building is more willing to accumulate the off-peak energy than another building with worse thermal insulation. The solution guarantees both (i) convergence and (ii) high utilization of the available resources if needed. From certain point of view this two properties might be antagonistic, but the algorithm which starts with a search for a suitable, which is then iteratively being improved maximizes the alignment of these aspects.

A pilot adoption of this approach has been tested on a model of the cluster of eight buildings that is located within the ENEA Casaccia research center. The experiments have demonstrated usability of the approach for the intended use-case and the obtained heating strategies agreed with the common sense expectations. The future work will be focused on transfer of the developed solution on embedded devices (PLCs, industrial PCs, etc.) in order to enable utilization of this approach for practical building automation applications.

Acknowledgments. This research was supported by institutional resources for research by the Czech Technical University in Prague, Czech Republic.

References

1. Heating and cooling no longer majority of u.s. home energy use. http://www.eia.gov/todayinenergy/detail.cfm?id=10271 (accessed: 2015-03-20)
2. Atthajariyakul, S., Leephakpreeda, T.: Real-time determination of optimal indoor-air condition for thermal comfort, air quality and efficient energy usage. Energy and Buildings **36**(7), 720–733 (2004)
3. Bellifemine, F.L., Caire, G., Greenwood, D.: Developing Multi-Agent Systems with JADE (Wiley Series in Agent Technology). John Wiley & Sons (2007)
4. Djuric, N., Novakovic, V., Holst, J., Mitrovic, Z.: Optimization of energy consumption in buildings with hydronic heating systems considering thermal comfort by use of computer-based tools. Energy and Buildings **39**(4), 471–477 (2007)

5. Ferreira, P.M., Ruano, A.E., Silva, S., Conceição, E.Z.E.: Neural networks based predictive control for thermal comfort and energy savings in public buildings. Energy and Buildings **55**, 238–251 (2012)
6. Qiao, B., Liu, K., Guy, C.: A multi-agent system for building control. In: In proceedings of the IEEE International Conference on Intelligent Agent Technology, pp. 653–659, December 2006
7. Yang, R., Wang, L.: Optimal control strategy for hvac system in building energy management. In: 2012 IEEE PES Transmission and Distribution Conference and Exposition (T D), pp. 1–8 (2012)
8. Yang, R., Wang, L.: Development of multi-agent system for building energy and comfort management based on occupant behaviors. Energy and Buildings **56**, 1–7 (2013)

Big Data Semantics in Industry 4.0

Marek Obitko[1(✉)] and Václav Jirkovský[1,2]

[1] Rockwell Automation Research and Development Center, Pekařská 695/10a,
Prague, Czech Republic
{mobitko,vjirkovsky}@ra.rockwell.com
[2] Czech Technical University in Prague, Zikova 4, Prague, Czech Republic

Abstract. The Industry 4.0 is a vision that includes connecting more intensively physical systems with their virtual counterparts in computers. This computerization of manufacturing will bring many advantages, including allowing data gathering, integration and analysis in the scale not seen earlier. In this paper we describe our Semantic Big Data Historian that is intended to handle large volumes of heterogeneous data gathered from distributed data sources. We describe the approach and implementation with a special focus on using Semantic Web technologies for integrating the data.

Keywords: Industry 4.0 · Cyber-Physical Systems · Big Data · Semantics · Internet of Things · Industrial automation · Heterogeneity

1 Introduction

One of the issues that the automation industry has to handle more and more is the amount of data that needs to be processed and analyzed for rapid decision making for improved productivity. The need for smart analytics tools is emphasized by so called "Industry 4.0", which is a transformation towards the fourth industrial revolution. It is an effort led by Germany with the vision to connect physical systems, such as manufacturing plants, with virtual models in computers, which will allow and provide automation in the scale not seen earlier. This movement can be in short described as the "computerization of manufacturing."

In this paper we discuss our contribution that we call Semantic Big Data Historian which is intended to handle large volumes of heterogeneous data gathered from distributed data sources, such as sensors. Following the "computerization of manufacturing" we use the technologies for handling Big Data and semantics used by internet companies and apply them to physical systems such as manufacturing plants.

This paper is organized as follows: first, we discuss the components of Industry 4.0, especially the Cyber-Physical Systems. Then we provide a description of Big Data features and also discuss Semantic Web effort together with a related ontology for sensor data. The main contribution of the paper is the following description of Big Data Historian – its motivations and goals, description and gathering of data, including a sample case study. We conclude the paper with conclusions and outlook.

© Springer International Publishing Switzerland 2015
V. Mařík et al. (Eds.): HoloMAS 2015, LNAI 9266, pp. 217–229, 2015.
DOI: 10.1007/978-3-319-22867-9_19

2   Industry 4.0 and Cyber-Physical Systems

The Industry 4.0 is the term used for fourth industrial revolution, following the three previous industrial revolutions. One of the differences from the previous revolutions is that this movement is predicted and in fact pushed a-priory – in other words, it is not observed ex-post. The economic impacts are predicted to be huge due to operational effectiveness, new business models, services and products. Some technologies, such as Internet of Things (IoT), Internet of Services (IoS) were introduced earlier than the concept of Industry 4.0, but are critical for Industry 4.0. On the other hand, Cyber-Physical Systems (CPS) were introduced as a paradigm within this context.

Clear and exact definition of Industry 4.0 is not provided, but it is usually characterized by its vision and description of basic technologies and selected scenarios [6]. The main design principles are as follows:

- Interoperability – companies, CPS and humans are connected over IoT and IoS. Standardization and semantic descriptions are important.
- Virtualization – CPS are able to monitor physical processes. In other words, the data from sensors are linked to virtual and simulation models.
- Decentralization – it is difficult to control inherently distributed systems centrally, so individual agents have to make decisions on their own and propagate only failures or complex decisions to higher levels.
- Real-time capability – the constant data analysis is needed to immediately react to any changes in the environment, such as routing or handling failures.
- Service orientation – service oriented architecture (SOA) allows encapsulation of various services to combine them together and to facilitate their utilization.
- Modularity – it is needed to be able to easily adjust or add modules and to utilize new modules immediately.

According to literature review in [6], the Industry 4.0 can be also characterized by its main components. Let us briefly review the components.

2.1   Cyber-Physical systems

Cyber-Physical systems (CPS) are "integrations of computation and physical processes. Embedded computers and networks monitor and control the physical processes, usually with feedback loops where physical processes affect computations and vice versa" [9]. The CPS provide the fusion of physical and virtual world, i.e., integration of computation and physical processes. This can be achieved by unique identification (for example RFID tags), both centralized and decentralized storage and analytics, with many sensors and actuators communicating over a network.

An example is a virtual battery [10] – a battery in electric car has its virtual counterpart updated in real time, which allows diagnostics, simulation, prediction etc. for better customer experience. The battery pack is one of the most significant components of an electric vehicle and the uncertainty in the driving range, the reliability and life of batteries, including safety concerns, are all challenges that must be overcome.

Therefore monitoring and processing of various factors of batteries is needed to provide for example failure prediction and for the possibility to improve the health of batteries. The individual monitoring of individual batteries separately is only the first step in usefulness – connecting the physical system to a virtual system where the data from many data sources can be combined together allows solutions such as prognostics, visualization, simulation and predictions at a higher level with combined data. This can help individual vehicles to improve the usage of batteries, but also provides help to battery manufacturers. It is expected that longer term data acquisition and analytics would allow further detailed study and improvements of batteries in electric vehicles in general.

Another example discussed in [10] is predictive health monitoring solution for industrial robots in an assembly line. Again, long term acquisition of data and connecting them in virtual world and models allows for monitoring, simulation and predictions.

2.2   Internet of Things

The Internet of Things (IoT) [1, 4] is a network of physical systems that are uniquely identified and can interact to reach common goals. The "things" in IoT are sensors, actuators, communication modules, devices that can cooperate together with neighboring smart components to reach goals that could not be achieved without this cooperation. In other words, the IoT can be described as a network where CPS cooperate with each other through unique addressing schemas.

An example is a Smart Home where connected devices such as various environmental sensors, components of heating and ventilation system and for example mobile phones are connected to provide more comfort. The visions of smart homes are currently expanded from the user-friendly automation of environmental conditions such as temperature and humidity to connecting even more devices together, such as kitchen equipment devices. Similar examples are Smart Grids and within the context of Industry 4.0 especially Smart Factories which are discussed in detail later.

2.3   Internet of Services

The Internet of Services (IoS) is the concept of offering the services over Internet so that they can be combined into a value-added services by various suppliers. The IoS consists of the service vendors providing the services themselves, infrastructure for services and business models. The formed services are then accessed by consumers. The applicability of this approach ranges from single manufacturing plants to networks of factories to allow special production technologies.

An example is forming virtual production technologies and capabilities by combining individual services as needed to carry out a complex task while combining different skills and observing time or financial restrictions.

2.4   Smart Factory

Smart factories are often mentioned as a key feature of Industry 4.0. In fact they are the realization of the other mentioned components in the context of a factory. The basic principle is that information coming from physical and virtual world is used to provide context and assistance for people and machines to execute their tasks. By context information such as position or status is meant – the information from environment is important as well, and was not usually considered much in the earlier approaches.

The work of a Smart Factory is driven by customer demands and utilizes CPS, IoT and IoS to satisfy the orders. An example of Smart Factory component is intelligent work piece carrier. These carriers are able to route the work pieces based on both required destination(s) and conditions in the transport system [15].

2.5   Other Components

Other Industry 4.0 components that we will not discuss in detail here include:

- Smart Product – the realization of CPS in a product. The Smart Product is situated, personalized, adaptive, pro-active and aware of business and location constraints. A Smart Product is smart from the time of its manufacturing, through the time of its time use by a consumer, till the end of its life. Additional services are provided in addition to a physical product.
- Machine to Machine (M2M) – communication between devices of the same or similar type. The communication between machines thorough IoT spans from one-to-one connections to a system of networks. It is expected that OPC UA (OPC Unified Architecture[1], as developed by OPC Foundation) will play important role here.
- Big Data – the amount of collected data requires new ways of handling the data. There are also other features beyond the volume of data that we discuss later in this paper.
- Cloud – handling of large amounts of data as mentioned in the previous point and also requiring additional computational capacity can be handled in cloud based solutions, especially in the cases, where the required computational capacity is changing often and is hard to be predicted.

2.6   Summary

Based on the above we can describe Industry 4.0 as a collective term for technologies and concepts of value chain organization [6]. Within the Smart Factories, CPS monitor physical processes, create a virtual copy of the physical world and make decentralized decisions. They communicate and cooperate over IoT, and both internal and cross organizational services are offered and utilized via the IoS.

---

[1] https://opcfoundation.org/about/opc-technologies/opc-ua/

3   Big Data

The term Big Data is used for datasets that are growing so that it becomes difficult to manage them using existing database management concepts and tools [14]. The growth that is bringing the difficulty is usually categorized into the following three dimensions: volume, velocity and variety.

As for **volume**, it is predicted that data will grow 50 times during next 5 years. The systems are moving to processing petabytes and larger amounts of data. This growth is brought by new opportunities to gather data from many sources together. This growth and the new ways of management of such large volumes of data was pioneered especially by internet companies, however the data are growing in other areas as well – medicine, biology, chemistry are just selected examples. Also, the Internet of Things is bringing the necessity to gather and process larger volumes of data – in addition to the distributed nature of proposed solutions, it is also beneficial to provide the overall view to a selected system, for which it is helpful to gather distributed data together.

The other dimension, **velocity**, is also demonstrating fast growth. It is not long time ago when state of the art system for processing data were working in batch mode. For example, analysis of data gathered from various business units proceeded in multiple steps: first, data were collected at a given time, then batch processing of the data pre-computed other views of the data (such as data cubes) and only after that it was possible to view the data in the desired way to understand the implications. Such processing is no more acceptable for certain uses. An example is again the real time processing by internet companies, where immediate reaction for serving appropriate webpage is required, however this trend is again coming to any other domains – for example, credit card fraud detection has to be processed almost immediately as well.

The last major dimension is **variety**. The variety of data is not surprising with the processing of almost anything in computers – well-structured data in relational databases are accompanied by texts, photos and other images, video and audio recordings etc. The challenges are coming when trying to integrate even well-structured data, and the problem of data integration in general is a big research question where even the understanding of the problem is still not developed. Data variety is causing issues even in smaller scale, in small volume and with small velocity – even without the other requirements of big data this problem is hard to solve. Several studies mention that the main problem in Big Data is not the "Big", but the heterogeneity of data. We can for example cite "It's about variety, not volume" [12] as a feedback from industrial use.

3.1   Big Data in Manufacturing Industry

In the text above, we have mentioned primarily the examples from internet companies. While it is true that this domain helped to advance the Big Data technologies, the question of handling large datasets with the properties discussed above is coming to virtually all areas. The domain of industrial automation is no exception – for example, an example application in a consumer packaged goods company generates 15,000 data samples per second [5], which may correspond to 70TB per year. The data gathered from an assembly plant exhibit all the properties mentioned above – they are large in volume, they are coming and need to be processed quickly, and they require integration of various data sources in different formats. For example, imagine gathering data from various sensors, information about the state and configuration of different machinery, data from suppliers such as various inputs including their specific quality, orders from customers including configurations and other requests, environmental and other similar conditions that can affect the production, information about shifts and holidays etc. The analysis of all such data may bring significant competitive advantage to the companies that are able to meaningfully process such data.

In addition to the discussed dimensions of Big Data there are other aspects that need to be considered, including for example veracity, validity, security, privacy etc., which are all relevant to the industrial domain as well. The challenges related to industrial automation are discussed in [13], including overview of the Big Data levers across the manufacturing value chain with examples such as energy and water consumption and production (Smart Grids mentioned earlier in this paper), transportation and logistics, Internet of Things, plant data processing, etc.

As already mentioned, the main problem of Big Data is the variety of data. From the summary of the use of Big Data in industrial automation in [13] it follows that there is a significant overlap with the Industry 4.0 components and challenges:

- Data integration from various sources while resolving their heterogeneity
- Providing means for efficient decision making – search, visualization, exploration and other analysis means
- Executing actions based on decisions – this is an important counterpart to data collection and integration

4   Semantic Web

Semantic Web is an activity led by World Wide Web Consortium (W3C) to enrich documents available on WWW so that they would have meaning understandable to computers. The languages such as Resource Description Framework (RDF) [11] and Web Ontology Language (OWL) [16] allow us to describe the data in a way that they can be easily integrated and queried. A well-known application of these languages on the web are Linked Data that demonstrate data integration in large scale (tens of billions of RDF triples) [2].

The Web and Internet in general provide means for handling unique addressing schemas in a large distributed system – ranging from IPv6 to Uniform Resource Identifiers (URIs) – which can be successfully used also in IoT and IoS as we discussed earlier.

4.1   Semantic Sensor Network

The W3C Semantic Sensor Network Incubator group (SSN-XG) developed Semantic Sensor Network (SSN) Ontology[2] to define sensors and observations [3]. This ontology is expressed in OWL2 [16] and describes sensors capabilities, measurements, observations, and deployments. The key concepts and relations, split by conceptual modules, are illustrated in the Fig. 1.

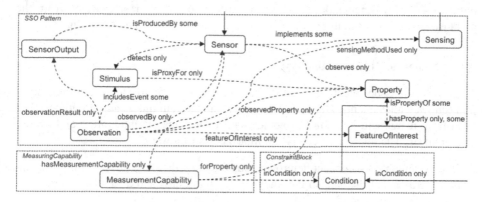

Fig. 1. SSN Ontology structure [3] – selected part

5   Semantics and Big Data in Industrial Automation

As discussed earlier in the paper, the important component of Industry 4.0 is the collection of data from physical sensors and their analysis together with the virtual models. The CPS assume both distributed and centralized handling of data. The autonomous decision making at the level of individual sensors or devices (that can be represented by agents) is an important feature that allows decentralized solutions. However, in the rest of this paper we are focusing mostly on the distributed data gathering to a data store for further data integration and analysis. We present our solution for handling semantics and larger volumes of data in so called Semantic Big Data Historian.

5.1   Manufacturing Plant Data Processing

The volume and velocity of data to be processed in a manufacturing plant are increasing. The traditional historians focus on achieving fast scan rate for collecting time series data, including the speed of storing data to collections for later analysis. Simple retrieving of data as well as basic data processing such as detecting trends and outliers is usually not an issue. However, the challenges for traditional historian software come when the data volume grows significantly over the order of GBs, when advanced analytics is needed and especially when it is needed to integrate various data sources.

---

[2] http://purl.oclc.org/NET/ssnx/ssn

During data analysis, single retrieval of time series data point, such as "what was the temperature at 1:23:45PM on March 15, 2015", is usually not an issue. On the other hand, task such as "what was the temperature trend during afternoons of this week, plus compare it to previous similar weekdays, holidays, after it rained, when different suppliers were used etc." is a more complex analytics task, especially in the context of large data volumes. The samples of needed data processing include pattern recognition and matching for example for predictive maintenance, key performance indicators (KPIs) benchmarking, clustering similar machines (for example from the point of view of their failures) and of course real time statistics and reporting.

5.2   Semantic Big Data Historian

To address the issues mentioned in the previous section, we are implementing a solution that we call Semantic Big Data Historian – a historian that is able to process Big Data from manufacturing plants, together with their semantic integration and further data analysis. The main goals can be summarized as follows:

- Handle semantics – connect heterogeneous data together. We are providing semantic description of the data so that they can be integrated and analyzed together, including their relations.
- Handle Big Data – be able to work with larger volume of data. We are using state of the art frameworks such as Hadoop to store, retrieve and analyze larger volumes of heterogeneous data.

The typical historian software focus is on time series data. We are extending this focus to include also other types of data, such as information about supplier, orders, shifts, external environmental conditions, various annotations etc. This will allow achieving analytics that was not possible when analyzing only sensor measurements on manufacturing machines.

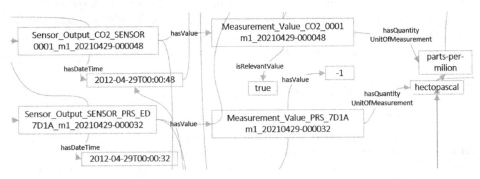

Fig. 2. Illustration of representation of sample data and sensors in RDF

5.3   Description of Sensors and Data

The core data we are storing are data from sensors. For describing both the sensors and data we use the SSN ontology [3]. We have extended existing concepts and relations to capture the data we need to process. The resulting ontology describes sensors, what they measure etc., together with the observations, including physical units, time, data quality etc. The data are then expressed in RDF/OWL [11, 16] using this ontology, as illustrated in the Fig. 2. The particular observations are stored directly as RDF triples and are linked together. For querying, the SPARQL language can be used.

5.4   Architecture

The overall architecture of our Semantic Big Data Historian, including sensor data gathering, is illustrated in the Fig. 3.

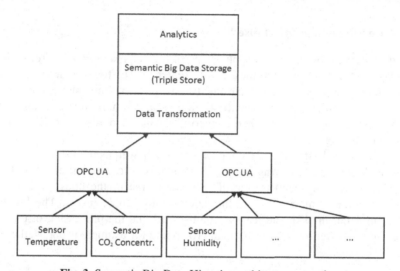

Fig. 3. Semantic Big Data Historian architecture overview

The data are collected through OPC UA, which is an industrial M2M communication protocol developed by OPC Foundation. One of the main advantages of OPC UA over the previous version is that an information model is provided for more detailed description of data semantics. This means that data can be fully described at the place where they are originating – in smart sensors. The attached description of data is then propagated together with the data. This allows efficient distributed data gathering – adding a new sensor means that the sensor itself describes its type, where it resides, what its features are, and when the sensor is connected, all of this information is provided to be stored in the triple store without additional configuration anywhere else then in the sensor. This is very important for achieving scalable data gathering.

The Data Transformation component transforms the data, including their semantic description into the OWL format. This includes pre-processing, mapping into the shared ontology and conversion to RDF triples.

These triples are then stored directly into a triple store running under Apache Hadoop[3], which is an implementation of the Map-Reduce framework. For working with triples in Hadoop we use Apache Jena Elephas[4]. The triple store can be then accessed via SPARQL querying language to get required subsets of data.

The top layer, Analytics, is to provide means for analysis of data. So far the queries and data processing that were beyond SPARQL capabilities (or that would be inefficient in SPARQL) were implemented directly in the Map-Reduce framework (see next section). However, we plan to use the Apache Mahout[5] that provides machine learning algorithms running on top of Hadoop.

The focus of our work so far was to integrate various data sources – data files in various formats including CSV or Excel files, live data access to sensors, or reading information such as current weather conditions from HTML pages. The OPC UA based architecture (implemented using FreeOPCUA[6]) helps with easy adding of new data sources, as well as with the description of the sensors.

5.5   Case Study – Passive House

Let us describe briefly one of the applications of this approach on data from a passive house. The data were obtained in files as historical data. The focus of the measurements was to control and improve indoor air quality – so the environmental parameters such as temperature, carbon dioxide concentration, relative humidity and air pressure were measured. The data were then converted using the ontology to RDF/OWL as illustrated in the Fig. 4.

To verify the usability of the Hadoop framework as well as the use of the Semantic Web technologies, the following sample analysis tasks were identified: complex querying using SPARQL, identification of relaxation time of the house, the impact of sunlight on indoor temperature and the detection of people inside. The last task is discussed in detail in [12], and it was demonstrated that the processing of the data in Hadoop cluster is significantly faster than processing for example using Matlab.

6   Discussion

We have discussed the Industry 4.0 components and have shown our approach for handling heterogeneity in data, while not neglecting the volume of data. As discussed earlier, the heterogeneity of data is an important factor that is often identified as the most important one. It is true that during our implementation we have found existing and usable solutions for handling large volume of data, there are also approaches to cope with the increasing velocity of data (that we did not discuss in detail), but the heterogeneity is something largely unsolved, or at least something that is hard to be transferred across different domains.

---

[3] https://hadoop.apache.org/
[4] https://jena.apache.org/documentation/hadoop/
[5] http://mahout.apache.org/
[6] https://freeopcua.github.io/

In order to have scalable solution, adding new components or reconfiguring existing components must be made without additional effort anywhere else than in the
place where the change occurred. This is why we pay special attention to the configu-
rability of sensors and of meaning of their data at the place where the data originate
and not at the level of data store. The OPC UA information model is an important step
forward to achieving the transportation of semantic information. We have discussed
only one direction of the data transport – from data sources to analysis. However, in
order to have CPS that reacts appropriately based on the decisions, the other direction
needs to be covered as well – to be able to control actuators (or states of agents) depending on the decisions made at higher level. For this we assume to use OPC UA
based communication as well. The overall approach of distributed data gathering will
have to be extended to also include data that do not come directly from sensor measurements, but from other sources, such as MES/ERP (Manufacturing Execution Sys-
tems/ Enterprise Resource Planning) systems – information about suppliers, orders,
shifts etc.

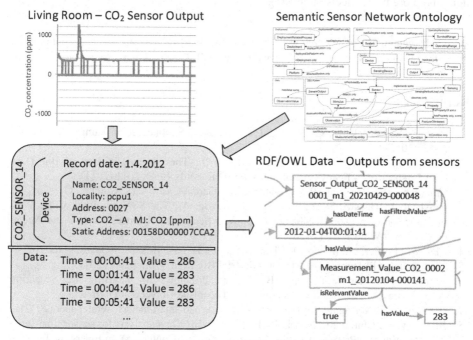

Fig. 4. Raw data conversion to RDF to be stored to triple store

It is also clear that to achieve Industry 4.0 visions both distributed and centralized
approaches will be needed. The small scale (M2M) data processing will exist together
with large scale (cloud) data processing. We have discussed data processing only for
the case of large scale collected data, however, the origin of data collection including
the description of the data is pushed to individual sensors.

7   Conclusion and Next Steps

We have summarized the Industry 4.0 with the focus on processing collected manufacturing plant data including coping with their heterogeneity. We have presented our approach to data storage, processing and analysis in Semantic Big Data Historian. The implementation is ongoing, but we have presented some first promising results.

Once we have the data integrated from different sources, our next steps include developing the infrastructure for efficient decision making, both automated and assisted by humans. This includes not only implementing the machine learning algorithms, but also visualization and exploration of data and analytics results.

As we have shown, the Big Data paradigm and technologies are useful for handling large volumes of data, however, coping with the variety of data is still unsolved – that is why we have presented the Semantic Big Data Historian implementation. The processing of data collected from various different and distributed data sources is an important feature for the realization of the Industry 4.0 visions, to allow more efficient and more useful decision making.

Acknowledgements. This research was supported by the Rockwell Automation Laboratory for Distributed Intelligent Control (RA-DIC) and by the CVUT institutional resources for research.

References

1. Becker, A., Sénéclauye, G., Purswani, P., Karekar, S.: Internet of Things. Atos White Paper (2012)
2. Bizer, Ch., Boncz, P., Brodie, M.L., Erling, O.: The Meaningful Use of Big Data: Four Perspectives – Four Challenges. SIGMOD Records **40**(4), 2011 (2011)
3. Compton, M., Barnaghi, P., Bermudez, L., Garcia-Castro, R., Corcho, O., Cox, S., Graybeal, J., Hauswirth, M., Henson, C., Herzog, A.: The SSN ontology of the W3C semantic sensor network incubator group. Web Semantics: Science, Services and Agents on the World Wide Web, **17** (2012)
4. Chui, M., Löffler, M., Roberts, R.: The Internet of Things. McKinsey Quarterly (2010)
5. GE Intelligent Platforms: The Rise of Industrial Big Data. Whitepaper (2012)
6. Herrman, M., Pentek, T., Otto, B.: Design Principles for Industrie 4.0 Scenarios: A Literature Review. Working Paper 01/205, Technishe Universität Dortmund
7. IBM Software: Managing Big Data for smart grids and smart meters. Whitepaper (2012)
8. Jirkovsky, V., Obitko, M., Novak, P., Kadera, P.: Big Data analysis for sensor time-series in automation. In: Proc. of the 19th IEEE International Conference on Emerging Technologies and Factory Automation (ETFA), Barcelona (2014)
9. Lee, E.A.: Cyber physical systems: design challenges. In: 11th IEEE Symposium on Object Oriented Real-Time Distributed Computing (ISORC) (2008)
10. Lee, J., Bagheri, B., Kao, H-A.: Recent advances and trends of Cyber-Physical Systems and Big Data analytics in industrial informatics. In: Proceeding of International Conference on Industrial Informatics (INDIN) (2014)
11. Manola, F., Miller, E. (eds): RDF Primer. W3C Recommendation (2004)
12. NewVantage Partners: Big Data Executive Survey 2012. Consolidated Summary Report (2012)

13. Obitko, M., Jirkovský, V., Bezdíček, J.: Big data challenges in industrial automation. In: Mařík, V., Lastra, J.L., Skobelev, P. (eds.) HoloMAS 2013. LNCS, vol. 8062, pp. 305–316. Springer, Heidelberg (2013)
14. Singh, S., Singh, N.: Big Data analytics. In: 2012 International Conference on Communication, Information & Computing Technology (ICCICT), Mumbai, India. IEEE Press (2012)
15. Vrba, P., Tichy, P., Marik, V., Hall, K.H., Staron, R.J., Maturana, F.P., Kadera, P.: Rockwell Automation's Holonic and Multiagent Control Systems Compendium. IEEE Transactions on Systems, Man, and Cybernetics, Part C: Applications and Reviews **41** (2011)
16. W3C OWL Working Group: OWL 2 Web Ontology Language Document Overview, 2nd edn. W3C Recommendation (2012)

Agent Simulation of Traffic Optimisation with the Use of Complex Networks Analysis and Voting

Jarosław Koźlak$^{(\boxtimes)}$ and Małgorzata Żabińska

AGH University of Science and Technology, Kraków, Poland
{kozlak,zabinska}@agh.edu.pl

Abstract. In the paper we present a model of the universal system for traffic control. The model comprises elements responsible for identification of key crossroads and decomposing of road network into sub-areas associated with given key crossroads. Different versions of key crossroads identification and network decomposing algorithms are shown. Some of these algorithms use voting by crossroads to distinguish the most important ones. Experiments carried out prove that the used approach improves efficiency of road traffic control.

Keywords: Traffic optimisation · Traffic light algorithms · Complex networks

1 Introduction

Cost and travel times optimisation is a crucial problem for traffic, which concerns both transit within large cities as well as transfer between distant points in a country or a continent. Traffic management may refer to a range of distinguished areas either geographically close or having similar traffic specificity. For the sake of traffic behaviour changes, it may be useful to carry out such decomposition into areas in the automatic way. One of fundamental mechanisms of traffic management is traffic lights application. Taking into consideration changes of traffic behaviour, it is justifiable to use adaptive algorithms for the choice of duration of given light phases. At the significant traffic intensity, a similar treatment of lanes, independently from the vehicle flow on them may lead to substantial jams on key road sections.

In the paper we propose merging of adaptive road traffic control algorithm with dynamic computation of road section significance and automatic determination of key crossroads by voting agents associated with given crossroads. It is assumed that key crossroad identification influences the calculation of minimal green light duration for the related road section and on the weight of parameter calculation of indicator switch, applied in the adaptive algorithm. The proposed mechanisms enable automatic adaptation to the state of traffic and on this basis to define key crossroads and network areas associated with them. We assume

© Springer International Publishing Switzerland 2015
V. Mařík et al. (Eds.): HoloMAS 2015, LNAI 9266, pp. 230–241, 2015.
DOI: 10.1007/978-3-319-22867-9_20

that areas in the neighbourhood of key crossroads should adopt lengths of their traffic light phases in such a way that it relieves traffic on the sections with their high volume. To evaluate our concept the simulation system was implemented and the new results were obtained.

2   Research Domain Description

The paper applies concepts used in some other domains: road traffic models, adaptive control of traffic lights, defining nodes measures in a graph with the use of complex and social networks analysis techniques as well as voting in multi-agent systems.

Modelling and optimisation of traffic is a popular application of multi–agent systems [3]. Traffic models may be classified as macroscopic approach (single vehicles are not modelled, general characteristics are defined, which describe traffic on a given section as traffic density, velocity, flow) or microscopic one (given vehicles are modelled). An example of microscopic models is Nagel-Schreckenberg model [9] and the ones which are its extensions. Adaptive algorithms of traffic lights control comprise among others SOTL algorithms [4] SOTL (Self-Organising Traffic Lights) exists in some versions [5–7]. Its fundamental element is subsequent calculation, for each road with a red light is switched on, leading to a crossroad, a product of vehicles number and time of red light duration. If the product excesses a given threshold value, then the road may request a green light. Moreover, to avoid too frequent traffic lights switching, the minimal time of green light duration is defined.

One of the significant problems to deal with is the identification of the critical crossroads with the highest traffic. For example, in SCOOT system [1] the volume of traffic is used to obtain this functionality. In our approach we decided to use methods of complex network analysis and social networks for the identification of key crossroads. To assign the importance of the given nodes, a directed weighted graph is taken into account, with traffic intensity as weights of single edges. For given edges, the values of Betweeness Centrality are calculated as follows: it is the ratio of the number of the shortest paths between all pairs of graph edges, that run through the given edge to the number of all the shortest paths between nodes in a graph.The measure PageRank was also used to assign the importance of the vertex, that takes into account importance of vertices which are connected with the vertex by edges entering it [2].

Voting issues, especially voting in agent systems are widely examined. Different protocols are applied, such as: the choice by voting of one or more preferred alternatives, plurality, binary or Borda protocols [11].

3   System Model

During our research we have developed several traffic modelling and simulation systems with modules using different algorithms for traffic modelling and traffic light management [8,10].

The goal of the created system is to obtain such traffic control to enable vehicles the best travel conditions from the start location to the end, i.e. provide the lowest travel time, the shortest travel distance or the highest possible average velocity. For this purpose, the system should discover or anticipate the fact of difficulties in traffic (jams formation) and choose the best method to solve a problem for a given situation (e.g. by choice of the traffic light control algorithm or its configuration, or by choice of methods of distribution of information regarding current and predicted states of the traffic on given roads).

The multi-agent environment comprises the road network with given road sections and crossroads. Road network is represented by a directed graph, whose nodes represent crossroads or selected locations - points of generations or destination of vehicles, whereas edges represent roads. Roads consist of traffic lanes and are represented by cellular automata. There exist a possibility to apply different traffic model. A traffic light system, functioning according to the selected algorithm, may be associated with crossroads. The main decisions provided by traffic light systems are: decision when a phase of a traffic light should be switched and which phase should be the next active one. Fundamental algorithms of traffic light control used in the created environments are SOTL [4] and RL [12]. The environment is composed of the simulation layer, responsible for vehicle traffic and the control layer, responsible for traffic light management and transfer of information about the traffic state. The paper focuses on the control layer description. The simulation system consists of controlling and simulation layers as well as auxiliary modules (see fig. 1).

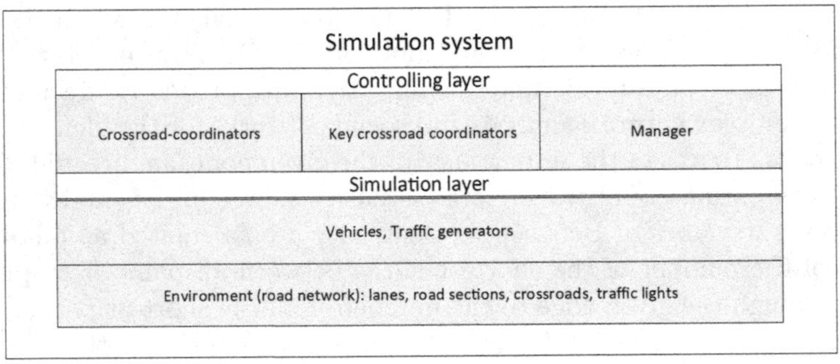

Fig. 1. System architecture

Simulation Layer. It comprises the set of Agent Vehicles generated in starting points and moving to destination points, according to the given probability distributions. The system environment is represented by a road network (graph of road sections and crossroads) and additional elements linked with it (road lanes, traffic lights).

Controlling Layer. The main task of the controlling layer is an improvement, from the point of view of given characteristics, the quality of vehicle traffic flow modelled in the simulation layer. The considered part of the multi–agent system is responsible for traffic control by appropriate management of traffic light phases. The system adapts to the current local state of traffic, taking into account also the most important crossroads globally defined. The layer consists of the following agent types: agent-crossroad coordinators, agent-key crossroad coordinators (as a distinguished group of agent-crossroad coordinators) and agent-manager. Below, the given types of agents are described in more detail, taking into account their goals, tasks, states, knowledge and performed actions.

Agent – Crossroad Coordinator. Its goal is to provide the best possible traffic flow on a given crossroad and its neighbourhood. Thus its tasks are:

- calculation of the current flow evaluation for given roads and lanes on crossroads,
- evaluation of the importance of other crossroads,
- sending crossroad evaluations to agent-manager and obtaining from agent-manager the information about key crossroads,
- correction of lengths of minimal phases duration and coefficients of traffic flow evaluations according to the given indications of key crossroads agents sent by agent crossroads.

State of agent crossroad coordinator ACC_{AccId} comprises following elements:

- number of active phases of traffic lights ($NPTL_{AccId}$),
- current phase of traffic lights ($curPTL$),
- current evaluation of the lanes, which defines the necessity of green light switching on, represented by set of values calculated for each input lane of the crossroad $LV_{AccId} = \{LV_{AccId}^i : i = 1 \ldots Lane_{max}\}$ for each lanes i,
- defines the threshold values of lanes for which the green light should be switched on (TV_{AccId}^i)
- minimal durations of traffic light phases on incoming lanes (MD_{AccId}),
- information about crossroads currently belonging to given sub–networks ($SubNetsSet$)

Knowledge of agent crossroad coordinators contains:

- current number of vehicles numbers on lanes ($VehN_{AccId}^i$), where i describes a number of lane, $i = 0 \ldots lane_{max}$
- modifier of traffic lane evaluation, which increases or decreases easiness to switch on the green light on this lane, ($ModTV_{AccId}^i$)
- set of all possible traffic phases $TPSet_{AccId}$, where traffic phase describes a colors of all traffic lights on the crossroad in the considered time,
- describes the lights switched on for the given road lanes (LLC_{AccId}^i) and their priorities for the given traffic lane switch (LLP_{AccId}^i)
- tables representing volumes of traffic between directly connected crossroads $trafTab$ and distances between crossroads $distTab$,
- sets of crossroads ($CRSet$), key crossroads ($KCRSet$) and measures calculated for the network ($RN_{measures}$).

Actions performed by agents are described by input parameters passed to the actions and output parameters set or produced as results of action execution. The agent performs actions from 3 groups. Communication actions are:

- sending crossroad evaluation to agent manager,
  $Send(in : CRId, in : AgentManager, in : LV_{AccId})$
- receiving network measure values from agent-manager,
  $Recv(in : AgentManager, out : RN_{measures})$
- receiving information on distinguished key crossroads from agent manager,
  $Recv(in : AgentManager, out : KCRSet)$
- receiving information from agent manager regarding belonging to the given sub-network.
  $Recv(in : AgentManager, out : subNetSet_{CRId})$,
  where $subNetDes_{CRId})$ represents sub–network to which $CRId$ belongs.

Perception actions are:

- identification of number of vehicles on traffic lane $LaneId$ in a given distance from the crossroads.
  $Perception(in : LaneId, out : VehN^{LaneId}_{AccId})$,

Decision actions contain:

- definition of the minimum duration of traffic light phase and evaluation coefficient of the given lane,
  $SetDuration(in : AccId, out : MD_{AccId})$, $SetEvalCoeff(in : AccId, in : laneId, out : LV^{LaneId}_{AccId})$
- switching on the phase of the traffic light to the phase which switches on the green light for the lane with the highest value of the parameter evaluating lane state,
  $switchToNewPhase(in : LV_{AccId}, in : TPSet_{AccId}, inout : curPTL)$
- change of the lane evaluation coefficient performed as a results of adjustments of the duration of traffic phases with key crossroads,
  $changeLaneEvalCoeff(in : LaneId, inout : ModTV^{LaneId}_{AccId}, in : SubNetSet)$
- change of the lane evaluation value, caused by the used traffic light control algorithm,
  $calLaneEvalVal(in : LaneId, in : VehN^{LaneId}_{AccId}, in : ModTV^{LaneId}_{AccId}, inout : LV^{LaneId}_{AccId})$
- calculates evaluation of crossroads importance from the point of view of the given crossroad
  $calCRRank(in : CRSet, in : trafTab, in : distTab, out : rankOfCR_{AccId})$

Key Crossroad Coordinator Agent. The agent is a crossroad coordinator agent with some additional properties. Its goal is to provide the best possible traffic flow on the given crossroad, in its neighbourhood and a part of the road network associated with it. Its tasks comprise the tasks of agent crossroad coordinators, and additionally:

- calculation of corrections of minimum duration times of traffic light phases and coefficients of flow evaluations for themselves and of other crossroads belonging to the given area,
- sending calculated modifications of traffic light phases durations and flow evaluation coefficients to other crossroads.

State and knowledge are similar to the ones for crossroad coordinator agents. In the scope of actions the performed actions are similar to actions for crossroad coordinators, and additionally the following communication and decision actions may be performed. Communication actions:

- sending modifications of traffic light phases durations and flow evaluation coefficients to other crossroads,

$sendModLightPhDur(in : CRId, in : CRSet, in : TLPDurCors)$
$sendModFlowEvalCfs(in : CRId, in : CRSet, in : FlowEvalCfCors)$
Decision actions:
- computation of corrections of minimum durations of traffic light phases and flow evaluation coefficients for crossroads in the given area.
$calTLPDurMod(in : CRSet, in : trafTab, in : distTab,$
$out : TLPDurCorsSet)$
$calModFECfs(in : CRSet, in : trafTab, in : distTab,$
$out : FEvalCoefCorsSet)$

Agent Manager. The main goal of agent manager is to define a key crossroad for the given traffic states in the road network. The following tasks are distinguished:

- calculation of measures describing road sections and crossroads,
- sending calculated measures to the given agent crossroads coordinators,
- leading voting concerning key crossroads,
- defining ranges of road network areas assigned to the given key crossroads,
- sending information on the current set of key crossroads and division of a road network into areas to other crossroads.

State of agent-manager contains:

- set of key crossroads identifiers ($KCRSet$),
- set of crossroad identifiers on road network areas associated with each key crossroad ($subNetSets$).

Knowledge of the agent consists of:

- frequency of execution of the algorithm for the identification of key crossroads and areas around them ($frecKCRcal$),
- values of traffic intensity for the given road sections ($trafTab$) and distances between crossroads ($distTab$).

Among its actions one can distinguish communication and decision ones:. Communication actions:

- receiving information about the current traffic flow,
  $recInfCurTrafFlow(out : trafTab)$
- receiving results of crossroad voting regarding key crossroads,
  $recResultsOfCRVoting(in : setOfVots, out : rankOfKCRVots)$

- sending information on key crossroads and assignment of network areas to crossroad coordinator agents.
  $sendInfoKCR(in : KCRSet)$
  $sendInfoAssOfNetAreas(in : KCRSet, in : subNetSets)$

Decision actions:

- calculation of graph measures,
  $calOfGraphMeasures(in : RoadNetwork, in : CRSet, out : RN_{measures})$
- identification of key crossroads,
  $identOfKCR(in : KCRVotings, out : KCRSet)$
- assignment of road network areas.
  $assignNetAreas(in : KCRSet, in : CRSet, in : trafTab, in : distTab, out : SubNetSets)$

4   Applied Traffic Management Algorithms

It is useful to decompose road network areas because of huge complexity of traffic control systems. In the model, dynamic division of a graph into areas taking into account the current state of traffic was introduced. The algorithm, executed every given interval of time, consists of the following steps:

1. Identification of the importance of given crossroads using methods of complex network analysis:
   - creation of weighted directed graph, for each road section representing its total traffic intensity,
   - computation of measure values describing importance of crossroads for the considered traffic state.
2. Identification of key crossroads considering their global and local importance:
   - given crossroads compute importance of crossroads in the system from their point of view, taking into consideration measures calculated in step (1), modified by a factor defining distances of given crossroad from the evaluating crossroad
   - performing of the crossroad voting concerning the choice of key crossroads, applying one of the voting algorithms presented below. Announcing of the voting results by agent manager.
3. Decomposition of the road network into areas associated with the given key crossroads:
   - areas are organised in such a way that each crossroad is assigned to the closest key crossroad.
4. Corrections of traffic lights control algorithms

- For key crossroads:
  - identification of the traffic lanes with high traffic intensity,
  - identification of the traffic lanes with low traffic intensity,
  - extension of the green light phase for lanes with high intensity by the fixed weight coefficient,
  - shortening of the green light phase for the lane with low intensity by the fixed weight coefficient.
- For crossroads with distance x (x =1; x=2; x++) from key crossroads
  - Identification of traffic lanes leading to and from key crossroads, with high traffic intensity,
  - Extension of the green light phase for lanes connected with key crossroads and shortening green light phase for other lanes.

The process of traffic light phase extension or shortening for the given lane may be performed in two ways - either it is assumed that the obtained value evaluating the given lane is multiplied by the weight coefficient (greater than 1 for privileged lanes or less than 1 for other lanes), or the minimal guaranteed time of the traffic light phase duration is changed (extended for privileged lanes, shortened for other ones). It is also possible to apply both modifications together. The principles of communication between agent crossroads coordinators in the algorithms are shown in figure 2. After distinguishing three key crossroads (crossroads KI_1, KI_2, KI_3) the appropriate areas of a road network were assigned to them (Area1, Area2, Area3) taking into account the distance to the key crossroads and traffic intensity in road sections being the shortest connections of the given crossroad and the key crossroad.

Algorithms of key crossroads identification are following:

Version Without Voting (V0). Key crossroads are chosen on the basis of their measures values of social networks (*BetweenesCentrality* or *PageRank*). Number of key crossroads equal to the number defined at configuring is selected. Such approach causes that very often the crossroads situated close to each other are chosen which makes the next step of such road network decomposition more difficult.

Versions with Voting. To increase distribution of key crossroads, voting crossroads on key crossroads was introduced. Used types of voting may differ by the number of crossroads which one node may vote for as well as the way of ranking calculation. Each note participates in voting. One node may vote for one candidate. Key crossroads are assigned on the basis of the number of votes. The node chooses the crossroad, which it votes for dividing the value of the social network measure (PageRank or BetweennesCentrality) by the assumed measure of a distance and selecting the node with the highest value obtained this way. The distance may be calculated in two ways: as the minimum possible number of crossroads in the route connecting the given node with the node - candidate (version V1.1) or defined as the cheapest path between two nodes, where the cost of the given road section is calculated as the product of vehicles density multiplied by the constant coefficient (version V1.2).

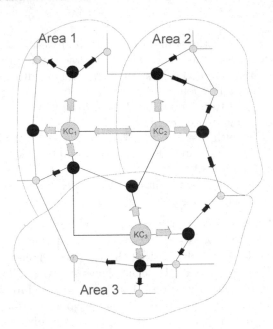

Fig. 2. Principles of areas distinguishing traffic light phases duration adjustments

5   Example

To justify profits offered by the proposed approach a simple graph representing road traffic shown in fig. 3 was considered.

Road traffic between nodes N1, N3, N7 and N10 was taken into account. From each of given four nodes to other three nodes the constant and equal vehicles intensity was directed. Only a large vehicles flow (5 times higher than others) was directed between nodes N7 and N3.

Algorithms described in sections 3 and 4 were executed to perform key cross-roads identification, dynamic division of a graph into areas connected with key crossroads and calculation a set of different modified adaptive algorithms controlling traffic lights. Algorithm of key crossroads identification with the use of voting indicated crossroads N6 and N8. A basic configuration of SOTL algorithm for N8 node assumed three settings of traffic lights: green for N (N7-N8, N8-N6 and N8-N9), green for E (N9-N8, N8-N7 and N8-N6) and green for W (N6-N8, N8-N7and N8-N9). During time unit 0,1 from N there are in average 7 vehicles arriving, from W - 4 vehicles, whereas from E - 3 vehicles. Minimal time of phase duration was assumed as 0.5 of the considered time unit. Correction of SOTL algorithm based on identified key crossroads and traffic between identified areas may run in the following way:

1. increase of the weight of switching factor for the N green light by 20 %, and decrease by 10 % of E and W,

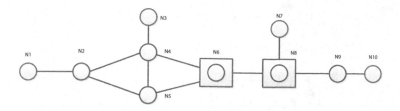

a)

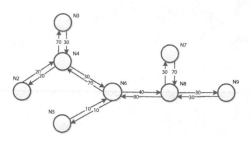

b)

Fig. 3. Road network a) organisation b) the part with traffic marked

2. decrease of the minimal green light duration time for N by 40 % and decrease by 20 % for E and W,
3. introducing both corrections simultaneously,
4. increasing the weight of N green light switching factor by 40%, and decreasing by 20% for both E and W,
5. decreasing green light minimal duration time for N by 80 % and decreasing by 40% for E and W,
6. introducing both corrections 4) and 5) simultaneously.

To evaluate every solution, the calculated number of vehicles waiting in each direction as well as their total number was assumed.

We can notice (fig. 4) that the best results (minimal numbers waiting in average for the given lanes, and the weighted average for all the lanes, i.e. all the vehicles flows) are obtained for combination c) with a modest correction of both weights of switch factors and the minimal frequency of traffic lights duration. When applying only single modifications and stronger modification stimuli, the worse solutions were obtained. We can assume that such a way of configuration modification gives better chance for the best traffic quality.

6   Results

With the use of the created simulation system written in Java, the series of experiments were carried out for different levels of traffic intensity and different configurations of the used algorithms.

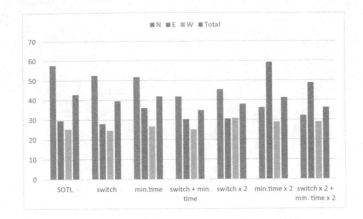

Fig. 4. Average number of waiting vehicles for different configurations of the traffic lights control algorithm

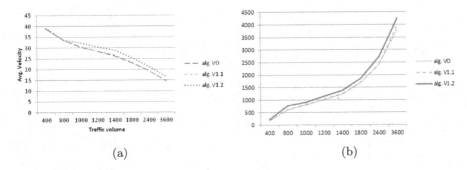

(a)   (b)

Fig. 5. Dependency of a) average velocity b) number of vehicles which finished their travel from traffic intensity and version of key crossroads choice algorithm

In fig. 5a, dependency of average velocity from traffic intensity (described by a number of vehicles travelling between each given starting node and destination) and a version of the used algorithm was presented. Three configurations of the algorithm were applied: a basic version without voting (V0) and two versions of the algorithm with the choice of key crossroads by voting (V1.1 and V1.2).We can notice that version V1.2 gives the highest average vehicles velocity.

Fig. 5b shows the number of vehicles, which finished their travel up to the given simulation course. One can notice that vehicles finish their travel with the shortest time in case of algorithm in version V1.2.

7   Conclusion

The created environment to simulate road traffic enables a wide range of simulation, applying different traffic models, algorithms of traffic lights control and their configuration. The applied way of decomposition enabled improvement of traffic management functioning, especially the results of traffic lights algorithms functioning. The performed experiments proved advantages of adaptive algorithm of traffic lights control, taking into account importance of the given crossroads.

The approach applied to calculation of the global importance of crossroads on the basis of analysis of complex networks and local importance based on voting of agents proved their usability. At huge costs generated by traffic jams, even a little percentage of parameters improvement (the average velocity increase, the decrease of travelling vehicles number and the travel time) enables significant savings.

References

1. The "SCOOT" Urban Traffic Control System. http://www.ukroads.org/webfiles/tal04-95.pdf
2. Carrington, P., Scott, J., Wasserman, S.: Models and Methods in Social Network Analysis. Cambridge University Press (2005)
3. Chen, B., Cheng, H.H.: A review of the applications of agent technology in traffic and transportation systems. Trans. Intell. Transport. Sys. 11(2), 485–497 (2010). http://dx.doi.org/10.1109/TITS.2010.2048313
4. Gershenson, C.: Self-organizing Traffic Lights. Complex Systems, 29–53 (2005)
5. Gershenson, C., Rosenblueth, D.A.: Self-organizing traffic lights at multiple-street intersections. Complex 17(4), 23–39 (2012)
6. de Gier, J., Garoni, T.M., Rojas, O.: Traffic flow on realistic road networks with adaptive traffic lights. Journal of Statistical Mechanics: Theory and Experiment 2011(04), P04008 (2011)
7. Helbing, D., Lmmer, S., Lebacque, J.P.: Self-organized control of irregular or perturbed network traffic. In: Deissenberg, C., Hartl, R. (eds.) Optimal Control and Dynamic Games, pp. 239–274. Springer, US (2005)
8. Koźlak, J., Dobrowolski, G., Kisiel-Dorohinicki, M., Nawarecki, E.: Anti-crisis Management of City Traffic Using Agent-based Approach. Journal of Universal Computer Science 14(14), 2359–2380 (2008)
9. Nagel, K., Schreckenberg, M.: A Cellular Automaton Model for Freeway Traffic. Journal de Physique I 2(12), 2221–2229 (1992)
10. Nawarecki, E., Koźlak, J., Dobrowolski, G., Kisiel-Dorohinicki, M.: Discovery of crises via agent-based simulation of a transportation system. In: Pěchouček, M., Petta, P., Varga, L.Z. (eds.) CEEMAS 2005. LNCS (LNAI), vol. 3690, pp. 132–141. Springer, Heidelberg (2005)
11. Sandholm, T.W.: Multiagent systems. chap. Distributed Rational Decision Making, pp. 201–258. MIT Press, Cambridge (1999)
12. Wiering, M., Vreeken, J., Van Veenen, J., Koopman, A.: Intelligent Traffic Light Control. Tech. Rep. Technical report UU-CS-2004-029, Utrecht University (2004)

Author Index

Adam, Emmanuel   59, 84
Andrén, Filip   195
Axinia, Emilian   22

Barbosa, José   59, 133
Bekrar, Abdelghani   108
Bendul, Julia   96
Blunck, Henning   96
Bründlinger, Roland   195

Chepegin, Vadim   133
Colombo, Armando Walter   73

da Silva, Robson Marinho   35
De Mazière, Patrick A.   120

Farid, Amro M.   3
Filho, Diolino J. Santos   35

Giret, Adriana   11

Harcuba, Ondřej   145

Jimenez, Jose Fernando   108
Jirkovský, Václav   217

Kadera, Petr   206
Kazanskaia, Daria   157
Klíma, Martin   145
Koźlak, Jarosław   230

Lakhin, O.I.   169
Lauss, Georg   195
Leitão, Paulo   59, 108

Lepuschitz, Wilfried   22
Lobato-Jimenez, Alvaro   22

Macaš, Martin   206
Madsen, Bjorn   157
Mařík, Vladimír   145
Merdan, Munir   22
Meridou, Despina T.   133
Miyagi, Paulo E.   35
Moraes, Eduardo Cardoso   73

Obitko, Marek   217

Papadopoulou, Maria-Eleftheria Ch.   133
Polnikov, A.S.   169

Shepilov, Yaroslav   157
Silisteanu, Andrei-Octavian   47
Simonova, E.V.   169
Skobelev, P.O.   169
Strasser, Thomas   195
Svec, Philipp   195

Trentesaux, Damien   11, 59, 108

Valckenaers, Paul   120
Vrba, Pavel   145
Vyatkin, Valeriy   181

Wajid, Usman   133
Wermann, Jeffrey   73

Żabińska, Małgorzata   230
Zhabelova, Gulnara   181

Printed in the United States
By Bookmasters